What reviewers say about *The Human Quest*—

". . . One of the best books currently available on the relationships between science and evangelical Christian faith. The questions discussed are important, the treatment is reasonable and informative, and the style of writing is understandable.

Richard Bube addresses those who have rejected the Christian faith without knowing what it means and those who have rejected science without understanding. This type of parallelism is a distinctive feature; the meanings of revelation, evidence and objectivity are explored for science and then for Christian faith. . . . Excellent to loan to a skeptic or troubled young person."

Eternity

"A must for Christian secondary school libraries. . . . The author considers all the significant issues in the light of Christian faith and competent science."

Library Materials Guide

"Bube understands science. It is refreshing to read what a Christian who knows what he is talking about has to say about the methodologies and limitations of science. . . . *The Human Quest* is exciting reading . . . an intriguing mixture of philosophy and educational psychology. . . . Bube, a physical scientist, [relates] true Christian faith to *real* science and all that science implies, including such topics as universal origins, the consistency of classical physics, the uncertainty of quantum mechanics, evolutionary theory, population control, environmental maintenance, racism, anti-intellectualism, and science as a service to man."

Christianity Today

"The serious reader can find much to stimulate his thinking concerning the science-Christianity interface. In his style of writing, in the provocative and probing questions following each chapter, in an extensive bibliography, Bube is a master teacher. The scope of each question is broadly considered and a tentative response provided, yet the reader is left with the freedom to make his own choice. In this age of specialization, few evangelicals can effectively encompass and provide integration for such broad areas of thought. In this book Richard Bube has provided real direction."

The Reformed Journal

". . . Combines scholarship with a high view of Scripture, a scientist's unwillingness to see everything in mutually exclusive contrasts of black and white, and the courage to deal with controversial subjects in this effort to show the consistency between science and the Christian faith. . . . [The author] takes both the Christian faith and science seriously, a good example for all of us following. . . . The final chapter on 'Social Implications' should be read by all thinking Christians."

The Evangelical Beacon

"I have high praise for Bube's book. It is clearly written with a smooth flow of argument. He is a thoroughly committed evangelical who is not afraid to use his intelligence to wrestle with the root problems of our time. All too often, Christians, in wanting to be faithful to the Bible, have then lapsed into a weak-kneed anti-intellectualism which disavows hard thinking on current issues. Bube will have none of this. He attacks problems in a refreshingly forthright manner. . . . I recommend *The Human Quest* to those interested in examining the various dilemmas—intellectual and social—engendered by modern science. Bube's answers won't please everybody but he raises the issues in a clear and non-irritating manner."

Provident Book Finder

The HUMAN QUEST

a new look at science and the Christian faith

WORD BOOKS, PUBLISHER, WACO, TEXAS

THE HUMAN QUEST: A NEW LOOK AT SCIENCE
AND THE CHRISTIAN FAITH

ISBN 0-87680-835-6
Library of Congress catalog card number: 70–160294
Printed in the United States of America.

First paperback printing, October 1976

In prayer
That those who sincerely search
May indeed find their answers
In Jesus Christ,
And with gratitude
For those who have

Contents

Foreword

The human mind seems to have an inveterate tendency to extremes, and no question better serves to illustrate this tendency than the one to which this book is addressed: how are the findings of natural science related to the affirmations of religious faith. So sharply polarized are those who take sides on the issues that writers in the past have even spoken of the "warfare" between science and theology.

In view of this unhappy circumstance, the book which Professor Bube has written is to be commended for its moderation and balance. Too often the Christian thinker is either threatened into overreaction and defensiveness by the results of scientific inquiry or else embarrassed into abject compromise of the Christian faith by accommodation to the repressive role of the Church against free inquiry. Probably no one ever completely escapes this imbalance in his thinking; but, in my judgment, the author of this book has achieved a goodly measure of success in setting forth a plausible and stimulating integration. In his statement of Christian doctrine, he is biblical; in his analysis of scientific theory, he is informed and up to date.

Along with moderation, the reader will find this book characterized throughout by a practical concern to meet the needs of today's college and university students. Each chapter closes with a series of questions under the heading "topics for discussion." These questions, reflecting the author's own encounter with the inquiring student mind, will enhance the usefulness of the work as a textbook for classroom and study-group use. As one whose whole life has been spent as a student and teacher, I should be hard put to frame a significant question which today's student is asking about science and the Christian faith which is not found in this book.

Finally, I wish to mention two specific items which are worthy of particular notice. The first has to do with the author's model for understanding the universe in terms of levels of meaning. This approach, set forth early in the book, is a most original and provocative contribution. Faced with the question, Has modern science made faith—specifically, Christian faith—impossible? Professor

Bube answers no. And he gives such an answer because of his dimensional epistemology. Secondly, the book concludes with a statement on the social implications of the scientific enterprise. In a day when so many scientists have assumed the neutral role of technicians, obsequiously serving the industrial-military complex (where the money is), it is encouraging to have a scientist leave his specialized sphere of competence and speak out on the larger human issues with candor and Christian insight.

PAUL K. JEWETT
Professor of Systematic Theology
Fuller Seminary

Preface

I will not say that I have never met a person who understood the Christian faith and yet rejected it. But I will say that I have met many indeed who have rejected Christian faith without ever understanding what it is. So many have stopped their religious thinking at about the second grade level. It is little wonder that their religious views seem ridiculous when compared with their university-level understanding of the sciences and the humanities. It is hardly surprising that they accept almost without question the presupposition that science has done away with the necessity and even the possibility of Christian faith. Even a Christian, while he is sorry for the error of their conclusions, can only commend such persons for rejecting that poor caricature of Christianity which they carry with them as a vestige of childhood. It is for such men and women that this book is written. To them I would say simply, "At least *know* what it is you are doing when you turn your back on the Christian faith."

Neither will I say that I have never met a person who understood the nature and purpose of science and yet rejected it. But I will say that I have met many indeed who believed that the claims of science were largely the illusions of atheistic scientists, which could therefore be dismissed before the clear revelation of the Bible. So many do not appreciate the coherence and internal consistency which provides the corrective guidance to science in the effort to describe the world. It is for such men and women also that this book is written. To them I would say simply, "At least *know* what it is that you are doing when you turn your back on scientific understanding."

When a person attempts to face life without a balanced perspective, whether he tends to overrate or underestimate science, he is likely to find himself asking questions without meaningful answers. A meaningless question invites a meaningless answer; a meaningless answer often provides the basis for a meaningless problem. A meaningless question is one that is asked on the basis of presuppositions which are themselves false. "Is the moon made out of limburger or swiss cheese?" is a meaningless question because it assumes that the moon is indeed made out of some kind of cheese.

This question is of course trivial, but I hope to show that questions of this kind are at the root of many pitfalls and difficulties in relating science and Christian faith. To ask meaningful questions is a common concern within the scientific disciplines. It is all the more important when scientists and Christians ask questions that seek to penetrate the meaning of the whole of life. The fact that the Christian believes he has the ultimate *answer* to all of life's deepest questions in Jesus Christ does not make less urgent his understanding of the nature of these questions.

In order to ask meaningful questions about science and Christian faith, it is necessary to have a reasonable understanding of the character, purpose, and limitations of each. To develop such an understanding it is necessary to discuss science and Christian faith separately, stressing major differences as well as many similarities. Discussion that follows this procedure is sometimes criticized as leading to a compartmentalized view of science and Christian faith which tries to avoid conflicts by keeping the combatants out of contact. It is certainly no intention of mine to offer a compartmentalized view of life as the solution to whatever difficulties exist in the encounter between science and Christian faith. The Christian of course believes that his ultimate commitment is to God and not to science and that his Christian faith must rule his whole life in and out of science. But to assert this unifying position does not solve the problem, for it must still be decided what one's ultimate commitment to God requires as far as one's immediate commitment to science is concerned. It is like deciding that one ought to teach physics from a Christian point of view and then finding out that after all Christian physics is really nothing else than *good* physics. The Christian approach to science provides a mandate to do good science. What it means to do good science in the various areas of inquiry is not immediately answered by taking the position.

The material gathered together in this book has come from many sources and stimuli. I cannot properly thank in person the many individuals whose ideas and questions have been involved in this writing. Certainly my association with members of the American Scientific Affiliation, personally and in local and national meetings, has provided a constant source of inspiration and incentive through the years, particularly those associated with me in the writing of *The Encounter Between Christianity and Science* (whose technical judgment I continue to rely on in many places in this book) and in the publication of the *Journal* of the ASA. I had the benefit of reactions from a group of adults in a three-month series on these topics at the Menlo Park Presbyterian Church and the provocative comments of several groups of bright and questioning students who took part in seminars on "Issues in Science and Religion" which I led over the past several years as part of the General Studies program at Stanford University. I have also profited greatly from a week's visit to Fuller Theological Seminary to discuss these subjects. My special thanks go to readers of the manuscript; to Drs. Paul K. Jewett, John Sommerville, Peter F. Lindquist and Frank Fishman; and to Gary Patterson, Evans Harrell, and Harry Kwok. My thanks are also due to my students, my children, and certainly my wife, who were all called upon at various odd and uncertain times to react to some particular formulation or idea. I think particularly of young people as I write this book and hope that in some way I have been able to appreciate their questions and help them to be able to see that perhaps after all there is an Answer.

Stanford, California
October, 1971

Chapter One

A Look at Some Questions

There are three basic questions that every man seeks to answer for himself. Science alone cannot supply a fully satisfying and meaningful answer to any of them.

Three Basic Questions

The first question is *"How can I know?"* Those who argue that science is the only route to knowledge are forced to answer that I can know only what I experience. Sometimes this conclusion is restricted still further to say that I can know only what I experience through sense interaction with the world. Scientifically my knowledge is limited to objects and relations between them. Purpose, meaning, love, hope—these kinds of concepts have only a materialistic basis.

Those who would go beyond science toward a humanist's point of view enlarge upon that answer. They argue that in addition to sense knowledge there is also a kind of cultural or intuitive knowledge which is possible for man as part of his social system. Still, my knowledge is limited to the capabilities and vision of man alone.

To sense knowledge and intuitive knowledge, both recognized as valid and valuable, the perspective of Christian faith adds the possibility of knowledge through revelation by God. The Christian maintains that man need not be restricted to knowing only those areas that can be treated as things or that fall within the possibility of man to conceive and propose by himself. The reality of purpose and meaning in life even above man's conception can be known nevertheless, because *God has spoken.*

The second question is *"Who am I?"* From the domain of his science, the scientist replies that I am a composite of biochemical processes, a complex organic computer. If it is argued that science is the only route to knowledge, then, to be consistent, it follows that I am *only* biochemical processes, *only* a computer—and nothing more. My individual consciousness and apprehension of personality are essentially an illusion. As an individual I have no intrinsic value or worth.

The humanist tempers this harsh evaluation. He concludes that I have value as a member of society, but he still is likely to maintain that my value and the reality of my personality are the direct products of my social identity.

Christian faith affirms the physical, biological, psychological, and sociological aspects of man, but it goes further. It declares that the reality of the personality of man and the intrinsic value of the individual is firmly grounded in the fact that God made man in his own image. The personality of man is thus rooted in his existence as the creation of a personal God.

The third question, *"What's the matter with me?,"* deals with the problem of evil and of the source of man's inhumanity to man. The man for whom science is the only source of knowledge is forced to the conclusion that nothing is wrong, simply because the categories of "good" and "bad" cannot exist within his framework. Man's inhumanity is not "bad"; it simply *is*. If science seeks to extract guidelines for "good" and "bad" from within its discipline, the best it can do is to conclude that what is, is good. Except for this groundless assumption, science is unable to provide the framework for ethical decisions.

The humanist concludes that what troubles me is my finiteness, my inability to cope with a complex world. Thus he is likely to feel that my trouble is basically metaphysical. I'm too little and the world is too big. Since my finiteness is not something that can be changed, my problem is essentially insoluble on either the personal or the collective level. The best I can do is to adjust to it.

Christian faith places the trouble in the world in the moral category, not only in the metaphysical. Christian faith propounds

Figure 1

CHARACTERISTIC RESPONSES TO BASIC QUESTIONS

	Scientism	*Humanism-Agnosticism*	*Christian Faith*
GOD (What is He like?)	Nonexistent (Meaningless)	Unknowable (Impersonal)	Knowable as He reveals Himself (Personal)
KNOWLEDGE (How can I know?)	Empirical (Sense experience)	Empirical and intuitive (Social consciousness)	Empirical, intuitive and revelational (God has spoken)
PERSONALITY (Who am I?)	Illusion (A complex machine)	Socially derived (A member of society)	Intrinsic (Created in the image of a personal God)
EVIL (What's wrong with me?) (What do I do about it?)	Meaningless (Nothing) (Let what *is* be the guide for what should be)	Metaphysical (I'm finite) (Adjust to it)	Moral (I'm in rebellion against God) (Accept God's offer to provide the help needed)

the view that the suffering and trouble of the world have their roots
in a personal rebellion which seeks to set up Self in the place of God.
Each individual man is by nature involved as he tries to give to the
creature the role that belongs only to the Creator. Furthermore,
Christian faith affirms that, in view of this moral dilemma, God
himself has provided a way through Jesus Christ by which man's
rebellion can be overcome, his violations of a proper relationship
with God forgiven, and a relationship of love and trust reestablished.

Has Science Made Religious Faith Impossible?

The three foregoing questions and their proposed answers are an
integral part of this whole book. At this initial stage of consideration, the comments that have just been made may seem to be un-
fair, incomplete, simplistic, or unsupportable. Many people respond, "I would like to believe the claims of Christianity, but I
can't. The world and life view that would allow an intelligent,
educated person to accept the Christian claims no longer exists
today. Our increase in scientific understanding has made it impossible to hold onto the old outdated comforting dogmas." There
was an era of joyful exultation in the liberation which science provided from religious superstition. This day has passed away. Now
there is instead a kind of sad nostalgia for the good old days of the
infancy of the race when it was still possible to believe in Santa
Claus, the Easter Rabbit, fairies, and all that Bible-creation-salva-
tion story.

One of the big questions today is simply this: Is it really true
that science has made religious faith impossible? Is it really true
that science has made unacceptable the foundations of the faith
of the saints of the past and present? Most of the world accepts this
as a foregone conclusion, not so much to be investigated as to be
endured. But it is just possible that they are wrong. Perhaps what
science has really done is to make it increasingly clear that certain
caricatures of Christianity are no longer adequate (if they ever
were), that the only thing able to stand today's pressures is the
genuine commitment of oneself to God in Jesus Christ.

Questions Asked in Objection to Christian Faith

Objections to Christian faith frequently take the form of questions. Most of these objections are not new. Perhaps none of them are. The questions too are the same ones people have been asking for centuries. The latest breakthrough at the frontiers of avant-garde theology turns out to be nothing but a heresy of the second century dusted off and rephrased. Perhaps these same questions are raised so frequently because the questioner already knows that no immediate answer is available. (Is it possible that these questions do not have meaningful answers?) Perhaps the asking of the question provides a convenient way of avoiding the immediate thrust of the claims of Christ. But such questions cannot be dismissed glibly. There are sincere questioners, and there must be sincere answerers.

In his book *How to Give Away Your Faith*, Paul Little, who talks to student groups all over the world, points out that he is always confronted by the same set of about seven questions.[1] These seven questions can be conveniently grouped into three major categories.

The Character of God

1. What about the heathen who never heard of Christ? Is it just to punish them for a chance they never had?
2. Why do the innocent suffer if God is both good and powerful?
3. Why do Christians insist that Jesus Christ is unique rather than just an outstanding example?
4. Won't a good moral life be enough to satisfy God?

God's Interaction with the World

5. How can miracles be possible in a world of scientific order?
6. Isn't the Bible full of errors and hence not a reliable revelation at all?

The Nature of Explanation

7. Isn't Christian experience only psychological and hence only one of many equivalent experiences?

---

[1] Paul E. Little, *How to Give Away Your Faith* (Chicago: Inter-Varsity Press, 1966), pp. 67–80.

(The sixth question might be listed under this third category as well.)

These questions are not the kind that can be ignored. Until one grapples in depth with each one and comes away enlightened but still tinged with awe, it cannot be claimed that the heart of Christian faith has been touched. Our concern in this book will be primarily with the latter two categories above, the first category having a basically theological rather than scientific orientation. To these latter questions we might add several more that focus particularly on issues directly related to the interaction between science and Christian faith.

8. Is there any reliable guide to truth except the scientific method?

9. If the universe obeys natural law, how can God act in nature?

10. Is man only a complex machine? How are mind and matter, body and soul related?

11. What is the significance of evolution for the reliability of the Bible, the nature of man, and the doctrine of a personal God?

12. What is the significance for religious faith if life is found in outer space, or if life is created in the laboratory?

13. Can a single individual be both a scientist and a Christian without involving himself in personal hypocrisy, delusion, or a compartmentalized approach to life?

14. Can science replace religion in human life and thought?

Evidence Against Christian Faith: The Church

When the question is asked, "What poses the greatest threat to Christian faith in the world today?" the surprising answer frequently heard is "The church itself." Now this is an exceedingly grave and unfortunate charge; yet it is not one that can be dismissed as simply groundless. Whenever people have looked to men, even if to professing Christians, rather than to Christ, they have found their vision obscured.

In this book, therefore, I will generally refer to "Christian faith," or perhaps occasionally to the less desirable term "Christianity," but will not in the same context refer to the "Christian church." This is not because I desire to downgrade the church or to minimize its contribution to individuals and society over the last two thousand years. So many books on the market have chosen this task (whether for tearing down or building up the church) that another is not needed at the moment. My intention is rather to distinguish between the "Christian faith" as set forth in the Bible and characterized by the heart of the message preached and defended by Christians of all kinds, and any form of institutionalized or denominationalized version of this message. I am in effect calling upon even the reader who is a lifelong member of a particular church to realize that the "Christian faith" is wider and broader—and possibly purer and more powerful—than the emphases characterizing a particular branch of the church. And I am urging anyone who has rejected "Christian faith" on the basis of his partial experience with some particular church body to explore the possibility that the claims of Jesus Christ transcend his very limited experience.

A Look at Some Answers

Having raised almost every conceivable question in objection to Christian faith, I would be remiss not to indicate at least the direction some of the proposed answers are going to take.

The questions that have been listed in the category dealing with the character of God can be answered only out of the midst of a Christian relationship, known and experienced, between a man and God. No amount of objective research is going to settle these questions to everyone's satisfaction. But it is wrong to think of them as even being that kind of question. Their answers arise from the depths of the nature of God and his relationship to man. They are answers that can be apprehended at all only if given to us by the revelation of God. And that we should in turn believe and accept this revelation of God is something that comes out of our personal experience of a relationship with God. Thus in a sense these are questions that no one without a relationship with God can ever hope to perceive satisfactorily. Even those in relationship with God can hope at best to understand just enough to make the answers acceptable although far from complete.

1. *What about the heathen?* Every man is a creature of God

who owes to God the supreme allegiance of his life. Certainly every man falls short of the standard of perfect love which is appropriate for him as a child of God. Not only this, but each man has a standard of his own by which he judges the lives of others, from which he himself constantly falls short, and by which he would be forced to condemn himself. God has shown both his justice and his mercy in Jesus Christ for all the world to receive and be restored to open communication with him. Such justice and mercy can be trusted to deal fairly with those who have never heard of Christ. Such justice and mercy can be trusted to judge a man according to what he does with what he knows, not according to what he does not know. This question is interesting because it can never be directly pertinent to the one who asks it. A person cannot ask this question unless he has heard of Christ himself and is therefore not part of that group of "heathen" concerning whom he is asking.

2. *Why do the innocent suffer?* Which is the case, that God cares and isn't able to stop the suffering of the innocent, or that God is able to stop their suffering and doesn't care? First of all, note that, from a purely intellectual perspective, the simultaneous existence of a good and all-powerful God and of evil in the world cannot be put into the form of a logical contradiction; that is, it cannot be stated in such a way as to force one to affirm that A is *not*-A.[2]

We may then categorically declare that the suffering of men is never consistent with the divine purpose of creation. We live in a world where evil and suffering are real facts of life. But because the world is a creation of a good God, the world itself is intrinsically (by design and when functioning according to design) good. The real evil and suffering in the world are the result of a violation of the character of the creation. In a sense they are aberrations on a good world. As members of the human race, we participate in and contribute to this general suffering, but such suffering is not out of control for the Christian. God cares. He showed us this by entering into this suffering himself in the person of Jesus Christ, innocent as no other man can claim to be, and by suffering even death at the hands of men in order to free man from the deeper suffering of

---

[2] Alvin Plantinga, *God and Other Minds* (Ithaca, N.Y.: Cornell University Press, 1967).

separation from God. In the lives of those who belong to God, suffering can be turned to strengthen faith and to produce the kind of
perseverance that can face any trial.

Evil and suffering in the chaos of the corrupted world may often
seem devoid of any positive significance. They are bound to have
this appearance to a man who is separated from God. What could
seem more pointless and meaningless in this sense than the legalized murder of Jesus of Nazareth, a man who preached peace and
went about healing the sick and doing good to all? But even the
apparent meaninglessness of suffering can be turned into the meaningfulness of faith in the life of a man committed to God. God took
the meaninglessness from the death of Jesus the Christ on the cross
and turned it into the ultimate meaningfulness of the way of
reconciliation between man and God.

But why does God not simply stop the suffering and evil by
removing all causes of these from the world? Perhaps because to
do that would mean that there could be *no* world at all where men
are free to choose and be responsible for their choices. If I am
really honest, I must admit that if God were to remove every cause
of evil from the world, he would have to start with me.

3. *Why is Jesus Christ unique?* The Christian bases his belief in
the uniqueness of Jesus Christ on his person and on his work. His
person was unique; there has never been another like it. His work
was unique; it accomplished what no other man could ever do. His
person is unique because he is the incarnate Son of God, preexistent and active in the creation of the world, risen from the dead,
ruling now and coming again to judge the living and the dead. No
other religion has a founder who escaped the final end of death;
Jesus conquered death and lives today. His work is unique. It is on
the basis of his life, his death, and his resurrection that it is possible
for men to be reconciled to God. No other religion has a founder
who has been able to provide for the salvation of any other man;
Jesus makes it possible for man's rebellion to be overcome and
man's creation-ordained place in the universe to be recovered. The
uniqueness of Christ must be not only intellectualized but experienced.

4. *Won't a good moral life satisfy God?* Yes, a good moral life
will satisfy God. Who lives one? A good moral life by God's

standard is one in which a person loves God with all his heart and mind and soul, and loves his fellow man as much as he does himself. A good moral life like this does satisfy God. But since it is evident that judgment by God's standard can only condemn us, we need to consider what provisions God has made for those who fall short of a "good moral life" and thus cause their own separation from God. That provision is to be found in Jesus Christ. He loved us so much he fulfilled the life of righteousness for us and made it possible for us through him to be forgiven and accepted by God.

We have dealt with these first four questions at some length here because our major concerns in the following pages will be with the other questions. As far as they are concerned, we introduce here two basic theses which appear to be foundational and indispensable if questions concerning God's interaction with the world and concerning the nature of scientific and religious explanation are to be understood adequately.

Two General Theses Relating Science and Christian Faith

THESIS I. *The universe exists moment by moment only because of the creative and preserving power of God.*

THESIS II. *There are many levels at which a given situation can be described. An exhaustive description on one level does not preclude meaningful descriptions on other levels.*

Thesis I. The emphasis of the first thesis is that everything that happens in the world is possible only because God is active at all times in maintaining and guiding the world. In a sense, then, this is a radically different perspective from the traditional one that pictures God as having created the world and its laws at some point in the past, after which they later became essentially self-sustaining except for God's occasional intervention to cause something special.

The implications of this thesis are widespread and powerful. On many occasions I have asked a group, "What would happen to the world and us if God should suddenly 'turn himself off'?" Admittedly this has to be a "thought" experiment, for it is clearly contrary to the nature of God to "turn himself off." Answers to this question usually fall into the following types.

(a) Nothing would happen.

(b) At first nothing would happen; then things would start to fall apart.

(c) Natural laws would start to break down and nature would become chaotic.

(d) Nothing much would happen to the physical world, but morality and love would not be present any more.

If analyzed consistently, these replies imply in order: (a) the existence of us and our world is independent of God, (b) we exist independently of God but we need him to keep things running smoothly, (c) God keeps only the natural laws running smoothly, (d) the physical world is independent of God but the moral or spiritual world depends on him.

We propose here that a full understanding of the nature of the interaction between God and the world permits only one answer. If God were to "turn himself off," everything would *cease to exist!* Without God there are no laws, no world, no us; to attempt to distinguish between physical and spiritual in this case is impossible. Not only do we rely upon God as the Creator at the beginning, as the Source of order and purpose in the world, as the personal Father who gives meaning to love and depth to personal relationships; we rely upon God constantly for our very existence.

There is a broad biblical basis for this position. A few of the relevant passages may be quoted here to indicate the nature of this support.

"By faith we understand that the world was created by the word of God, so that what is seen was made out of things which do not appear" (Heb. 11:3).

"He [Jesus] reflects the glory of God and bears the very stamp of his nature, upholding the universe by his word of power" (Heb. 1:3).

"He [Jesus] is before all things, and in him all things hold together" (Col. 1:17).

"In his hand is the life of every living thing and the breath of all mankind" (Job 12:10).

"In him we live and move and have our being" (Acts 17:28).

". . . there is one God, the Father, from whom are all things and for whom we exist, and one Lord, Jesus Christ, through whom are all things and through whom we exist" (1 Cor. 8:6).

As an analogy, Donald M. MacKay has offered the model of a

television screen.[3] Personalities appear on the screen and interact
with one another according to the laws of the world and of life.
They love, they fight; if they step off buildings, they fall (barring
children's cartoons!); if they are cut, they bleed. But what happens
if the plug of the set is pulled out? Do the laws of nature in the
events on the television screen begin to fail? Do the characters begin to be less loving and considerate? No, when the power is removed—when the plug is pulled—the very source of existence is
gone: the personalities on the screen in their life and story context
simply cease to exist.

Some of the other dramatic effects of this thesis can be summarized, to be discussed in more detail later on.

All such phrases as "God intervenes in the natural order," "God
uses natural processes," and "God works through natural law" are
ruled out. The natural order exists only because God is constantly
active in upholding it. God does not use natural processes as if they
existed without him. God does not take advantage of natural laws to
accomplish his will as if the laws existed without him. We see
immediately why the question "Can God intervene in a world
ruled by orderly laws?" is meaningless. There *is* no world ruled by
orderly laws except that one constantly maintained in existence by
the activity of God.

It is as if one were to cut a watermelon down the center and let
the left exposed face represent the world and the right exposed face
represent God. When the two parts are placed together to express
reality there is a point-by-point connection between the half on
the left and the half on the right. Every aspect of the physical
world, every atom, every gamma ray, every cell, every synapse of the
brain, is *on* the interface with God, constantly maintained in existence by him.

Or it is as if our existence were describable in terms of a two-
dimensional circle, the points on the circle representing elements in
our life. For a two-dimensional creature to enter our life, it would
be necessary to enter the circle and proceed in it to the desired spot.
But for a three-dimensional creature, every point on the circle, every
aspect of our life, is open constantly and simultaneously for access
from the third dimension of distance above the circle.

[3] See for example Malcolm A. Jeeves, *The Scientific Enterprise and Christian
Faith* (London: Tyndale Press, 1969), pp. 23, 24.

If thesis 1 is accepted, it also becomes immediately clear why the question "Does God exist?" is a meaningless question. If there were no God, nothing would exist. Instead of the classical argument for human existence, *"Cogito, ergo sum"* (I think, therefore I am), we might almost substitute, *"Sum, ergo Deus est"* (I exist, therefore God is). If we exist and can meaningfully debate whether or not "god" exists, we are not talking about the God of the Christian faith, the God of the Bible, at all. The possibility that I may exist without God is unthinkable. The possibility that matter exists independently of God is also unthinkable.

We can also see why the question often asked by children, "Where did God come from?" is a meaningless question. If God is truly the source of all existence, the "ultimate ground of being itself," as Paul Tillich puts it,[4] it follows that to ask where God came from is equivalent to asking where the basis of existence came from. But the basis of existence can only be; it cannot come into being.

To fail to appreciate the significance of thesis 1 is to open oneself to the possibility of all kinds of problems and misconceptions with respect to the interaction of God and the universe. We will be considering these as we go into more detail on various apparent problems between science and Christian faith. The idea of God as a completely separate Being, operating on the world—a completely separate assemblage of matter with independent existence—leads to many difficulties. The occurrence of miracles in a regime of natural law assumes a difficulty it need not have. There is a tendency to seek to find evidence for the existence of God only in those areas where man is currently ignorant. An increase in natural understanding causes a decrease in theistic understanding, and false dichotomies arise like that between creation and evolution, or between mind and matter or between body and soul.

Thesis II. We are all familiar with the fact that reality has many levels and that different kinds of concepts and language are used to describe reality at each level. If a child reads *Gulliver's Travels* and then describes how much he enjoyed reading about little men climbing across the stomach of Gulliver, he is giving a true descrip-

---

[4] Paul Tillich, *The Shaking of the Foundations* (New York: Charles Scribner's Sons, 1948).

tion on that level. An adult sociologist reading the same story might comment on his delight in the social satire symbolized by some of the events in the story; he is also giving a true description on that level. Although this kind of example is clear enough, we sometimes lose sight of the possibility of true description of the same event or phenomenon on several different levels. When this happens, we conclude that a description on one level excludes or invalidates descriptions on other levels. Since what is really needed for a coherent and ultimate understanding of the nature of reality is a description on *all* levels, the neglect of description on some levels can only diminish our total understanding.

It is possible to describe reality on several levels corresponding to the physical sciences, biology, psychology, sociology, and theology. The intent of thesis 2 is to assert that *every* phenomenon that occurs in the world can in principle be described on *every* one of these levels; and not only this, but also to assert that an *exhaustive* description is possible on every level without detracting from or invalidating descriptions on other levels. An exhaustive description is one in which there are in principle no unknown or unknowable gaps, using *only the particular categories of a given level*. Complete knowledge, in this view, requires an exhaustive description on every level.

In order to make this argument somewhat less theoretical and abstract, consider the following analogy. Let the subject matter for consideration be that of language, in particular the sentence, "I love you." As that sentence is examined, four principles should become apparent. (1) There are many levels on which this sentence can be described. (2) An exhaustive description on each level is in principle possible and in practice attainable at least at the lower levels. (3) An exhaustive description on any one level does not affect the significance or the necessity of an exhaustive description on another level. (4) A complete description of the sentence requires descriptions on every level.

The lowest (least complex, most axiomatic, least interaction) level on which the sentence "I love you" can be described is the level of the *alphabet*, the level of letters. The sentence contains eight letters. It is in the English language and all the letters are defined in the English alphabet. There are no symbols among these eight that are not part of the alphabet. On the level of letters, the

Figure 2

THE STRUCTURE OF LANGUAGE

Level Representation*

Ultimate
Meaning

Personal
Meaning

Meaning

Objects

Ultimate Content

Context

Grammar
Words

Phonetics
Letters

* Dashes mark qualitative changes.

Concentric Representation*

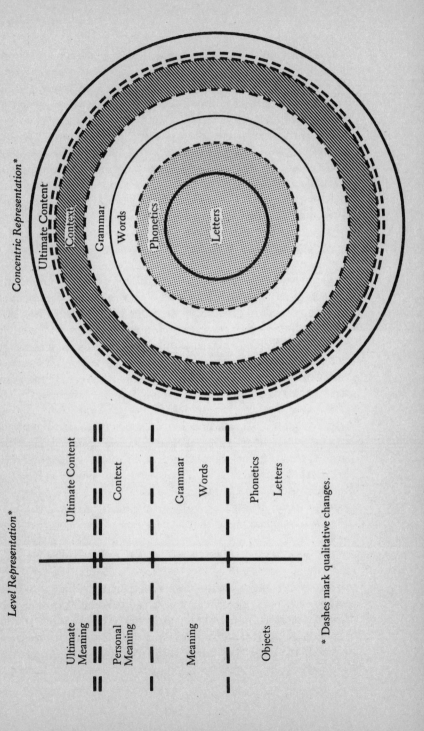

sentence is completely described. Nothing further need or can be said than that the sentence is composed of letters number 5, 9, 12, 15, 21, 22, and 25 in the English alphabet, arranged in the order 9 12-15-22-5 25-15-21. This is an exhaustive description on this level.

The next level on which the sentence "I love you" can be described is the level of *phonetics*, the level of letter sounds, of fundamental interactions between letters. We note the long-*i* sound, the liquid consonant *l*-sound, the short *o*, the voiced fricative consonant *v*, the silent *e*, the palatal semi-vowel *y*, and the diphthong *ou*. In the spoken sentence "I love you," all of these phonetic rules are followed, and an exhaustive phonetic description of the sentence has been given. Note that it is the combination (interaction) of elements on the lower level which gives rise to the elements on the higher level.

The next higher level on which the sentence can be described is the level of vocabulary, the level of *words*. Letters interacting together according to the laws of phonetics form words. Our sentence contains three such words, two pronouns and one verb. Each of the words is an accepted English word and can be found in an English dictionary. Furthermore, each word has a *meaning*. Thus a new aspect enters; as a result of the interaction between letters according to the rules of phonetics, meaning becomes possible.

The next level of description is that of *grammar*. Words interact with one another according to certain rules to form sentences. Sentences are made up of elements like subjects, objects, verbs, phrases, etc. In terms of grammar, the sentence "I love you" can be described exhaustively. The subject is "I," the object is "you," and the verb relating the subject and object is "love." The interaction between words to form a sentence enhances the meaning. All of these words appear in the sentence in their correct form as required by grammar.

The next level of description is that of *context*. In order to understand the meaning of a sentence, we must take the grammatical configuration of the lower level and see where it is found, that is, in what context of sentences and paragraphs. A new depth is provided to the meaning of the sentence, a personal depth, as it is spoken by one person to another to convey mutual commitment and trust. The sentence "I love you," read abstractly in the context of a book, has a quite different meaning from the same words heard from the lips of a loved one.

The final level of description is that of *ultimate content*. How is loving ultimately to be defined and realized? What does it mean really to love someone? In our hierarchy of levels this level is the highest (the most complex, the product of the most interactions), but in another reference system it is also the deepest. In fact, as our levels become higher, they also become deeper in overall content and import. Perhaps this picture of height and depth should be forsaken for a picture of concentric spheres of influence, with each higher level with its deeper import embracing all lower levels. For the Christian, this highest (deepest) level is to be defined in terms of the character of God, who biblically is not only the Author of love, but is himself love in its purest form.

It is the claim of thesis 2 that the kind of relationship described in this analogy exists also in the world at large, in the description of the world on the various levels possible. The constituents of all matter are the atoms and the subatomic particles of physics that interact to form the molecules and nonliving matter of the physical sciences. As these elements continue to interact in more complicated patterns, a qualitatively new characteristic emerges: the characteristic of life. Biology traces the life processes, the properties of cells, and the interaction between cells to form the "higher" types of life. As these higher types of life interact with one another, psychology and sociology provide the categories consistent with their description. Another characteristic emerges in this process: the human personality. The ultimate interpretation of the meaning of the human personality can be made only in terms of the relationship between that personality and God, the relationship between a personal creature and a personal Creator. As word meaning, personal meaning, and ultimate meaning developed out of more complex and more intricate patterns of interaction in the analogy of language, so it is proposed that matter, life, and human personality in the world as a whole develop out of more complex and more intricate patterns of interaction.

Because it is possible to describe a process exhaustively on the level of the physical sciences does not mean that the levels of biological, psychological, sociological, and theological categories have

Figure 3

THE STRUCTURE OF THE UNIVERSE

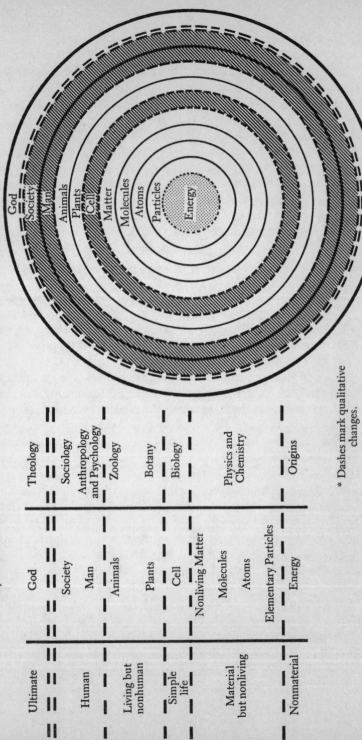

*Level Representation** *

Ultimate	God	Theology	
Human	Society	Sociology	
	Man	Anthropology and Psychology	
Living but nonhuman	Animals	Zoology	
	Plants	Botany	
Simple life	Cell	Biology	
Material but nonliving	Nonliving Matter		
	Molecules	Physics and Chemistry	
	Atoms		
Nonmaterial	Elementary Particles		
	Energy	Origins	

*Concentric Representation**

God
Society
Man
Animals
Plants
Cell
Matter
Molecules
Atoms
Particles
Energy

* Dashes mark qualitative changes.

no meaning or can be readily dispensed with. A complete description is needed on every level for a complete understanding.

Because descriptions on every level are valid and meaningful, it is neither proper nor necessary to exclude descriptions on some levels. The theologian need not exclude the description in terms of physics and chemistry out of fear that such a mechanistic description would invalidate his theological description. Nor need the scientist exclude the description on the theological level out of fear that such a mystical description would do violence to his experimental data.

It is true that descriptions in terms of the categories of the higher levels will deal with questions in a more ultimate way. Nevertheless, it is improper to make a choice of one description over another on the grounds that one is more nearly true than the other. To argue, for example, that cosmological theories involving collapsing nebulae are a more satisfactory (preferable) description of the origin of the universe than the statement that in the beginning God created the universe is like claiming to prefer English grammar over Shakespeare.

On the basis of thesis 2, false dichotomies are removed in many areas. It is no longer necessary to debate whether Christian conversion is a psychological or a theological experience. Christian conversion can be understood only when described as a psychological *and* a theological experience, as well as a biological, biochemical, and biophysical experience. It is no longer necessary to debate whether man is a machine or a person created by God. Man can be understood only when described as a machine *and* as a person created by God, created with real personality in the image of a personal God but functioning on the biological, biochemical, and biophysical levels according to the laws that govern the rest of nature as well.

Summary

In this first chapter we have tried to give a summary of some of the ideas that will be pursued in greater depth and detail in the remainder of this book. Many of them have been presented without much supporting evidence, primarily to get them on the record and to show the kind of presuppositions that influence our further discussion.

We have argued that science does not now—and indeed cannot by its intrinsic limitations—provide a fully satisfactory answer to certain basic questions. These questions are of such fundamental significance that it is improbable any man has gone through life without forming at least an unconscious answer to them. They have to do with what kinds of things we can know, what our identity is, and what the cause is of the evil and suffering in the world around us.

Next we faced up to some of the questions asked repeatedly as objections to Christian faith. We saw that some of these were basically theological questions that could be responded to in a meaningful way only out of an existing relationship between an individual and God. Others dealt with the interaction between God and the world, and with apparent conflicts between scientific and theological explanations for the same events.

In preparation for answering the latter kinds of questions, we introduced two theses, together with a few words about their implications with respect to some of the basic problems to be raised. The first thesis proposed that the interaction between God and the world could be understood only on the basis of a moment-by-moment dependence on God for its very existence. The second thesis proposed that any event in the world could be described in terms of the categories of a number of different levels. Description on one level did not eliminate the need for description on other levels, and in fact a total understanding would require a complete description on every level.

Topics for Discussion

1. Do you *know* that the earth goes around the sun once a year? Describe the basis for this knowledge. Do you *know* that some particular individual loves you? Describe the basis for this knowledge. Compare the ways in which you come to know things in these two instances.

2. Describe who you are to another person in the group. What kinds of categories do you have to use? Does the other person know

who you are from what you've told him? Do you know who you are?

3. Think of ways that what "ought" to be done might be decided on the basis of scientific investigation alone. Pick some of the most urgent problems of your town or country. Does your personal opinion of what ought to be done agree with the conclusion you reach by scientific investigation? If not, why not?

4. Make a record of ways that members of the group may feel that science has made religious faith impossible. Keep the record to be consulted in connection with later discussions.

5. Are there other questions not listed in the chapter that may be raised in objection to Christian faith? If so, keep a record of these as well for future discussion.

6. In your experience, do different branches of the Christian church have different attitudes toward problems relating science and Christian faith? Can you suggest reasons for these differences?

7. If before reading this chapter you had been asked the question "What would happen to us and the world if God were 'to turn himself off,' " what would you have answered? What do you answer now? Analyze the implications of your answer as far as the interaction between God and the world is concerned. Do some of your problems relating science and Christian faith arise because of your view about this interaction?

8. How would you answer the question, "What was God doing before he created the world?" Or to the question, "How long was he doing it?"

9. If scientists were to create life in the laboratory, would it affect your religious faith? Why, or why not? Suppose scientists were to create a man in the laboratory, starting with nonliving chemicals and putting them together in the *exact* way that a man is put together. Would your religious faith be troubled? Would the scientists' creation be a real man?

10. Is there anything man can find out that will make it impossible to believe in God?

11. Construct an analogy for levels of description using the structure of music as the relevant area.

Chapter Two

The Pattern of History

Many of the issues involving science and Christian faith in potential conflict are not new but have been encountered in different forms through the years. Still, it would be foolish to deny that developments in science and philosophy have aggravated certain areas of conflict. As the popular view of the world has changed, there has been a continuous and dramatic shift in the outlook of the common man toward science and Christian faith. Today the attitude so frequently found is that science has made religious faith impossible. How this has happened is more understandable in the light of the historical developments involved. At this point, therefore, we shall take a brief overview of the changes in thinking over the last several hundred years.

Explanation in Terms of Purpose

The Greek philosopher Aristotle, whose perspective ruled the world of thought for such a long time, explained natural events in terms of purpose. His concept was that objects fall to the ground when dropped because they seek their natural resting place. Acorns grow in order to become oaks. Rain falls in order to nourish the crops. Explanations of this kind are termed *teleological*. Obviously they are quite different from the mechanistic explanations that modern science would give for these same events.

As a whole, teleological explanations of natural events and theological explanations of the world go well together. If the world is the creation of a purposeful God, then the working out of his purposes in the events of the natural world constitutes the ultimate explanation. Such descriptions are not testable by experiment, and in fact the very idea of experimenting to understand the natural world was formerly an alien concept. The explanation is inferred by looking back at the completed process and deducing the purpose that was fulfilled by it. In spite of the claim by most modern scientists that teleological elements should be purged from scientific explanations, some attempts to explain specific structures and functions through an evolutionary mechanism border on this kind of explanation.

God was viewed as the Supreme Good, a combination in the hands of Aquinas of Aristotle's Unmoved Mover and the Bible's personal Father. God was active in the events of the world, causing all things to fulfill his purposes, working both directly and indirectly in many different ways. Man, the special creation in the image of God, was properly at the center of the created universe. The earth, the stage for the drama between God and man, was properly the central point about which the other heavenly bodies revolved.

Reason and revelation were complementary, revelation having the ultimate position. The truths of God, given in the revelation of the Bible, were apprehended and applied through reason. In this context it was a natural ambition for a man to be a minister of the church and an almost unthinkable choice for him to be associated with the science of the day—a mixture of magic, sorcery, and astrology, identified with attempts to obtain power over the evil forces resident in nature.

World history unfolded in a linear fashion with time, marked by the five "C"s of God's intervention: Creation, Covenant, Christ, Church, and Consummation.

Galileo's New Sciences

Galileo (1564–1642) and his work are the symbols in history of the development of two new ingredients in man's attempt to understand nature: the combination of mathematical reasoning with experimental observations. The perspective which these changes introduced differed greatly from that of Aristotle. Aristotle's view held that a moving cart came to rest because rest was its natural state; Galileo's view held that a moving cart would continue in motion forever (that was its "natural state") except for the effects of friction that stopped it. Aristotle's view was that a swinging pendulum would come to rest in time because rest was its natural state; Galileo's view again was that the pendulum would continue to swing forever except for the effects of friction. Aristotle saw in the stopping pendulum the outworkings of a grand teleological pattern; Galileo saw rubbing on the axis. The shift in the nature of the explanation carried with it a logical shift in the nature of the questions to be asked by the new science. The ultimate teleological "why" questions were replaced by the immediate mechanistic "how" questions. Models to describe natural processes took the form of matter in motion; scientific explanations would involve predominantly the categories of mass, space, and time.

The effect of Galileo's research on the relationship of the earth and the sun is, of course, a landmark all by itself in the history of the interaction between science and Christian faith. It contains within it most of the characteristics of many such painful interactions to follow. The church leaders of Galileo's day had accepted a view of the universe with which they were comfortable. To their minds it provided beautiful consistency between their interpretation of the Bible and the scientifically accepted Ptolemaic astronomy which placed the earth at the center of the universe. It is difficult for us today to appreciate the gravity of the situation. The geocentric position was supported by long scientific prestige, by well-accepted traditional interpretations of the Bible, and by certain particular proof texts from the Bible, such as the sun standing still for Joshua. The Roman Catholic church was joined by the fathers of the Protestant Reformation in the attack on Copernican astronomical interpretations. They argued that if the Bible were wrong on *this* crucial point, then it was wrong on every crucial point; in fact, God was a liar and Christ had died a meaningless death as a political martyr. Since their position was indefensible, it was only a matter of time before the most conservative churchmen ceased to be troubled by the shift in astronomical emphasis. They came to realize in a slow and painful way that the truth of God and the meaning of Christ's life and death were not at stake but that the validity of men's interpretations were. Several lessons can be learned from this historical sequence of events:

1. The implication of particular passages of the Bible, so far as mechanistic or modern-scientific descriptions of the world are concerned, is far from clear. Any definite correlation must depend upon a human interpretation and hence be susceptible to change and reinterpretation.

2. Currently accepted scientific theories (the Ptolemaic system, in this case) need not be a reliable guide to the mechanistic or modern-scientific implications of particular Bible passages.

3. Whether any passages of the Bible should be expected to provide mechanistic or modern-scientific descriptions is itself a question that must be seriously considered.

4. Sometimes a defense of Christian faith is based on the assertion that the validity of the whole biblical message rests on the ability of a particular interpretation of the Bible to provide a mechanistic or modern-scientific description that is true. When this is the case, the defender must not be surprised if the ultimate overthrow of his interpretation is understood by the world as a whole as an overthrow of Christian faith itself.

Unfortunately, subsequent events in the history of the interaction between science and Christian faith indicate that these lessons are not easily learned.

The change in perspective that came with the new sciences had profound influences on the way in which both God's and man's place in the universe were viewed. With the transformation of teleological explanations to mechanistic explanations, the symbolic image of God shifted from that of the First Good to that of the First Cause. With the new astronomy, man was removed from the central spot in the universe to become only a spectator on a minor speck in the vast solar system.

The Newtonian World Machine

Sir Isaac Newton (1642–1727) was a religious man. It is ironic that the applications of his contributions to science were to intensify the loss of a sense of personal relationship between man and God.

As the combination of mathematics and experiment was pursued further, it was found that many phenomena in the natural world could be described in terms of a set of simple basic laws. It should perhaps have been expected that the world would be thought of as a law-abiding machine. The picture of a man as a special creation of a personal God, living in the bosom of his good and purposeful Father, was drastically altered. Now man was a small creature in a great machine run and maintained by a Great Machinist. This concept of the world as a complex but completely predictable machine following unchanging laws did not trouble Newton's own religious convictions, but it was ultimately to help overthrow the very perspective he held dear.

As the growth of technology encouraged mechanical models, the descriptive model for God became that of Divine Clockmaker. As a master craftsman puts together the intricate details of a fine clock so that all the pieces work in unison to produce an accurate timepiece, so God could be viewed as putting together the elements of the world in such a way that they would follow a set of natural laws in mutual harmony. In this model God becomes separated from the world; in the extreme deist interpretation, God's participation in the activities of the world is limited almost to the act of creation alone. The sense of God's immediate and moment-by-moment activity in the world, commonly described in terms of the concept of Providence, was largely lost. Providence became only preservation.

As human success in describing the world by scientific methods increased, it might be expected that religiously committed men would try to draw a connection between the findings of science and their Christian faith. What they sought to do out of their personal faith, namely, to provide an objective and scientific basis for Christian doctrines and ethics without reference to revelation, eventually led others to the denial of that very faith. As natural theology (the attempt to derive knowledge of God from a scientific investigation of the world) flourished, the need for supernatural theology (the understanding of the revelation of God given in the Bible) decreased. The more man was able to derive what he considered to be the truths about God, the world, and himself from his scientific enterprises, the less he needed the special revelation of God in the Bible. The result was an exaltation of human reason. God, especially the deistic God, was relegated to a position of an almost irrelevant hypothesis, and there was a general optimism in man's own ability to solve all his problems by himself through reason and the scientific approach.

Through all this change in perspective, man still held a position of special eminence. Although he was no longer at the geometric center of the created universe, his striking intellectual achievements in the new sciences supported the belief that he was indeed a very special creature. All the universe around him might be only a vast and complex machine ruled by mechanistic law, but he and God were excepted. If the world was indeed only a machine, man was at least the ruler of it.

The positive connection between Christian faith and the rise of science should not be overlooked in this brief historical survey. The basic convictions of the Judeo-Christian tradition coupled with the principles of Greek thought provided the philosophical foundations upon which modern science is built. The difference between religious perspectives of the East and the West must be accorded a principal role in determining differences in the development of science in the two halves of the world. The Judeo-Christian doctrine of creation taught that the creation was understandable by man, that it was basically good since it was fashioned by a good God, and that man's dominion over nature was part of his mandate as a child of God. Science is based on the presupposition that the world is orderly and knowable and that the investigation of the world is a good pursuit to follow. In an Eastern religious context, where commonly it is held that the material, finite aspects of life are only hindrances to the experience of ultimate unity with the Divine, science did not have the impetus to develop.

The Romantic Reaction
(Late 18th and Early 19th Century)

The mechanistic, sterile mold into which deism cast religious thought was acceptable only to individuals with a highly developed degree of intellectual abstraction. A reaction calling for a realization of the importance of emotional and imaginative aspects of life was soon mounted against this extreme emphasis. The impact of immediate experience, of freedom and individuality, of dynamic change and novelty, were all underrated in the deistic view. Religious revivals emphasized the importance of personal experience as opposed to intellectual dogma and the expression of Christian faith in a devout life instead of only in a defensible creed. Like most reactions, reversal of approach can also be easily taken to extremes. When, in reaction to an excessively rationalistic and objective presentation of Christian faith, an irrational and wholly subjective position is advanced, the ultimate destruction of Christian faith is equally likely.

Two Philosophical Positions

In the eighteenth century two men, David Hume (1711–1776) and Immanuel Kant (1724–1804), made major contributions to the philosophical basis for the interaction between science and Christian faith.

Hume argued that all reliable knowledge is based only on sense impressions. He was, in modern terms, an empiricist. The function of the human mind in treating these data is *only* to record, rearrange, and compare. Hume attacked natural theology in general and the argument for the existence of God as First Cause in particular, maintaining that a cause can never be deduced from its effect. Because of his empirical emphasis, he also attacked the power of human reason and religious faith in the form of deism.

Kant, in contrast to Hume, argued that the human mind plays a fundamental role in interpreting sense data. He proposed that what we call knowledge is the result of both sense data inputs and the structure of human consciousness, which organizes and interprets in terms of its own categories. Because of the role played by the individual mind, we can never know how the world really is; we can only know how the world appears to us.

Each of these lines of reasoning in its own way opened wider the separation between science and religious faith. Empiricism like that of Hume left little rational ground for the operation of religious faith, since religious knowledge is not commonly acquired through sense impressions. That which could be learned through sense impressions could be said to be *known*; that which could not be derived from the senses could only be *believed*. Kant, on the other hand, concluded that science was adequate for treating the objects, the things of the world, but that it was not adequate for treating the world of thought or faith. Thus science and religious faith were accorded separate realms; because there was no real interaction or competition between these realms, there was no cause of conflict. On the surface this may seem to be an agreeable solution to the problems that arise when science and religious faith are considered as part of the same or interacting realms. Its ultimate effect, however, is destructive of religious faith since it divorces it from any objective or historical confirmation.

The Darwinian Revolution

The publication of *Origin of the Species* by Charles Darwin in 1859 marked a new era in man's perspective on God, the world, and himself. Darwinian evolution quickly became a revolution. The extrapolation of the restricted theory of evolution—that living creatures change by natural selection in response to their environment—to the general theory proposing the origin of all living creatures from a common ancestor abruptly deposed man from his previous position. Fallen from his high position as ruler of a complex machine, man now became just a part of that very same machine. The dignity ascribed to man because of his uniquely human station was seriously questioned when he was viewed as only the most highly developed animal.

Other implications of the general theory of evolution are so numerous they cannot all be given here. Nature is to be viewed not as the static product of a fiat creation but in terms of a dynamic process. The importance of change, of interacting and interdependent forces, was emphasized. The argument for the existence of God from the design evident in living creatures was threatened because this design could now be attributed to the workings of the evolutionary mechanisms. The Providence of God was replaced by the progress of evolution. The whole validity of the Christian faith based upon a fiat creation interpretation of the Bible was called into question, and the astronomical controversy of Galileo's day was resurrected in evolutionary form with life-or-death intensity.

Once again the assertion was heard, "If evolution is true, then the Bible is false and God is a liar." The response, as might be expected, was, "Evolution is true and therefore the Bible is false and the God of the Bible is dead."

Evolutionary theory has been extended back before the biological period to deal also with the evolution of matter, planetary bodies, stars, and life on earth; it has been extrapolated beyond the biological realm to treat social, cultural, political, and religious evolution. In a little over a century it has assumed the proportions of a major religious faith, sometimes being cited as the major opposing faith to Christian faith.

Modern Theology and Philosophy

The most common point of agreement among modern versions of theology and philosophy is the necessary separation between science and religious faith. There is a conviction that the consistent pursuit of science is at least partly to blame for having led to the conclusion that man is only a machine. Man's personal consciousness and experience rebels at accepting this view of himself. In order to extricate himself as a man from the restrictions apparently imposed on him by science, he concludes that religious faith and values must be sought in the realm of the irrational and subjective that science does not touch.

Karl Barth, frequently called the father of neo-orthodoxy, arrived at the conclusion of a necessary separation between science and religious faith from a relatively conservative theological perspective. Disillusioned with the perspective of liberal theology which often tended to equate God with evolution, Barth reacted with an extreme exaltation of special revelation and a categorical rejection of all natural theology. He argued that man can know nothing apart from the special revelation of God's Word. Thus science can contribute nothing of significance to theology.

From their own somewhat different perspective, the existential philosophers (e.g., Jaspers, Camus, or Heidegger) and theologians (e.g., Bultmann) emphasize the ultimate significance of present experience as opposed to any objective, historical, or scientific basis for philosophical or religious truth. Such existential experiences cannot really be communicated from one person to another, nor can their validity or meaning be tested by objective or scientific criteria.

Summary

General trends resulting from the interpretation of science have had a profound impact on the way in which man views the relationship between God, the world, and himself. In this chapter we have attempted to trace this relationship in quite a superficial way. It has been our purpose to indicate the kinds of historical influences that underlie the present convictions of most of our contemporaries.

As a teleological mode of explanation gave way to a mechanistic mode in terms of matter in motion, the concept of God as the Supreme Good was altered to that of the First Cause. Increases in mechanistic-type descriptions led to the picture of God as the Divine Clockmaker and ultimately to the deistic view of God as the vague, almost irrelevant, impulse behind the beginnings of things. The concept of a self-sufficient, law-abiding universe makes any activity of God in the present both difficult and unnecessary. Providence, becoming only preservation, finally is identified with evolutionary progress. As the gap between objective and verifiable events and the concepts of theology widens, God becomes unknown, unknowable, and, ultimately, dead.

Man once considered himself as a special creation of a personal God, placed at the center of the universe where he was the focus of attention and concern. His geometrical position was lost when astronomical investigation revealed that the earth was not the center of the universe. The depersonalization of his universe was accelerated by the evidence that the universe could be regarded as a massive complex machine. His special position as superior to the machine was lost when evolutionary theory placed him as a part of that machine. The "death" of God means that the human man has been replaced by the "man-machine" and that in a sense the human man is also dead.

In the context of teleological explanations of natural events, science and religious faith were closely related. Success in attempts to provide mechanistic explanations for natural events stimulated the effort similarly to derive religious concepts, doctrines, and ethics. Insofar as this effort was considered successful, the necessity of special revelation in religious thinking was minimized. Reason was exalted over revelation, man's ability over his basic moral dilemma. Theology was transformed into anthropology. When experience showed that the exaltation of human reason led only to disillusionment and the denial of the reality of humanity (the man-machine problem mentioned above), release was sought in separating science and religion into noninteracting, independent realms. To science was ascribed the area of objective, rational, and empirical observation and deduction; to religion was ascribed the area of subjective, irrational, and mystical experience. If science led consistently to the picture of man as a machine, then religion could be invoked to provide the basis for purpose and meaning, even if it meant that all ties with history and physical reality had to be severed to accomplish it.

The question to which we must now address ourselves in the remainder of this book is how inevitable *are* these changes in perspective? If an assessment of the interpretation of science is undertaken on the basis of all that we know today, must we be forced to these same conclusions? Or is it possible that these deplorable and hopeless conclusions are not really derived from all the evidence available but, rather, express the results of inappropriate presuppositions and the effects of imperfect interpretations? We hope to show how we can profit from the lessons of history without at the same time repeating the mistakes of the past.

Topics for Discussion

1. Are teleological and mechanistic descriptions necessarily exclusive? Discuss Matt. 5:45 from the standpoint of modern meteorology. How about James 5:17,18?

2. Discuss problems that might be encountered in the development of science in a completely atheistic context. Why should it be assumed that science is even possible?

3. How would you handle the use of anesthetics to ease pain during childbirth, or the development of methods for painless childbirth, in view of Gen. 3:16?

4. Do you think that modern scientific descriptions of natural events are revealed in the Bible? Why or why not? Suppose that the general theory of evolution were completely true; how would you rewrite Genesis 1?

5. Does Rom. 1:20,21 provide the biblical basis for the development of a natural theology?

6. Attempt to describe Creation and Providence in such a way that a clear distinction is made. What characteristics of the world are implied?

7. Do you think that Christian faith needs to have direct connection with history and the physical world? Why or why not? If your answer is yes, suggest some points of connection.

8. Is the Darwinian view of a world in dynamic process a more adequate representation than a static view of the world produced in a single fiat act? Need a fiat view lead to a static world?

9. What kind of evidence would be needed either to prove or disprove the general theory of evolution? What are the chances of getting these?

10. Have you ever had a "mountaintop" experience of religious intensity? Describe it to somebody else. Are you sure you really had it?

Chapter Three

If This Is
What Science Is Like...

These next three chapters have a common purpose.
It is, quite frankly, to suggest that although science and religion
may seem to be quite different in terms of everyday experience, they
are actually not at all mutually exclusive. In fact, if we define science
and religion broadly enough, it becomes evident that science is a
kind of religion and religion a kind of science. Such definitions may
indeed be too general to be genuinely useful, but we are so condi-
tioned to thinking of science and religion as contrary approaches to
life with nothing in common that a small amount of semantic
shock therapy may be a good thing.

Consider the following excerpt from a letter to the editor of
Physics Today. It is an example of the kind of statement heard so
often that it becomes an apparent truism.

> A science-conditioned student looks at religion, sees that it is
> founded on belief, not facts, rejects it and fails to find anything
> to fill its place. Unless he searches further and finds a philosophy
> that is, for him, scientifically acceptable, he grows up to hate
> science for emptying his existence of purpose.[1]

In order to check and to challenge the validity of this perspective,
we shall attempt to discuss in turn the nature of science, the nature
of religion and Christian faith, and the regions of overlap between
these two areas which show that the common dichotomies constructed to separate them are of only limited accuracy.

---

[1] D. J. S. Hockey, *Physics Today*, American Institute of Physics, 21, no. 5
(New York, 1968), p. 9.

Some Definitions

Consider first three terms: science, natural, and supernatural. What do we mean when we use these words?

The first meaning given in many dictionaries for the word *science* is simply *knowledge*. Though this definition is consistent with the meaning of the Latin root in the word *science*, "to know," it is not specific enough really to be helpful. Even in the most general terms, our common use of the word *science* implies at least two aspects. Science is both (a) a way of knowing, and (b) a body of knowledge derived from the systematic interpretation of facts. The dynamic nature of science is emphasized in an often-quoted definition by James B. Conant.

> Science is an interconnected series of concepts and conceptual schemes that have developed as a result of experimentation and observation and are fruitful of further experimentation and observation.[2]

Science is a way of knowing. It is a way of knowing by sense interaction with the world. There may be other ways of knowing, or there may not. This question is not settled by science, which simply asserts that everything that can be known by sense interaction with the world (seeing, hearing, feeling, smelling, tasting—and the many sophisticated ways in which machines and instruments extend these basic sense impressions) is in the domain of scientific knowledge. Some people do argue that scientific knowledge is the *only* kind of knowledge there is. This position is not derived from science, however, but is added to science on the basis of the individual's own basic presuppositions or assumptions about life. We might argue, therefore, that the assertion that scientific knowledge is the only kind of knowledge is itself a nonscientific statement and thus cannot be known!

Science is a way of knowing. This way is commonly referred to as the scientific method. Sometimes it is thought of as a rigid sequence of logical steps involving observation, hypothesis, experiment, confirmation or correction, and prediction. All of these elements do enter the exercise of the scientific method in one way

---

[2] James B. Conant, *Science and Common Sense* (New Haven: Yale University Press, 1951), p. 25.

or another, but what characterizes the scientific method is more an attitude and a frame of mind rather than an automatic process. Consider an analogy from the field of painting. The practice of science is more like the production of an original oil painting than it is like the completion of a rigidly defined paint-by-number picture. Ingredients like intuition, inspiration, frustration, and plain hard work must be included to get a reasonably accurate idea of what it means "to do science." It is also necessary to remember that science is done by people, not by machines; to say that science is being done where scientists themselves are not personally involved is probably inappropriate.

To stress the dynamic characteristics of science in the emphasis on science as a way of knowing is not to overlook the way in which the word *science* is used to refer to a body of knowledge obtained as a result of applying this way of knowing to the world. Still, it would probably not be appropriate to think of a scientific library, with all its accumulation of journals, books, and manuscripts, as *containing* science. Such a library contains the records of science, the results of science, the words of scientists, but the scientist feels instinctively that science itself is a living activity, not a static repository. If science is also to be a body of knowledge, it is a dynamic, almost existential body of knowledge, based on the investigations of the past but changing and being shaped anew with each passing moment.

Because science is a way of knowing on the basis of sense interactions with the world, its descriptions are in terms of natural categories. To expect science to give a supernatural description would involve a contradiction in definitions. Before we can unambiguously use these words *natural* and *supernatural*, we must give some thought to the ways in which they are used.

There are two possible ways of looking at these words: (a) operationally in relation to the scientific enterprise, and (b) interpretationally in relation to the significance of an event. In an operational sense, we may define *natural* as describing an event or an observation that can be represented in terms of known scientific understanding. A natural event is one that occurs in accordance with known scientific mechanisms. In this same operational sense, *supernatural* may then be defined as describing an event or an observation that cannot be treated in terms of known scientific understanding.

A supernatural event is one that occurs through a mechanism which cannot be described by known science.

In the interpretational sense, a natural explanation is one that involves only scientific mechanisms and categories and does not attempt to relate the event to God. In this sense, a supernatural explanation is one that seeks to set forth the significance of the event in terms of its relationship to God.

When used in these ways, which I believe are consistent with ordinary practice and common experience, the terms *natural* and *supernatural* are not necessarily exclusive of one another. A natural event in an operational sense, for example, the beginning of rain at the end of a drought, certainly has a natural explanation in an interpretational sense, that is, pressure and temperature changes in moving air masses. But it may also have a supernatural explanation in an interpretational sense, as God's answer to prayer by his people in need. A supernatural event in an operational sense, for instance, a case of psychosomatic healing in biblical times, may well have a natural explanation which is unknown to the contemporaries, and a supernatural explanation as well, in this case God's healing power in response to faith. In an ultimate sense every event has both a natural and a supernatural explanation, although one or both of these may not be known or understood at the time. Considerations of this kind bring us back once more to thesis 2 of chapter 1, which proposes that to be complete a description (explanation) must be made on many different levels.

The Purpose of Science

What is science for? Often we can understand the nature of something better if we understand what it is really supposed to do. We saw in chapter 2 that, early in the development of science, descriptions of natural phenomena were teleological in nature; in seeking to answer questions asked, they assumed a basic purpose to the universe. When experimental and analytical science became established, the nature of the questions asked changed and the conception of the basic purpose of a scientific investigation also changed. "Why" questions became "how" questions. It was recognized implicitly that sense interactions with the world were not going to provide the answers to "why" questions in any ultimate sense (for example, Why is there a world? Why am I here? Why does an electron have a charge?) but that this methodology was adequate for answering "how" questions in terms of scientific mechanisms (friction, gravity, electromagnetic fields, evolution and the like).

The purpose of science, as understood for the last several hundred years, therefore, is to *describe* the natural world. It is the goal of science to develop that combination of scientific mechanisms that will permit a description of a given phenomenon with sufficient accuracy to give reasonable agreement between the theoretical description and actual measurements. The scientific description of a pendulum, for example, involves a given mass acted upon by gravity, constrained to remain at a fixed distance from a point, the motion of the pendulum resulting in friction at this point. Science produces a conceptual construction of its own that is satisfactory as long as it adequately describes measured phenomena in the natural world.

There are, of course, underlying motives for the drive of science to describe the world. Efforts to produce such description are motivated by a desire to obtain a more complete *understanding* of the world and a desire to be better able to *control* the phenomena that interact with our lives. The more completely a description fits the observable events of the world around us, the closer it brings us to an understanding of what the world is probably really like. The better we are able to control the phenomena that affect our lives, the more likely we are to improve the quality of life and its potentialities for expression and fulfillment.

Both of these motivating aspects for science have religious roots. When the world is viewed as the creation of God, the understanding of the world becomes the understanding of God's work, and hence by implication, of certain aspects of God himself. To understand the world is one of the basic steps in fulfilling the role ascribed to man in the Genesis account.

> And God blessed them, and God said to them, "Be fruitful and multiply, and fill the earth and subdue it; and have dominion over the fish of the sea and over the birds of the air and over every living thing that moves upon the earth" (Gen. 1:28).

Therefore to do science becomes an honorable activity, even a sacred responsibility. But, as the Bible never separates knowledge from life, so also in this case the understanding is to be in order to control for the welfare of all creation. The term *control* sometimes rings falsely on modern ears; it sounds too much like *manipulate* in a cold, calculating and impersonal way. This should not be the case. When we heal disease, when we fertilize fields, when we make traffic laws, we are in the process of controlling the world. *Control* in a religious sense can be translated into *service*. There are human needs in the world; in the act of serving the world by meeting these needs, it becomes necessary for science to learn to control the world. The power to control carries with it a great responsibility. Anyone who interprets the words *subdue* and *have dominion* from the Genesis record above in a selfish or exploitive sense has not grasped the divinely given responsibility to care for the world and to safeguard it as a loan from God himself.

Faith and Science

The doing of science is based upon a certain faith with respect to the world. Like all faith, this faith underlying scientific activity is not derived by logical deduction from any prior considerations, but still is essential for the very doing of science. The successes of science may strengthen one's conviction that this faith is well grounded, but they do not remove it from the area of presuppositions accepted without proof.

The impact of this faith can perhaps be more completely appreciated if viewed in the following way. The complaint is frequently leveled against the religious perspective that if one wants to check the truth of a statement in science, all one has to do is perform a suitable experiment; on the other hand, if one wants to check the truth of a religious statement, there is nothing one can do except to accept it blindly in faith. For example, it is argued, what objective test can be proposed for the existence of God? By contrast, the existence of gravity, electrostatic attraction, optical interference, electronic charges, and the like, can all be shown by an appropriate experiment that is able to settle the question once and for all. This claim itself might be debated, but let us grant it. The problem in this comparison is that one must ask a comparable question in science before one sees the inescapable faith foundation. If the question "Does God exist?" is our sample question from religious thought, the analogous question in science does not deal with incidental concepts within science. The analogous question in science must be, "Is science possible?"

The basic faith that science is possible is of course a prerequisite for the doing of science. What it means to accept in faith that science is possible might be elucidated in a variety of different ways. One way of enumerating the presuppositions that underlie science is to say that

1. The universe can be understood by a rational process.
2. Patterns of order can be discerned in the universe.
3. Phenomena observed here and now are also valid there and then.
4. Conceptualizations of the human mind are suitable for the description of the universe.

Each of these propositions must be assumed before it can be assumed that science is possible. Science itself provides no a priori basis for their assumption. They are accepted in faith, and the scientist proceeds on the basis of them to construct a description of the world. But, it may be objected, the scientist knows that these faith assumptions are justified because his experience on the basis of them provides a consistent picture. But then is not the same kind of answer valid for the Christian?—I know that my faith assumptions are justified because of my experience on the basis of them. We may also note that the Christian teaching of God the Creator and of man as made in the image of the Creator provides a rational, integrated basis for the four ingredients of scientific faith cited above. It might be argued, therefore, that the scientific faith includes many of the ingredients of Christian faith, except for the fact that the scientist as such does not explicitly realize that God is the foundation for science to be possible.

Adjectives Describing Science

Our discussion about what science is like can be helped at this point by considering briefly the applicability of eight different adjectives which describe aspects of science and its limitations. They are each the completion of the sentence, "Science is . . . "

Natural. Every scientific investigation intends to discover some natural mechanism for the phenomenon of interest. A scientific description of an event must be in terms of natural categories. Unless the phenomena are susceptible to detection by the senses (aided or unaided), they cannot be investigated by science. If there is a supernatural realm, science can never detect anything about it except for effects in the natural world caused by interaction with the supernatural. Supernatural descriptions or explanations are ruled out of science by definition, not because of the lack of faith of scientists.

Limited. Science is an activity of human beings. Human beings are finite, temporal, and of restricted experience. The growth of science is correlated with the overcoming of many of the limitations on human beings. Still, in any ultimate sense, science is limited experimentally by the ingenuity of human beings and theoretically by the ability of human beings to conceptualize beyond their experience.

Not self-interpreting. Science is derived from the facts of experience by the process of human interpretation. One definition of science might be that it is a human interpretation of the facts of the universe. Although the equations, laws, and theories of science are based on experimental data (that is, upon facts), the interpretations of scientists (that is, science) are based upon the ideas of men. No fact is self-interpreting. Facts never speak for themselves. Each fact that a scientist establishes must be interpreted by him in accordance with his presuppositions and contextual perspective at that moment. Indeed, every experiment is already designed and planned on the basis of certain theoretical presuppositions which to some extent predetermine both the outcome and the interpretation of the experiment. *Good* science seeks to minimize these presuppositional effects; *real* science cannot exist without them.

Statistical. Many of the phenomena with which science is concerned have such a large number of complex constituents that it proves practically impossible to take individual account of each constituent. Still, it proves possible to describe the collective effects of all such constituents by a statistical averaging process. It would be practically impossible to describe individually the motions of the 10^{22} atoms per cubic centimeter that exist in a gas, but their average collective action in terms of pressure can be readily and accurately described. Life insurance companies manage to maintain financial solvency by predicting accurately the average life expectancy of human beings of a given age, sex, and culture, even though they would be completely unable to predict accurately the life expectancy of any particular individual person. Election predictions and opinion polls maintain a respectable record of accuracy by testing a selected sample and projecting these results on the national level, even though the specific vote of no particular individual is known. Scientific descriptions then are statistical for two reasons. There are situations where in principle a completely exact description could be given except for the overwhelming number of constituents involved but practically we are ignorant of the facts. In other situations the phenomenon itself is intrinsically probabilistic. In modern physics, for example, at the atomic level, the description of the motion of atomic particles must be done in terms of probability distributions and not in terms of exactly known positions and velocities. The present state of quantum theory treats this situation as intrinsic to the characteristics of matter on the atomic level. In an assemblage of 10^{19} radioactively decaying atoms, the time required for half of the atoms to decay can be exceedingly accurately measured, even though it is completely unknowable when any particular atom will decay.

Pragmatic. The test of scientific truth is the ability of a scientific description to conform to experimental measurements and observations, performed to check the description and its predictions. The fact that scientific truth is constantly changing, that what is true today may be false tomorrow, causes no embarrassment or confusion once it is realized that the criterion for scientific truth is primarily a pragmatic one. Nor does this recognition in any way minimize or depreciate the significance of scientific truth. It merely emphasizes the difference between scientific truth and absolute truth and warns against the fallacy that scientific truth is simply translatable into absolute truth. Of course, if scientific truth is the only truth, then there is no absolute truth at all. But once again we can note that the statement that scientific truth is the only truth is not scientifically derived. To be consistent in our reasoning it must therefore be false.

For the same kind of reasons, a *good* scientific description is one that works, that is, one that conforms to experimental measurements. A *bad* scientific description is one that does not work, that is, one that does not conform to experimental measurements. As long as *good* and *bad* are pragmatic terms, then no more problem is encountered with this description than with the description of scientific truth above. If, however, either a conscious or unconscious shift is made from pragmatic good and bad to ethical or prescriptive good and bad, note what happens. Since a pragmatically good description conforms to experimental measurements, it is fallaciously concluded that experimental measurements, that is, the way things are, prescribe how things *ought* to be. This is the basis for the common scientific approach to ethics: what is, is good. It is the result of an unconscious or deliberate transformation from a pragmatic to a prescriptive good without taking note of this shift.

A *human endeavor.* Activities which involve planning and interpretation by human beings are bound to be subjectively influenced in some way. Science is not an objective mechanical process unaffected by subjective presuppositions and perspectives of the scientist. Rather, it shows in some way the effect of his prejudices, training, conditions, and predisposition toward the problem. The interaction between the scientist and the experiment received graphic emphasis even in physics when the indeterminancy principle in modern physics emphasized the impossibility of obtaining some information about an atomic system without destroying other complementary information. If this kind of consideration is essential in the highly quantified and controlled areas of physics, how much more is it likely to be essential in the less rigorous, person-oriented sciences of psychology and sociology. There are many experiments that cannot be attempted with persons without dramatically affecting either their response or their subsequent position. There is the story of a man who was recovering from a very serious operation and who was under strict doctor's orders not to sit up under any circumstances. A friend who was not aware of the seriousness of the situation came to visit him. Walking into the room, he called out, "Well, how are you?" Delighted to see him, his friend sat up in bed, said, "Fine," and died.

Incomplete. A complete understanding of anything is strictly impossible. Certainly this is true of a scientific understanding, which is openly partial, changing, and fragmentary. It is possible to have reasonably complete scientific descriptions of certain diverse phenomena in terms of a more general construct. The claim, however, that a strictly complete understanding was at hand would require as thorough an understanding of this general construct in terms of more general constructs, and so on. It is possible to say that we understand the motion of the planets reasonably well in terms of the law of gravity, but a claim that this represents any kind of complete understanding has to reckon with the fact that we have only a vague notion of what gravity itself is.

Relative. The best available scientific descriptions we have of the world may be such gross approximations to the actual situation that we are seriously mistaken in believing them to be a faithful representation of reality. The scientist can only tell what the world may be like, not what it "really is."

The Scientific Model

A basic presupposition of our discussion is that there is such a thing as ultimate reality. We define ultimate reality as that which is. Similarly, we define truth as that which conforms exactly to ultimate reality, to that which is. This is an absolute definition of truth, quite different from that of scientific truth. Since a scientific description is an attempt to picture certain aspects of ultimate reality in terms of natural categories, scientific truth is always only an approximation to truth.

The real world is usually too complicated for the scientist to tackle directly. In order to treat any problem theoretically, he simplifies the problem by constructing a conceptual model drawn from the categories of his experience so that he may apply human concepts, methods, and mathematics to the solution of the problem. A model represents an actual situation and contains, it is hoped, the most important features of the real situation. Nonetheless, it omits many factors that are believed to be insignificant or that are unknown to the scientist. The value of such a model is judged by its ability to permit a description of the phenomenon that will agree with experimental data already available and to predict values for data that may be measured in the future, particularly those kinds of data not used in the formulation of the model in the first place. It is in the measurements that produce these data that the scientist is able to make contact with the real world. The legitimately measured data provide the checks on his model by comparison with the real world. (Of course, in certain scientific disciplines, it may be more appropriate to replace the words *experiment* and *measure* by *search* and *observe*.)

Models frequently increase in sophistication and in diversity from common experiential concepts as experimentation more clearly reveals the structure of the real world. The conceptual model for matter starts with a continuity-of-substance idea in direct agreement with our everyday experience of the impenetrability of matter. Then there are the particle models of matter involving molecules or atoms as small hard balls. Structure inside the atom is modeled as a miniature solar system with electrons traveling in orbits around the nucleus like planets around the sun. Finally, the model for the atom and its constituents becomes that of a wavelike system in which everyday concepts of position and velocity take on new and unexpected properties. Each of the more sophisticated models is capable of describing and predicting the properties which led to the simpler models. In actual practice all of these models are invoked in some measure even today, depending upon the actual aspect of the real world of major concern. For example, it is much more useful for a scientist interested in the strength of materials under stress to think in terms of a continuity-of-substance model to which he can apply the mathematics of continuum mechanics than it would be to think in terms of the details of the wave picture and quantum mechanics.

Although it is recognized that each model the scientist constructs is only a partial representation of the real world, it is a matter of faith—a reasonable assumption—that the more closely and comprehensively a model accounts for or predicts the results of a wide variety of experiments, the more likely it is that the principal features of the model have some correspondence to the principal features of the real world. Thus the scientist believes that, in spite of all the limitations we have discussed and in spite of the necessity to be constantly approximating reality through conceptual models, he is growing in a partial understanding of what ultimate reality is like insofar as such understanding can be described in natural categories.

Philosophical Attitudes Toward Science

The questions about what science is good for are hardly new. Because they are old questions, there have been a number of attempts to answer them in different ways from different historical positions and presuppositions. Since "science" as a concept may mean something quite different to various people, I have attempted to summarize these possible philosophical attitudes, with a personal evaluation, in figure 4. Anticipating our discussion in the following chapter on what religious faith is like, I have also included in figure 4 a sequence of closely related philosophical attitudes toward theology. The point of similarity is that, as science is the result of an interpretation of the scientific data (that is, the natural world), so Christian theology is the result of an interpretation of the revelational data (that is, the Bible).

Empiricists or *positivists* argue that science consists simply of the ordering and arrangement of sense data, with no correlation between this activity and the real world—a concept which is considered essentially irrelevant. Such an extreme position underestimates the theoretical side of scientific activity, the contribution of the scientist's creative ingenuity, and the significance of the scientist's presuppositions.

Idealists argue that the concepts and descriptions of science are purely subjective, being the creations of the mind rather than an objective description of the natural world itself. This extreme position underestimates the experimental side of scientific activity, the necessity of correspondence with experimental data.

Operationalists insist that the most important question is not "What is the meaning of a scientific statement?" as though the statement really had cognitive significance for the real world, but instead, "How is that scientific statement being used?" Thus, in an extreme position, the operationalist denies that science can lead to *any* knowledge. Gordon H. Clark writes,

> Operationalism identifies the purpose of science not as description but as manipulation. Laws are not cognitive statements about na-

Figure 4

PHILOSOPHICAL ATTITUDES TOWARD SCIENCE AND CHRISTIAN THEOLOGY

	Science	Christian Theology
EMPIRICISM	Knowledge consists only of isolated facts collected and assembled by the individual, who makes no contribution to them subjectively.	Knowledge consists only of isolated Bible passages collected and assembled by the individual, who makes no contribution to them subjectively.
	Ignores the interpretation that is intimately related to the search for and the appropriation of facts.	
IDEALISM	Knowledge is shaped by the constructs of the mind so that one can never have any assurance that the ideas of one's mind have any correlation to reality. Personal beliefs are independent of facts.	Knowledge is shaped by the constructs of the mind so that no interpretation of the Bible can be thought to have any authoritative value. Faith is independent of facts.
	Ignores the facts (whether natural or historical) which ultimately constrain any subjective interpretation.	
OPERATIONALISM	Words are used not to describe what is, but to prescribe a role of action. Statements about scientific reality are in truth only recipes for activity in the laboratory.	Words are used not to describe spiritual reality, but to indicate a style of life commitment. Statements about God are in truth only personal confessions of a life style.
	Ignores the necessary connection between words and that reality which influences which choice of words is adequate and useful.	
REALISM	The scientific method is a viable tool for coming to understand the nature of reality. Scientific findings and laws are directly related to the way things really are.	It is possible by interpreting the Bible (hermeneutics) to come to understand the full nature of spiritual reality. Statements about God and His dealings may be treated as literal statements of truth.
	Ignores the limitations that the human mind and human method imposes upon any attempt to describe or understand in a complete sense the nature of reality.	
CRITICAL REALISM	The scientific method is a viable tool for arriving at a limited and partial understanding of the nature of reality, incomplete and always changing, but increasing in its ability to describe what really is.	The interpretation of the Bible in order to arrive at the basic purpose behind the writings is a viable approach for arriving at a limited and partial understanding of God and His purpose. Although it is limited and partial, yet because it comes from God, it is sufficient.
	My choice.	

ture, but are directions for operating in a laboratory. They do not say what nature has done; they say what the scientists should do . . . . With or without a priori concepts, science is not a cognitive enterprise.[3]

This position underestimates the capabilities of science, the bona fide potentiality that science has of providing approximate knowledge, but definitely knowledge nevertheless. To say that science can lead to *no* knowledge is as wide of the mark as to say that science can lead to *all* knowledge.

Realists argue that science is a valid approach to finding out exactly what the real world is like. The constantly changing nature of scientific description and the inherent limitations of human experimental and theoretical capabilities make such an interpretation seem unacceptable.

Finally there is the position of what might be called *critical realism* (I would call it Christian realism). This position fully integrates the limitations and the potentialities of science. It recognizes that the scientific enterprise is limited by the finiteness of the human element and thereby recognizes that a scientific description must always be an approximate description. Critical realism recognizes that science must describe in terms of natural categories and thereby by definition excludes large areas of life and experience from its legitimate domain. It recognizes that science can never achieve the perfect understanding of the natural world that would be properly described as having attained the truth. But it also recognizes that science is a legitimate enterprise for establishing knowledge about the natural world in terms of natural categories and that this description comes progressively closer to a reliable description of the working of the natural world as science advances. Critical (Christian) realism thus acclaims science as a worthwhile endeavor in understanding the created order as well as in controlling it, affirms the mandate of Genesis to man to have dominion over the world, and prevents the profession of science from degenerating into a mere practice of technology.

---

[3] *The Philosophy of Gordon H. Clark*, ed. Ronald H. Nash (Philadelphia: Presbyterian and Reformed Publishing Co., 1968), p. 42.

Summary

Understanding what science is like should take away some of the aura of mechanical infallibility that is so often popularly associated with it. Understanding what science is like should also make it impossible to dismiss it casually as having no relevance for an understanding of what the world is really like. Understanding what science is like should show what strong common elements are shared with other aspects of life, including the practice of religious faith.

Although science is a way of knowing and a way of arriving at an approximate description of truth, it cannot be meaningfully asserted that science is the only way of knowing and the only way of arriving at truth. Such assertions cannot be derived from science. To be consistent to the same framework, therefore, they must be either false or statements of personal faith.

The purpose of science is to describe the world in natural categories in order to make possible a more complete understanding of the world and a more effective control of its resources. The presuppositions that make science possible are not derivable from the scientific enterprise itself; they are, however, a direct consequence of the Judeo-Christian biblical world view. It is no more possible to do science without the faith that a rational understanding of the world is a possible goal for finite human minds than it is to enter into religion without the faith that God exists. The faith statements of science are of the same kind as the faith statements of Christianity, except that the scientist may be unaware that the validity of his faith statements rests upon the Being of God.

In order to understand the kind of descriptions provided by science, the concept of a scientific model must be appreciated. A model is a picture or representation constructed by the scientist on the basis of his knowledge and experience in order to match the results of his observations or experiments. Models may be very simple or extremely sophisticated. The more comprehensively a given model can describe observed phenomena and the more successfully a given model can predict new results that are later confirmed by observation or experiment, the more adequately it is supposed that the model depicts the details of ultimate reality. The most comprehensive model is not always the most useful model for a particular application, and even the most successful model may still fall far short of describing the depth and richness of phenomena in the real world.

Philosophical attitudes toward science range over the whole spectrum. That attitude called critical or Christian realism is advanced as the most adequate way of looking at science. It involves an appreciation for the wide capabilities and potentialities of science in obtaining a reliable description and partial understanding of a portion of experience. At the same time it recognizes the limitations of science and the intrinsic necessity for science to produce descriptions in terms of natural categories only.

Topics for Discussion

1. Do you accept the idea that science is a kind of religion? If so, what plays the role of (a) deity, (b) worship, (c) prayer, (d) revelation, and (e) sacrifice?

2. Discuss science as a way of knowing. Discuss also the problem of knowing whether or not another person loves you. Can you solve this problem scientifically? If not, how do you solve it?

3. Describe the crossing of the Red Sea by the Israelites (Exod. 14:21-29) in terms of possible natural and supernatural descriptions and explanations. Do the same for the curing of the blind man in John 9.

4. Discuss the relevance of Gen. 1:28 to modern concerns about ecological exploitation and pollution of natural resources.

5. Do you think that it is possible to describe scientifically why a light bulb works? Try it, being careful to press your description back as far as you can to basic and elementary concepts. What do you end up with?

6. Is it possible to rationalize the exercise of scientific faith by an atheist?

7. If a scientist attempts to describe an experience of personal spiritual faith in a scientific manner, what kind of description will he come up with?

8. Consider the fact "I exist." Use this fact to explore the implications of the assertion that no fact is self-interpreting.

9. Consider this statement: "Before the times of Galileo and

Copernicus, it was scientifically true that the sun went around the earth." Discuss the validity of this statement in the light of the definition of scientific truth.

10. Consider this statement: "Most young people today have premarital sex; since this is the normal course of events, we ought to revise older, out-of-date notions of chastity." How much of this statement is in the realm of science (or might be if the facts were as stated)? What is the basis for the "ought" suggestion?

11. Discuss TV reporting of election returns in terms of a measurement that can seriously affect the outcome of the experiment. Is it possible that the outcome of the election might have been different if pre-election opinion polls and TV election return reporting had not been made public?

12. One model for ice would be that of an extended hard and impenetrable matter (as one experiences by falling while ice-skating). Another model for ice would be that of atoms arranged in an orderly array in such a way that most of the ice was "empty" space. Think of several occupations or applications of ice that would favor one or the other of these models.

13. Which of the philosophical attitudes cited comes closest to your own intuitive feeling about science?

Chapter Four

... And If This Is What Christian Faith Is Like...

Evidence of a religious consciousness is as old as the human race. Indeed, one of the criteria used by anthropologists for deciding the "humanity" of prehistoric creatures is to determine whether or not they took care to bury their dead in the expectation of a life after death. A man may escape reasonably completely from having a scientific view of life, but he can hardly escape from having a religious view of life. To speak of the religious element in life is to speak most generally of those ingredients of life that deal with the ultimate concerns of human existence. Though a man may argue that life is essentially meaningless, this viewpoint itself is a religious perspective of his life as long as he maintains his humanity. Even the man who stoutly maintains that there is no God is taking part in a religious activity. Only by denying his own humanity, only by accepting himself completely as only an animal or only a machine, can a man escape from religious experience. Perhaps this use of the word "religious" bothers the reader, because it is too general. Perhaps it is time for this chapter's definitions.

Some Definitions

What is "religious faith?" Let us first attempt a general definition that will reveal the essential characteristics of religious faith before we become more specific and consider the meaning of Christian faith.

Religious faith involves at least three ingredients and a general area of relevance. Religious faith requires belief, trust, and commitment, in an area that deals with matters of ultimate concern.

Belief is concerned primarily with matters of knowledge. No religious faith can exist in the complete absence of facts, interpretations of facts, teachings, doctrines, creeds, statements, perspectives, or dogmas. The importance of the belief ingredient in religious faith may be minimal, as in a religious perspective in which belief in a Supreme Power is the only thing that can be verbalized, or it may be extensive, as in a religious perspective with lengthy written creeds and doctrinal expositions.

Belief can be a wholly intellectual activity. To speak of trust in religious faith is to emphasize a response to the items of belief with the whole person. Not only does one believe certain things, but these things *matter*. They are of utmost significance for the understanding of life and the appreciation of its problems. They are worthy of being trusted as guides to fulfillment and meaning.

The final step in religious faith is to commit oneself to the items of belief and trust that form the religious perspective. It is not sufficient only to believe and accept wholeheartedly; it is necessary to throw oneself after one's beliefs, to prove one's trust by putting one's life on the line. To commit oneself is to be transformed from the passive to the active, from the spectator to the participant, from the disengaged to the completely involved.

The area which religious faith treats is the the area of meaning, purpose, depth, significance, and concern. Sometimes an individual can delineate the shape of his religious faith by asking himself the question, "What means enough for me to die for it?" Some people would die in the effort to save their material possessions. They believe that material things are ultimately significant, they trust these things to provide security and happiness, and they commit themselves to the possession and maintenance of these things. To such people material possessions are the items of ultimate concern in their life; in a sense, material possessions play the role of God in their perspective on life.

Other items of ultimate concern may shape the religious faith in other circumstances. Financial success, personal fame, public recognition and praise, power and political authority, a beloved animal or person, national patriotism, a radical cause, or a social ideal may all play the role of God in an individual's perspective on life. Religious faith is exercised in communism, Maoism, Nazism, Americanism, socialism, capitalism, and the Revolution, the more so as one of these ideologies is given the principal position in defining meaning for one's life.

Sometimes the question "What means enough for me to die for it?" can be helpfully replaced by the question "What means enough for me to live for it?" There are many circumstances where to live for a concern of religious faith is more difficult than to die for it. The event of dying for one's faith carries with it the conviction and glory of martyrdom whereas the daily living for one's faith in spite of trivial and undramatic inconsistencies and failures has none of this glamor.

A third question that might be asked to help determine the area of ultimate concern in an individual's life is, "What could I lose from my life without losing the meaning of my life?" That area which, if lost, would deprive life of meaning is certain to be a focal point of religious faith for an individual.

On the basis of the definition of religious faith discussed here, it can be concluded that there are no atheists in the world, no people without some kind of religious faith. But the reader may object that this is a small victory in view of the extremely generalized definition of religious faith we have proposed. The point of the discussion, however, is this: we do not have the option of choosing between having a religious faith and not having one; every man must choose some kind of religious faith in order to be a man. The man who rejects the God of the Bible in favor of the god of communism or capitalism has not made a wiser choice by basing his decision on fact rather than on fancy. He too has his faith presuppositions that cannot be derived or proved; he too adds trust and commitment to belief in the development of his own personal religious position.

Theology

When we begin to compare science and Christian faith, we ought to realize what the comparable ingredients in each area really are. For example, we ought to compare scientific *faith* with Christian faith, or we ought to compare science with theology. Science is a way of knowing and a dynamic body of knowledge derived from an interpretation of the natural world according to the scientific methodology, as we discussed in chapter 3. Theology is the way of knowing and the dynamic body of knowledge derived from an interpretation of the appropriate data for the theological methodology.

Theology is a way of knowing. There are in general two sources for theological knowledge: revelation and experience. As science is an interpretation of observations and experiments in the natural world, so theology is an interpretation of revelation and experience. Each discipline attempts to construct a unified perspective consistent with its methodology and purpose.

Revelation plays the role in theology of knowledge gained by personal communication. This is by no means a unique method of obtaining knowledge, since most of an individual scientist's knowledge has been acquired in the same way. The correspondence could be stretched still further by considering the natural world also as a revelation provided to the scientist, since he plays no role in its existence and yet accepts it as wholly reliable.

In theology, as in science, the interpretation of revelation is guided by experience, and the interpretation of experience is guided by revelation. Whenever a glaring conflict is apparent between an interpretation of revelation and an interpretation of experience, the theologian stops to examine which interpretation is in error. The scientist accepts the natural world as wholly reliable even when his interpretations of it are faulty and lead him into problems; the theologian accepts revelation as wholly reliable even when his interpretations of it are faulty and lead him into problems. Conflicts between science and theology arise when the scientist attempts to make his interpretations of his revelation (the natural world) preeminent over the theologian's interpretations of his revelation (sacred writings), or when the theologian attempts the reverse procedure. Aggravated grounds for conflict arise when scientist or theologian seeks to deny the validity of the other's source of revelation, that is, when the scientist denies that the theologian's sacred writings are genuinely revelatory, and the theologian denies that the scientist's natural world is genuinely revelatory.

Theology is also a body of knowledge, perhaps to a somewhat greater extent than this same description could be applied to science. Theological libraries, treatises, books, and journals contain correlated interpretations of revelation and experience of the past; therefore by our definition they contain theology. But like science, theology as a body of knowledge is also dynamically responsive to the needs and the concerns of the day. Now more than ever a correlation is being sought between the interpretations of revelation and past experience and the application of these interpretations to present living.

The Christian Faith

We have talked long enough in the preceding pages in generalities about religion and theology. Everything that has been said is true also of Christian faith and Christian theology, but we need now to outline the distinctives of the Christian position.

Creation. The God of whom the Christian speaks is the Maker of heaven and earth. The God who loves is identified with the God who creates. Thus is established at the beginning the relationship between the God of religious faith and the God of physical reality.

If God is the Creator of heaven and earth, out of what did he create it? There are three formal possibilities: (1) he created it out of preexistent matter, (2) he created it out of himself, or (3) he created it freely, neither out of preexistent matter nor out of himself. The traditional Christian doctrine that God created the world "out of nothing" is an affirmation of the last of these possibilities in order to deny the errors considered to be intrinsic to the first two possibilities. In maintaining that God did not create the world out of preexistent matter, Christian theology argues against the possibility of dualism, that is, that there is more than one ultimate basis for the world. It rejected the idea that creation meant the imposition of form on eternal matter, and it rejected the possibility that good and evil are coeternal characteristics of reality. The monotheism of the biblical revelation leaves no room for such manifestations of dualism. In maintaining that God did not create the world out of himself, Christian theology argues against the concept of pantheism, that is, that the created world is intrinsically divine, or that the sum total of the universe is identical with God.

To identify God as the Maker of heaven and earth is to emphasize his transcendence over the natural order, his immanence in the natural order, and his complete freedom of action. Because he is the Creator, his mode of existence is of necessity different from that of the finite spatio-temporal universe he makes, as well as being distinct from that of the universe. Because the universe is sustained moment by moment only by the continuing creative power of God, he is present in the natural order in the most profound sense. Because he is constrained neither by matter nor by any other power, he is free to act in accordance with his will.

Because God is the Maker of the universe, the universe is intrinsically good. This affirmation leads to several deeply significant conclusions. First, it provides a basis for the scientist's presupposition that the world is indeed understandable by rational processes. Since the world is the product of divine wisdom and since man himself is also a creature brought into being by that same divine wisdom, it follows that the world itself is orderly and capable of being understood and that this process of understanding is a worthy enterprise for man. Second, it means that, in spite of the uncertainties and contingencies of finite human existence, still it is possible to maintain that such existence has the possibility of ultimate meaning, the more so as it is related to the divine purpose which underlies the creation and sustaining of the universe. Third, it declares that evil is not a necessary ingredient in the world but that it is an aberration on a good creation, an intruder into a world in which evil is intrinsically an outsider. Finally, it affirms that the very real evil of daily existence can be overcome and that man can be brought by the power of God to the realization of his potentialities as a creature made in the image of God.[1]

Revelation. The God who made heaven and earth has not withdrawn himself from it. The biblical picture for the act of creating involves the speaking of a word by God, and the biblical picture for

---

[1] These themes are developed in detail in Langdon Gilkey, *Maker of Heaven and Earth: The Christian Doctrine of Creation in the Light of Modern Knowledge* (Garden City, N.Y.: Doubleday, Anchor Books, 1965).

the act of sustaining the world involves this same figure. God makes himself known to men through the revelation that he gives in the natural world, the events of history and their interpretations by prophets and apostles, and supremely in the person of Jesus Christ. The most significant record of this revelation for the Christian is that collection of books, biographies, poetry, and letters known as the Bible. This remarkable collection of writings, gathered and guarded by men who had experienced God in their lives, carries self-authenticating authority.

Thus the Christian contends that God has not left man alone in the world, without a witness to the character and will of God, but that God has spoken and continues to speak today through the words of the Bible and the lives of those who have committed themselves to him in Jesus Christ.

Evil. The Christian sees real evil in the world, and he also sees man as a participant in this evil because of his rejection of God and his exaltation of his own self-interest in an idolatrous act. Thus, although the mystery of the existence of evil in an intrinsically good universe remains ultimately just that, a mystery, the responsibility and potentialities for each man here and now are clearly set forth. Because evil and suffering in the world are not a necessary or proper aspect of reality, opposition to these forces is in accord with the divine will. The dimensions of the problem of evil encompass moral responsibility on the part of man and are not simply inevitable consequences of man's metaphysical situation.

Redemption. Because of man's self-idolatry, he has separated himself from God and is in effective rebellion against God in the ordering of his life and goals. The power to overcome this separation and to restore man to the position he holds as a creature made in the image of God is not something that man can call up for himself. It is something, however, that God has done for man. God has shown his love for man by acting on man's behalf. What God has done is to become incarnate in Jesus of Nazareth, called Jesus Christ because of his unique identity as the Son of God. In the person of Jesus Christ, God himself made it possible for the separation between man and God to be ended, the idolatry of man to be forgiven, and the creation-ordained relationship to be reestablished. As men accept for themselves the finished work of Jesus

Christ and commit themselves to him, they enter into the new life of a restored and forgiven relationship with God.

How this work of redemption was accomplished through the life, death, and resurrection of Jesus Christ remains a marvel that has depths no man can reach. The authors of the Bible used many different approaches to attempt to spell out the significance of this work. They spoke of salvation because the work of Christ brings healing to a spiritually sick man; they spoke of redemption because the work of Christ is like buying an enslaved man from slavery in order to set him free in new life; they spoke of reconciliation because the personal relationship between estranged man and God was reestablished; they spoke of victory because the resurrection of Jesus is the sign of the ultimate victory over the power of evil and death; and they spoke of sacrifice because Christ laid down his own life willingly in a demonstration of love that was both unique and an example to those who would follow him.

The work of redemption has significance for the individual in his own life here and now. The Christian looks in faith for a final redemption as well, in which the aberration of evil and suffering that infects the present world will be cast off and the healing work begun in Christ and carried on in the lives of Christians will be completed in the fulfillment of the creation purpose.

Our brief summary of aspects of Christian faith in terms of the categories of creation, revelation, evil, and redemption may be considered as the basic presuppositions of the Christian faith, similar to the presuppositions of the scientific faith discussed in chapter 3.

We may also see how the Christian faith fulfills the requirements of general religious faith, as set forth in the first section of this chapter.

The belief elements of the Christian faith include at least belief in God who creates, preserves, and redeems; in a revelation from God available in the Bible; in the rebellion of human nature against God with the result of a separation existing between man and God; in the incarnation of God in Jesus Christ; in the work of redemption achieved through the life, death, and resurrection of Christ, and appropriated by the individual through faith in Christ; in a life lived under commitment to God in Christ as Lord and Savior;

and in a future state of existence with God. Such belief elements are summarized in the creeds of Christianity and are expounded at greater length in various church confessional statements.

Simple intellectual assent to these belief statements, however, does not constitute Christian faith. Christian faith is based not only, or not even primarily, on faith *that* . . . ; it is based rather on trust and commitment *in* and *to a Person*—God in and through Jesus Christ. The only security in the Christian faith stems from the fact that God is trustworthy, that a man who commits himself to Jesus Christ, accepting him as Lord of his life, enters into a new personal relationship with the living Christ. The vitality of the Christian faith arises from the power derived from this new personal relationship which informs and transforms every aspect of life. A living Christian faith without a changed and committed Christian life is a contradiction in terms.

The Purpose of Religious Faith

What is Christian faith supposed to do? What are its goals and purposes? Understanding of the purpose of Christian faith must start with the realization that Christian faith is *not* a way to get something. As long as it is considered a mechanism or a technique, its real purpose will not be realized.

Quite simply, the purpose of Christian faith is to *restore broken relationships between persons*. Broken relationships characterize the human dilemma: broken relationships between man and God, between man and woman, between white and black, between brother and sister, between this man and that man, between you and me, between me and myself. From these broken relationships flow the estrangement, the alienation, the hysterical attempts at self-authentication, the insecurity, and the apparent intrinsic meaninglessness of the human situation. No amount of technology and scientific achievement fully meets these needs. No advance in intellectual accomplishments, no universalization of education, no dependence on psychological treatment alone restores these fundamental breaks in personal relationships. Unless it is realized that broken personal relationships underlie the whole structure of society and its sickness, attempts to deal with them will be limited to the treatment of transient symptoms without the diagnosis of the disease.

The Christian position put quite simply is something like this. Although each of us is a creature made by God in his own image, our own intrinsic rebellion against him and against our proper relationship with him make it impossible for us to respond to the genuine challenge of being fully human. This is not a situation that we can overcome by ourselves. Left to our own resources, we will shrivel in upon ourselves in this life with consequences that pursue us beyond the grave. But God has provided a way for this dilemma to be resolved. Through the life, death, and resurrection of Jesus Christ, the incarnate Son of God, he has made it possible for forgiveness, restoration, and healing to come to us. When we appropriate for ourselves what He offers to us and we commit ourselves wholly to Jesus Christ as our own personal Savior and our own personal Lord in life, it becomes possible for us to come home, to recover that relationship with God and with our fellow men that is intended for us as human beings made in the image of God.

The restoration of broken relationships naturally carries with it many other effects that we recognize as blessings in our life. The Christian context makes it possible to understand life more completely, and also to live life more fully. There are many analogies that we might invoke to illustrate such effects. Consider the way in which the reconciliation of parent and child, or of husband and wife, can enlighten aspects of their lives apparently far removed from the broken relationship.

Adjectives Describing Christian Faith

In our discussion of science in the previous chapter we attempted to clarify certain aspects of science by considering a series of adjectives that described the scientific enterprise. At this point in the present chapter on Christian faith, the same kind of approach is in order. Strict adherence to the same pattern will not be maintained where it is inappropriate, however. The following adjectives or phrases are completions of the sentence, "Christian faith is . . . ."

Personal. Christian faith is best understood on the personal level, since its most direct concern is with personal relationships. Images, analogies, and modes of expression best suited to describe Christian faith are those rich in personal connotations. In describing the content of Christian faith, we will expect the relationship between husband and wife to be more useful than the relationship between jeweler and watch, the relationship between father and son to be more expressive than the relationship between mechanic and automobile, the relationship between brother and sister to be more relevant than the relationship between dentist and teeth. Concepts of will, love, and person will be more adequate than concepts of law, mechanical relationship, and thing. Unless we recognize the personal elements of life—those aspects of life that have to do with depth, purpose, and meaning—we will never understand the place of religious faith in life.

Limited—but unlimited. The exercise of Christian faith is limited by the self-centeredness of man. The understanding of Christian faith is limited by the finiteness of man's comprehensive and conceptual ability. And the breadth of Christian faith is limited by the extent of the revelation that is available to him. The realistic Christian, therefore, will not expect to know all things or to have the answers to all conceivable questions. He will be on his guard against inconsistencies in his own life and against the constant danger of misreading his own prejudices as the will of God. But in another sense, Christian faith is unlimited. It rests upon the power of God, who is the Creator and Sustainer of all that is. The resources available to be tapped through Christian faith are indeed limitless.

Not self-interpreting. Given revelation and experience, the problem of interpretation cannot be overlooked. No passage from the biblical context and no experience with religious significance conveys its own interpretation without due regard for the total biblical or experiential perspective. In order for a man to apply to himself the content of revelation or experience, he must pass through the stage of interpretation. It is a difficult task many times to avoid the misconceptions and the presuppositions that shape his interpretation and to arrive at the actual content. I see what I want to see and I hear what I want to hear, no matter what happens. It requires discipline to break through.

Based on an absolute. Christian faith is based on the reality of an absolute. To speak of God is to speak of the Absolute. To consider that the dilemma of man is based on the moral guilt of his rebellion against God is to accept an absolute moral standard. The Christian absolute can be related to the concept of ultimate reality introduced in the last chapter. The Christian absolute expresses the nature of ultimate reality, insofar as this is known. To affirm that there *is* an absolute, however, is not to assert that it is or ever can be completely known. The Christian is engaged in the constant activity of coming to a better understanding of the meaning of the absolute in a particular finite context.

If a person admits to believing in an absolute, he is often accused of being committed to inflexibles, largely because human history has many cases where men have attempted to credit absolute status to relative prescriptions. Adherence to the absolute moral law does not lead to legalism unresponsive to the reality of a particular situation. The basic absolute principle in life is that man is to love God with his whole heart and more than any created thing or person, including himself. From this then follows the second absolute principle in life—that man is to love his fellow man as he does himself. There are no exceptions to these principles. Whenever the absolute of love is violated, the very structure of the universe is violated. Any life pattern that departs from love is a corrupted life pattern, one that falls short of the potentialities inherent in a good creation. The absolute to which Christian faith looks has the inflexibility only of ultimate reality. It describes the structure of life that is fully human. It can do no other; that is the way it is.

To be unable to say what someone else "ought" to do—to be able to say only that each person ought to do what seems right to himself—is to reflect one's lack of belief in the existence or knowability of an absolute. To believe in an absolute is to believe in reality. If there is a reality, there is an absolute. If there is no absolute, there is no reality except that which each individual creates for himself.

The scientist believes in reality. In his own way he believes also in an absolute. Not all the subjective desire in the world can prevent a man from falling if he steps off a high building. We say to him, "You ought not to step off that high building." What we mean is that the structure of reality is such that stepping off a high building will result in a violation of that structure and hence in an undesirable consequence to the stepper.

The Christian believes in reality. He believes in the ultimate basis for all reality, God himself, the only Absolute. Not all the subjective desire in the world can prevent a man from experiencing the consequences of violating the spiritual structure of reality. We say to him, "You ought not to steal." What we mean is that the structure of reality is such that stealing will result in a violation of that structure and hence in an undesirable consequence to the thief. The Christian, of course, also means that one's relationship to God carries with it certain responsibilities that flow out of a love relationship.

Realistic—not only pragmatic. Religious faith that makes no difference in the life of the one involved is a delusion. Christian faith works. Jesus and the New Testament writers repeat over and over again that a man who says he has faith and shows no signs of it in the concerns and deeds of his life is only fooling himself. Whatever faith he says he has is a *dead* faith, no real faith at all. But the test of Christian faith by purely pragmatic criteria is also unjustified, unless these criteria are very carefully selected in accordance with the biblical perspective. Because a particular mental or psychological frame of mind seems to make a person more happy or more successful does not validate that frame of mind as being based on Christian faith. The evidence of pragmatism is too limited in time, context, and depth of content to be reliable. The test of the reality of Christian faith to a person must be based on the degree to which he has achieved the goal of Christlikeness with its accompanying attributes of love, humility, justice, and righteousness.

Human. Although the source of Christian faith is divine, the exercise of Christian faith is human. That it is affected in many ways by the personality, abilities, life-style, and cultural heritage of the Christian, sometimes to its detriment, should be no surprise. Yet those who criticize the Christian faith most often direct their most outspoken barbs against Christian human beings who do not fully manifest the presence of Christ in their lives.

One of the most frequently experienced attributes of Christian faith is the ability provided by the presence of Christ to cut across racial, national, and ethnic differences between Christian individuals. In circumstances in which every natural background acts to prevent any kind of meaningful personal relationship between people, it is still common for Christians to sense immediately the spiritual unity of fellow Christians.

Incomplete. The understanding of the Christian faith is bound to be incomplete for the same reasons that it is limited. The finite limitations of human beings and the partial nature of the revelation available both contribute to this situation. Yet, knowledge need not be complete before it is true, understanding need not be comprehensive before it is satisfying, and insight need not be exhaustive before it is sufficient.

In addition, the Christian has the prospect of a continuously growing insight. In this life his understanding grows as he is obedient to the extent of understanding he currently has. And he holds to the promise that one day when he knows his Lord in the context of a new life after death he will have more perfect understanding.

Theological Models and Analogies

To confess that the God of Christian faith is transcendent is to confess that any description of God must be set forth in terms of analogies based on human experience. Such analogies may be called theological models, with similarities to scientific models.

Since the fact that God is personal is so central to the biblical representation of God, the picturing of God in terms of human analogies is a common practice. Thus the biblical writers refer to the eyes of God, the arm of God, and other anthropomorphisms. Perhaps one of the deepest meanings to be derived from this kind of analogy is the emphasis on the freedom of God and the fact that his activity is to be conceived in terms of the exercise of his free will rather than in terms of universal law by which he also is bound. It is helpful and indeed necessary to use this kind of language when speaking of God, but it is equally essential to avoid the fallacy of believing the analogy to be a fully adequate representation.

The relationship between God and man is described by a variety of different analogies: the King and his subjects, the Judge and the accused, the Husband and the wife, the Shepherd and the sheep, the Bridegroom and the bride, the Head and the body, the Vine and the branches, the Hen and the chickens, and the Father and the child. Each of these analogies truly depicts a facet of the relationship between God and man in the sense that man is led to understand this aspect of the relationship better. The relationship between God and man is truly like that between father and child. Yet, the relationship is not wholly like that between father and child, nor does the analogy of father adequately express the totality of the attributes of God.

The scientist constructs a model in order to simplify an actual system that is too complex for comprehensive description. As long as he uses the model properly, that is, as a device for predicting and describing experimental results, he does not fall into conceptual error. But if he presses the model beyond its proper limits and attempts to apply it where it is not appropriate as though it were indeed a faithful representation of reality, he runs into trouble. The theological model must be handled in the same way. It can describe what theological reality is like truly without describing what theological reality is like either wholly comprehensively or wholly accurately. When it is extended as though it were a wholly comprehensive or accurate representation, trouble is again the result.

Another factor to remember in using analogies is that it often requires the use of two or more analogies in order to do justice to the description of an actual phenomenon. Since a given analogy does an adequate job of describing only one facet of the phenomenon, a richly significant phenomenon may require a number of well-developed analogies to describe faithfully its essential characteristics. The story of the blind men who attempted to describe an elephant is well known; each by touch identified a particular feature of the elephant, and hence they concluded that an elephant was like a rope (tail), a pole (leg), a wall (side), a leaf (ear), and a hose (trunk). Each of the men gave a true analogy of what part of an elephant was like; the combination of all their analogies gives a somewhat better idea of what a whole elephant is like, but it still falls far short of establishing what an elephant is. This is also an example, therefore, of the fact that a combination of partial analogies should not be expected to give a fully adequate representation of the whole. Another common example of multiple analogies can be drawn from modern physics where it is necessary to treat an electron, for example, in terms of a particle analogy under certain circumstances and in terms of a wave analogy under others.

A striking example of multiple biblical analogies can be found in one of the central teachings of the Bible: the atonement made on our behalf by Jesus Christ. We mentioned in this chapter how the biblical writers used the terms salvation, redemption, reconciliation, victory, and sacrifice to describe different aspects of the atonement. If one studies theological writings, religious literature, and expressions of Christian faith in hymns, it is evident that there are three principal analogies to describe the atonement. The first analogy is sometimes called the moral influence model of the atonement. It emphasizes the demonstration of the love of God displayed in the willing death of Jesus Christ on the cross on our behalf. When estranged man comes face to face with that tremendous demonstration of love, he can do no other than renounce his rebellion and be reconciled to God. The second analogy is the *Christus victor* model of the atonement. It emphasizes the victory that Jesus Christ won over the powers of evil and death by passing through the powers of death himself and then indicating his victory by the resurrection. The third analogy is the judicial model of the atonement. It emphasizes the necessity for payment for the guilt of man's sin and the mercy of God in that he himself in the person of his Son paid this price in sinful man's place. Since the payment is made, man need do nothing further to pay for his sins; he need only accept the payment made for him by Jesus. Each of these analogies illuminates a different aspect of the atonement. The full impact of the atonement can be realized only by holding all three analogies at the same time and experiencing their truth in one's own life. To say that these analogies explain how the atonement works or comprehensively set forth the full meaning of the atonement is to miss the depths of this profound mystery in which the love, mercy, and justice of God meet.

There is, of course, one basic difference between the models and analogies the scientist constructs in order to further his ability to describe and picture the world and the models and analogies given to us in the revelation recorded in the Bible. The scientist's models are the products of his own mental processes; the biblical models are given to us as part of the verbal revelation of God. There is always a certain greater assurance, therefore, that the essence of the biblical models reveals the relationship between God and man truly, in accordance with ultimate reality. Somewhat less justification exists for treating the scientific models as being equally valid representations of ultimate reality.

Philosophical Attitudes Toward Theology

When we treated several philosophical attitudes toward science at the end of the previous chapter, we included in figure 3 some parallel considerations about theology. In particular, we gave the equivalent theological attitudes toward the interpretation of the biblical revelation corresponding to the scientific attitudes toward the interpretation of the physical universe.

In this framework it is possible to define the biblical empiricist as one who underestimates the role of personal interpretation in understanding the revelation given in the Bible. The theological idealist regards subjective experience as normative and underestimates the importance of God's revelation in and through specific historical events. The theological operationalist denies that God-language conveys information about God, and he underestimates the necessity of the correlation between language and reality. The theological realist considers that the biblical revelation is not only sufficient but also complete in the truth it conveys, and he underestimates the limitations imposed by finite minds and language. Finally there is the Christian realist, who recognizes that the understanding of the Bible involves human interpretation in a critical way. He is aware that the content of the biblical revelation can be determined and trusted, that God-language does convey truth about God and his relationship with man because it comes through his revelation, and that a sufficient but not complete understanding of God and his purposes can be obtained from his biblical revelation.

The close similarity of philosophical patterns in science and theology is evident from figure 3 and this discussion.

Summary

No human being can escape a religious perspective on life. Whenever he confronts issues of purpose, meaning, and the deep concerns of his life, he is compelled to adopt some kind of religious attitude. In other words, the basis of man's life-view must always rest upon a faith decision. It is false to suggest that a man has the opportunity to choose between an objective, scientific (certain) basis for his life-view and a subjective, religious (questionable) basis. The very choice of a scientific life-view would involve the tremendous faith that this approach could indeed meet life's needs. Furthermore it is the very fact that a scientific life-view proves inadequate to deal with the deepest concerns of life which has given rise to so many of the problems of today's science-age society.

Both science and theology are systems for interpreting data provided by revelation, the scientist dealing with the natural revelation provided by God's creative activity and the theologian dealing with the special revelation provided by God's inspirational activity in the authors of the Bible. Because they are both systems of interpretation, both are susceptible to human error. Science is in error if the scientist incorrectly interprets the natural phenomena encountered in his experience, and theology is in error if the theologian incorrectly interprets the biblical revelation in the light of his experience. When science is in error, the reliability of the natural world is not called into question; when theology is in error, the reliability of the biblical revelation is not called into question.

Christian faith addresses itself to the basic problem of man. Intended by creation to live in spiritual oneness with God and to serve him in joy and fulfillment, man can never find satisfaction and peace as long as he rebels against his position as a creature. When man is separated from God, he is also separated from his fellow men, and he is separated as well from his own true identity. To bring an end to this separation is not something that man can do for himself. But God has acted in history. By entering the stream of humanity in the person of Jesus Christ, he has made and continues to make it possible by his life, death, and resurrection for man to be reconciled to God, to be redeemed from the dominion of self, and to experience the victory won by Christ. When a man commits himself to God through faith in Christ, he acknowledges

that Jesus Christ is his Savior and the Lord of his life; he is transformed into a "new creature" restored to the position destined for
him by God's creation. No longer separated from God, and established in the security of his own identity as a child of God, he is
enabled to breach the separation between himself and others and
to endure the risk of rejection in order to bring to others the love of
Christ.

Major similarities and differences between science and Christian
faith are revealed by the types of adjectives used to describe them.
Both Christian faith and science are limited and shaped by the
human influences of their followers, but Christian faith claims an
unlimited resource of strength and wisdom in God and his revelation. The data underlying science and Christian faith are not self-
interpreting for either, and understanding in both areas must of
necessity be incomplete. Christian faith deals primarily in personal
categories, science in mechanical categories. Christian faith is predicted on the reality and discernibility of the absolute; science is by
nature relative. Christian truth is related to reality and therefore,
although it is effective, it is not exclusively pragmatic; scientific truth
is determined primarily by pragmatic criteria.

In order to describe reality, both science and Christian faith find
it essential to use models and analogies of reality. In both fields
these models are useful as long as their limitations and restrictions
are kept in mind, and dangerous if they are not. Philosophical attitudes found in the discussion of science and of Christian faith are
remarkably similar.

Topics for Discussion

1. Consider your own life and list in order of concern to you the
five items or areas of life to which you attribute ultimate concern.

2. Choose some broad secular ideal such as communism or the
American way of life and show how such an ideal can play the role
of religious faith in the life of an individual.

3. Martin Luther is quoted as having said that if he heard a
voice speaking to him and telling him, "Martin, this is the voice of
the Lord telling you that 2 plus 2 is 5," he would reply, "Get away
from me, Satan!" Comment on this story in the light of the inter-

action between the interpretation of revelation and personal experience. Under what conditions can personal experience be a valid guide to interpreting the Bible?

4. Scientists used to believe that the sun revolved around the earth; theologians used to believe the same thing. After Galileo was it harder for theologians to change their minds than for scientists? Why?

5. Many religious views consider that the Creation and the Fall are identical. What effect would such a position have, and how would it differ in basic ways from the Christian position?

6. Personal evil resulting from man's separation from God and manifesting itself as man's inhumanity to man can be interpreted as a misuse of freedom, a good gift in God's good creation. How then can natural evil, for example, disease, earthquake, flood, accident, death, be explained? Does Christian faith provide a way of responding to these natural evils?

7. Show that to make anything except God the ultimate concern of one's life is to take part in idolatry.

8. Do you think that there is a correlation between the extent that a particular church group or organization emphasizes intellectual correctness of belief and the warmth and outgoingness of the life lived by individual members? Are there cases of both positive and negative correlation?

9. Consider the difficulty of interpreting the biblical revelation apart from our personal prejudices by viewing Acts 16:30–33 through the eyes of a Presbyterian and of a Baptist; by viewing Rom. 9:10–13 through the eyes of a Calvinist and of an Arminian; by viewing Matt. 16:17–19 through the eyes of a Roman Catholic and of a Protestant; by viewing Isaiah 53 through the eyes of a Jew and of a Christian.

10. Consider the following inflexible laws. (a) If you walk off the top of a tall building without a parachute, you will surely die. (b) If you rebel against God in your heart and life, you will surely die (Gen. 2:16,17). Is there any reason to consider one of these laws to have good inflexibility and the other to have bad inflexibility?

11. Discuss the relationship between a theological analogy and a parable.

12. The church is described in the Bible as the Bride of Christ (Eph. 5:22–32; Rev. 19:6–9), the Body of Christ (1 Cor. 12:12–27;

Rom. 12:5), and the Building of God (1 Cor. 3:9–17; Eph. 2:19–22; 1 Pet. 2:5). Trace out the implications of these models for the church and show how all of them are needed to bring out different aspects of the nature of the church.

13. Consider the biblical models for the Holy Spirit. Show how they are helpful if properly used but how they can lead to questionable conclusions if pressed too far.

Chapter Five

...Are They Really
Exclusively Different?

In the previous two chapters we have attempted to sketch the principal characteristics first of the scientific and then the religious perspective on life. We have seen certain striking similarities and correlations between science and Christian faith when considered in their general aspects, and we have also noted certain radical differences. As a kind of conclusion to this aspect of our discussion, we turn our attention here to several specific comments usually made about the relationship between science and Christian faith, the basic sense of which is that these are two completely different and essentially exclusive approaches to life. In view of what we have already said, it is our contention that science and Christian faith have so many points of similarity that their differences must be considered to be of degree rather than of kind. Any perspective on life that does not recognize both the scientific and the religious aspects of life cannot possibly do justice to the richness of human experience.

Objective Facts versus Subjective Judgments

The science versus religious faith controversy is frequently cast into the context of objective versus subjective approaches to life. In this view, science is based upon objective facts and therefore has the reliability to be associated with a feet-on-the-ground approach to life. Religious faith, on the other hand, is pictured as incapable of proof, based on personal feelings rather than on logic, a matter wholly up to the whim of the individual.

Given these descriptions of science and religious faith, it is evident that there are ample grounds for an objective versus subjective disjunction. Real science and Christian faith, however, do not lend themselves to such a description.

We have already seen that the pure objectivity of real science is a myth. The subjective influences of the scientist are felt at every step along the way of a scientific investigation. It is perfectly true that it is the aim of science to eliminate the intrusion of this subjective element, but it is also true that this subjective element must constantly be reckoned with in order to evaluate a scientific position. Observations and measurements in science are made by men. Scientific theories are constructed by men. Experimental programs are designed by men. Data are interpreted by men. All of these activities are done by individuals with a particular cultural, academic, and scientific orientation. It is no surprise that when a scientist in one field tackles a problem in a quite different field, he will attempt to adapt models and analogies from the field of his experience to the new field.

There are, furthermore, situations in every branch of science where it becomes increasingly difficult or even impossible for the scientist to experiment in such a way that he does not affect the outcome of the experiment. In an experiment designed to determine both the position and the velocity of an electron at a given instant of time, the scientist cannot stay outside his experiment. His very attempt to measure the position imparts velocity to the electron; his attempt to measure the velocity destroys any information about the position of the electron. This is an example selected from physics, the most exact of the sciences. If such an influence of the experimenter on the experiment is found here, how much more likely is it to be found in the less exact and more human-oriented sciences?

It must also be mentioned that what ordinarily passes for science in the normal course of everyday events is not limited to specific facts and their careful technical interpretation by scientists. The mantle of science is cast popularly upon a whole area of extrapolations from scientific research, personal opinions, and deductions of scientists, and upon an interpretation of life ostensibly derived from

a scientific foundation. In this area of popular science and its pronouncements, it is no exaggeration to state that the subjective influences completely dominate.

On the other hand, Christian faith is based on solid historical
data. It is true that many religious writers accept a completely subjective basis for religious faith, leaving foundation, evidence, and
definition of that faith wholly to individual subjectivity. In such a
framework, all religious concepts become entirely relative. My God
and my doctrine are just as valid as your God and your doctrine—
even when mine are logically contradictory to yours—provided that
they "do something for me." Such a relativistic subjective religious
perspective is incompatible with science; it is significant that it is
adopted so frequently by those who are disenchanted with science
and who are seeking to establish a source of meaning in life while
rejecting the naturalistic conclusions of popular science.

One of the reasons the Christian faith receives so much opposition is that it is *not* relativistic and subjective. The Christian faith
does not allow the individual the freedom to construct whatever
kind of religious system he subjectively chooses. Instead it demands
that he subject himself to the objective reality of historical events.
The God of creation is the God who led the people of Israel out of
Egypt into Canaan. He interacted with this people in their religion,
life, and customs in order to reveal his nature and purposes to them.
He spoke to them through his prophets. He came to them himself
in the person of Jesus of Nazareth, called the Christ. He lived
among them, taught them, healed them, fed them, and warned
them. Men of his day, secure in their own wealth and power, could
not tolerate his exposure of them. Seeing in him a threat to their
own status, they arranged for him to be put to death. He was hung
on a cross outside the city of Jerusalem, with nails pounded through
his hands and feet. A sword was thrust into his side by a soldier and
he bled. He was unostentatiously wrapped for burial and placed in
a new tomb, which was sealed by rolling a large stone over its mouth.
On the first day of the week, three days later, that same tomb was
empty and Jesus of Nazareth was no longer dead. He was alive
again, and he met and taught his disciples for forty days after his
resurrection, meeting with groups from one to five hundred in
number. He left them then, promising that they would not be left
alone but would shortly experience the power of God's Holy Spirit

in their lives. On the festival of Pentecost the disciples did experience this great surge of power. It transformed them from fearful ignorant men of the country into fearless leaders and preachers of the message of salvation through faith in Jesus the Christ. They spread the message all over the world, and neither persecution nor suffering nor hardship could overcome the indomitable spirit they shared in the knowledge that their Lord had risen from the dead.

Let us put the dependence of Christian faith on historical data as strongly as possible: if Jesus of Nazareth, called the Christ, did not rise from the dead at a particular time in history, at a particular place in history, the claims and promises of the Christian faith are worthless.

A man who would ally himself with the Christian faith is bound by the objective historical data and by the insight given to us by Jesus Christ about the nature of God and the relationship between God and man. Christian faith is not a collection of philosophical platitudes or directions for living; it is allegiance to a Person—the risen Lord Jesus. This is the reason that Christian faith emphasizes the uniqueness of Jesus. It is of interest to note that the four questions raised in theological objection against Christianity (see pp. 23-26) all complain that the Christian faith is too objectively defined and contend for a more subjectively free interpretation of Christian data.

Objectivity in forming an opinion is characterized by weighing all the evidence available and coming to a rational conclusion. When, having considered only a portion of the available evidence, someone attempts to inject a subjective view as authoritative, science and religious faith respond alike. In both disciplines such a person is labeled a heretic, a "quack." Everyone who is involved in any discipline involving extensive training and understanding has at some time had an encounter with an individual of this type. Frequently these "quacks" are sincerely motivated individuals who strongly desire to gain recognition of some point they consider to be of vital interest and value. William Pollard aptly describes the situation from the standpoint of the physicist.

> In my own field of physics it is a common experience to receive privately published papers which develop all kinds of strange and bizarre theories about everything from the electron to the universe as a whole. . . . To the non-physicist they have as bona fide a ring

as a paper in the *Physical Review*. But to physicists they are immediately recognized as fundamentally different. They constitute in the strict sense of the word unorthodox or heretical physics. In subtle ways impossible to describe clearly to the world at large, they violate everything which has given the physics community power to slowly and painfully acquire real and dependable insights into the nature of things. They are lone wolf enterprises unchecked by the discipline of the community and unsupported by an essential loyalty to the enterprise of physics as a whole. Most often the authors of these papers are completely oblivious to these elements and suffer from a deep sense of persecution. They cannot see why their theories have not been given an equal hearing with those of accepted physicists. They cannot understand why the community consistently and repeatedly rejects them.[1]

In both science and Christian faith, the common experience of heresy emphasizes the role played by objectivity, as opposed to free individual subjectivism. In science a man is not free to deny the law of gravity; in Christian faith a man is not free to deny the resurrection of Jesus Christ. It is curious that no one would think of criticizing scientists for insisting that the law of gravity must be accepted, but popular opinion has always seemed to feel that Christians were being arbitrarily orthodox in insisting on the historical event of the resurrection of Jesus.

Heretics, whether in science or in religious faith, generally fulfill the following criteria: (1) they are certain that they have found the truth; (2) this truth is generally unknown to the world at large, but is of extreme significance; (3) their case is built upon selected bits of evidence without a consideration of the picture as a whole; (4) they are bitter at the community because it will not listen to them, and they attribute the basest motives to the members of the community for this reaction; (5) they are generally neither able nor willing to react to genuine criticism of their work; and (6) they do not consider themselves to be, nor do others consider them to be, members of the community.

Just as there have been Christians who sought to introduce scientific heresy by departing from the objectivity of science, so also there have been scientists who sought to introduce theological heresy by departing from the objective historical events underlying

---

[1] William G. Pollard, *Physicist and Christian* (Greenwich, Conn.: Seabury Press, 1961), p. 21.

the Christian faith. The existence and characteristics of both pseudoscience and pseudotheology provide clues for the identification of the genuine activities.

Rational versus Nonrational Attitudes

A second criterion men often attempt to employ in distinguishing between science and Christian faith is rationality. Science is represented as a process by which one rationally proceeds from data to conclusion. On the other hand, Christian faith is represented as requiring one to accept certain conclusions blindly on faith in what must be described as a nonrational, if not an irrational, procedure. Given this perspective, it is clear that science and religious faith are mutually exclusive. Admittedly, there are mystical approaches to religious faith to which such a representation can be applied. It does not apply, however, to real science and Christian faith.

The major breakthroughs in science occur much more often as the result of guesses, intuition, flashes of insight, or instances of serendipity than they do as the result of fully specified progress from data to conclusions. The concept of science's following logically and infallibly, step upon step, from one experiment to the next applies more to the routine pursuit of scientific evidence (if it ever really applies) than it does to the development of significant new scientific insights. But there is a creative mode in which the competent scientist can operate. In it he becomes aware of the totality of the problems of interest and is able to make some connection between that totality and the totality of his experience and knowledge. It is a kind of *Gestalt* mode in which the scientist responds to what he may call the beauty or elegance of a particular model. Suddenly he "sees" his answer and cries, "Eureka!" However the moment may be described, it belongs to the nonrational side of his experience in the sense that the scientist is not aware of the steps involved in arriving at the final understanding. Such phenomena are not peripheral to science but actually characterize what is meant by science as distinguished from technology or pure engineering. Training in creativity, still in an embryonic state, emphasizes this aspect of the scientific enterprise.

Christian faith, on the other hand, is a rational faith. Lest these two words seem to be mutually exclusive, let us consider what it means to act rationally. To act rationally in a given situation is to act upon a careful and logical assessment of all the available evidence. To act rationally does not mean to take only those actions that are connected by a series of logically provable links; indeed, if this definition were to be assumed, it would mean that most of our life would be consigned to nonrational behavior by definition. To act irrationally then means to act contrary to or in spite of the results of a careful and logical assessment of all the available evidence. To act meaningfully at all, whether in science or Christian experience, requires a rational act of faith.

Let us illustrate these definitions a little further. Suppose that early in the morning the sky is dark, the wind is blowing, thunder and lightning are heard in the distance, and the weather report on the radio says that rain is due in about an hour. To believe that it will probably rain and hence to take one's umbrella to work is to act on the basis of a rational faith. To put on one's best suit and to drive off in a convertible with the top down is to act irrationally. To believe that it will rain (or will not rain) without looking out the windows or listening to the radio at all is to arrive at a conclusion by nonrational means.

It is evident that science becomes possible because of a rational faith in the ability of man to describe the world according to orderly patterns conceivable by his own mind. It is likewise evident that Christian faith is a rational faith based on the totality of biblical revelation, historical events, and personal experience.

Let us consider how we come to believe anything at all, whether in science or in Christian faith. If all the possible ways of coming to believe something are analyzed, it is found that there are two major categories. We come to believe something either (1) because we accept the word of someone we trust (belief based on authority), or (2) because we have a personal experience sufficient to be convincing (belief based on personal perception). These two ways of coming to believe something are equally applicable to science and Christian faith.

Scientists are called upon to accept the testimony of other scientists as authoritative. Students in science spend a long time coming to believe things through the authority mode before they have the opportunity to check out for themselves the validity of even a fraction of the concepts to which they are introduced. It is probably no exaggeration to say that the belief of almost every university student in the general theory of evolution has been generated by the authority mode of communication. Nor is it an exaggeration to say that most of the knowledge of any kind that any one of us thinks he has, has come to us because we accepted the word of someone else we trusted. Of course, since scientists are fallible, it is healthy for science students to work at maintaining a certain degree of scepticism. But the generally rational choice for such a student to make is to accept the word of his instructor in faith, act upon this acceptance, and finally see in his own experience where this acceptance leads. If the science instructor is correct in his assessment of the scientific material and if the understanding he presents conforms reasonably well to reality, the student will confirm this in part in his own experience and his faith in the scientific method will be strengthened. If the instructor is misinformed, or if the particular scientific viewpoint presented is inadequate, the student may be fortunate enough to come to a better understanding of reality in his own experience because at least initially he acted in rational faith on the basis of the knowledge he did have.

Much of the above paragraph applies equally well to the area of Christian faith. The correlation between science and Christian faith can be made complete if the universe to which the scientist addresses himself for the accumulation of his scientific data is considered to be God's revelation in created form (something that God has made), and the biblical record to which the theologian addresses himself for the accumulation of his theological data is considered to be God's relevation in spoken form (something that God has told). The scientist accumulates his scientific data through his controlled personal experience; the theologian accumulates his theological data from the spoken word of God as enlightened by his personal experience. Thus the mode of belief by which one trusts the spoken word of a person considered to be worthy of trust in science involves only men and their interpretation of the natural revelation. The mode of belief by which one trusts the spoken word in Christian faith goes back one step further, however, to the acceptance of the revelation provided in verbal form by God himself. Thus there are two stages of the authority mode for arriving at belief in the area of Christian faith, whereas only one stage is explicit in the area of science. Nevertheless, science and Christian faith are not really different on this point, for the scientist trusts completely in the reliability of the natural world even as the Christian trusts completely in the reliability of God's word. The scientist does not accuse the natural world of lying to him as he questions it and probes it; the Christian does not accuse God's word in the Bible of lying to him as he questions it and probes it.

Empirical Evidence versus Interpretation Based Only on Faith

A variation of the objective versus subjective disjunction often claimed to exist between science and Christian faith is the claim that science is reliably based on empirical data whereas Christian faith has no real basis except individual preference. In science, so it is said, positions may be firmly founded on the rockbed of fact; in Christian faith, a leap of faith is necessary.

We do not need to repeat many of the arguments already advanced to show that both science and Christian faith have their objective and subjective elements. We have seen that the very existence and practice of science derives from an act of faith, that every interpretation of empirical data is faith-related, and that facts provide no interpretation of their own but must be given their interpretation by men. We have seen also that the validity of Christian faith requires empirical validation; such faith must be based on the "data" of historical revelation, on the witness of trusted men to their experiences, and on one's own experience both individually and in company with one's contemporaries.

Still, it may be argued that the test of a scientific viewpoint is more readily achieved than the test of a religious viewpoint. Such a distinction is most obvious when the tests of physics are compared with the tests of Christian faith. But, after all, physics deals with matter in motion and not with persons. This distinction is much less obvious when we compare the human-oriented sciences with religious faith. Are scientific viewpoints in psychology, for example, really so readily tested? How is it then that so many schools of psychological thought exist? How is it that the psychologically approved method of child-rearing, for example, oscillates back and forth between an authoritarian and a permissive framework?

The test of a basic scientific perspective, in the last analysis, rests on the agreement of the majority of practicing competent scientists. What is taken to be the position of science at a given time is what most scientists agree on. A lone dissenter from the consensus will ordinarily be ignored, or if he is persistent and relatively isolated from the scientific community, he will be labeled a crackpot (a heretic), as indicated earlier. Sometimes the two groups of scientists disagreeing on a basic scientific perspective each carry so much scientific prestige that the community as a whole is unable to declare itself clearly. For a time such a stand-off occurred between Niels Bohr, advocating the ultimacy of the statistical interpretation of quantum mechanics, and Albert Einstein, who for philosophical reasons could not accept an intrinsically statistical structure of the universe. Even though both of these renowned scientists are now dead, the controversy is unresolved. It appears that most of the scientific community leans toward Bohr's position, but there is enough constant unrest in the opposite direction to keep the issue alive. At the present time, there is no known experimental way to settle the question empirically.

Without undermining the validity of the biblical data in determining Christian faith, it may be maintained that the test of a theological interpretation of those data also rests on the agreement of the members of the Christian community. In theological terms, this is the activity of the Holy Spirit of God working in and through the community of Christians to make known the application of the essential truths of the biblical data to contemporary situations.

In both science and Christian faith, the interpretation of the data has to accord with the experience of the community and with a person's own present experience. As the scientist is constrained by the empirical facts from going off in a purely individualistic direction, so the Christian is constrained by the equivalent historical foundation of his faith and the facts of the biblical revelation from going off in a purely individualistic direction.

It therefore appears that a kind of testing based on the agreement of individual persons relating data, experience, and the pattern of knowledge available is common to both science and Christian faith. Though the testing is, of course, quantitatively different in these two areas, its nature is qualitatively the same. Such intersubjective testing comes into prominence in both science and Christian faith in areas where direct experimental tests are either impossible or inappropriate.

If it is objected that intersubjective testing is not very effective in religious areas as indicated by the multiplicity of denominations and religious sects, it should also be remembered that among physicists there are determinists and indeterminists, that among biologists there are evolutionists and nonevolutionists, and that among psychologists there are functionalists, behaviorists, intro-spectionists, Gestalt psychologists, Freudians and anti-Freudians, to give an incomplete catalogue. It may also be noted that psychologists of two different schools may well have less in common than individual Christians of differing denominational backgrounds who all confess to the Lordship of Jesus Christ.

Objective Independence versus Personal Commitment

The ideal of science is to be as objective and as independent of one's subject as possible. The scientist is an impartial observer who separates himself as an individual insofar as he is able from the progress of his scientific investigation. On the other hand, the ideal of Christian faith is to be as fully committed personally as humanly possible. The Christian is a committed individual who involves himself to the fullest possible extent in the progress of his Christian faith and life. Here at last there appears to be a crucial difference between these two areas.

The difference is indeed real, and it lies in the attitude essential for making progress. In science, I come to know by abstracting myself and regarding the rest of my subject as impersonally as possible. Whenever I treat anything scientifically, what I treat becomes an object. Only the scientist is the subject; everything (everybody) else is an object to be observed and manipulated in order to gain an understanding. Thus the scientist can never treat himself scientifically.

In Christian faith, on the other hand, I come to know by trusting God's promise in Jesus Christ, by committing myself wholly to him, and by being obedient to the word that he speaks to me. Religious knowledge can come from study of the biblical revelation; religious understanding comes only when I act on the basis of what little I may presently know.

But perhaps even this difference between objective scientific aloofness and personally committed Christian involvement is not as great as it seems at first glance. Though it is true that the scientist must not allow himself personally to affect the outcome of his scientific research, his research will be pointless if he is not personally committed to a search for a scientific understanding of the world. A scientist is by his very vocation a committed person; he believes that the world can be understood, that the mysteries of the universe can be resolved, and that he can come up with descriptions of the complexities of life that will be valid. A man not committed to this perspective can hardly make it as a practicing scientist.

Likewise, the intense personal involvement of the Christian cannot be permitted to completely subjectivize his faith. Self-examination to guard against self-deception and hypocrisy is an essential aspect of the Christian life. It is not the purpose of the Christian to have the kind of faith that lets him live a self-directed life according only to what seems right to him. Rather he must be able to serve God in the way that seems right to God. Thus the Christian is constantly testing the elements of his experience in the light of the biblical revelation and attempting to draw objective judgments. This attitude is implicit in the exercise of a rational faith, as described in an earlier section of this chapter.

Summary

An examination of the nature of science and Christian faith shows that the two areas are not mutually exclusive but that qualitatively the same ingredients are found in both. Although science sometimes appears to be more objective than Christian faith, it is also true that the subjective element is essential in science and frequently even dominates it, and that the basis for Christian faith lies in objective historical events.

Both science and Christian faith share the experience of heresy, the injection of a subjective view as authoritative when only a portion of the pertinent evidence has been considered.

The rational processes of science are enlightened by the moments of total awareness which always mark major advances in general perspective, moments which are closely related to aspects of religious experience. Christian faith is a rational faith, constructed on the basis of the evidence, just as the faith that science is possible is a rational faith, similarly constructed.

In both science and Christian faith, knowledge comes either through the words of one we trust, or through personal experience. A large portion of any scientist's knowledge has come to him through his trust in the words of other scientists. Christian faith has its foundation in a trust in the words of God given in the biblical revelation. Personal experience confirms the verbally acquired knowledge of the scientist; personal experience also confirms the verbally acquired knowledge of the Christian.

In the final analysis, the acceptance of a given scientific perspective at a given time derives not only from the facts currently available but from the agreement in the scientific community. Thus there are strong elements of intersubjective testing in the scientific discipline, even as there are in the Christian discipline as the Holy Spirit works out the growth of Christian understanding in Christian individuals and groups.

Both the scientist and the Christian are committed individuals. The scientist is committed to his faith in the possibility of science and the understandability of the world; the Christian is committed to his faith in the Person of Jesus Christ and the God who is his Father. Unless a scientist is wholly personally involved in his commitment to a scientific understanding of the world, he cannot be a good scientist. Unless a Christian is wholly personally involved in his commitment to God in Christ, he cannot live as a Christian should.

Both the scientist and the Christian exercise objective judgment in connection with their commitment. The scientist separates himself from the object of his research and attempts to draw objective observations and conclusions about that object. The Christian subjects his experience to the guide provided in the biblical revelation so that he can discern the working of God. He does not wish to deceive himself or to be unconsciously hypocritical. Because scientific knowledge can be increased only when the scientist treats the participants in his investigation as objects, personal avenues to knowledge are closed to the scientific method. Both objective and personal routes to increased knowledge and understanding are possible in Christian faith.

Topics for Discussion

1. Usually the introductory phrase, "Scientists today believe . . ." is invoked to give authoritative backing to a particular statement. Discuss examples where such authority is justified and others where it is not. What kind of criteria would you devise to distinguish between them?

2. We frequently hear the assertion, "All men worship the same God." Can this conclusion be reached from a rational faith? What does one do if the characteristics of one man's God are contradictory to those of another man's God?

3. List five teachings of the Christian faith that may be treated as culturally relative. List five teachings of the Christian faith that must be treated as objective revelation.

4. Scientific heretics have seldom, if ever, been burned at the stake. Many Christian "heretics" have been so treated. How do you account for the difference? How should a heretic be treated in science? In Christian faith?

5. What is intuition? Give some examples of experiences of your own where a sudden insight brought unexpected understanding or solution of a problem. Can this kind of experience be stimulated? How would you go about it? Use both scientific and Christian faith examples.

6. Choose any subject that you know something about. How much of what you know today is the result of someone else's telling you about it and how much the result of your own experience?

7. Devise criteria for judging whether or not to believe something that is told to you. Apply these criteria to an example in science and one in Christian faith.

8. Consider the scientific theory of evolution which states that all living matter has evolved from a common source, initially nonliving. What experiments would have to be done to prove it conclusively? To disprove it conclusively? Why is the consensus of the scientific community so strongly in support of it?

9. Discuss John 16:12–15 in connection with the treatment of intersubjective testing among Christians with respect to their faith.

10. Discuss why a psychoanalyst cannot treat himself. Does this have a lesson for us too in a more common context of everyday life?

11. Discuss Matt. 13:12 in connection with an increase in Christian understanding. Would the same kind of principle also apply in scientific research?

Chapter Six

What Do Science and Christian Faith Say about Each Other?

It is all very well to appreciate that science and Christian faith have many aspects in common, as we have done in the previous three chapters. But if science can never say anything of relevance to Christian faith, and if Christian faith can never say anything of relevance to science, we might just as well separate these two disciplines once and for all and forget about their similarities. Each can then be put into its own compartment, and we as individuals can proceed to sample one and then the other without ever being forced to face a conflict or a disparity between them.

It is evident that historically such a separation has not been made. Otherwise there would be little cause for the conflict between science and Christian faith which has been waged fairly continuously ever since empirical science was born. It may be, of course, that men have *thought* that science had something to say about Christian faith and that Christian faith had something to say about science, whereas in reality they did not bear directly on one another. It may be that all the conflicts to date have been fought for no reason, that they have been the result of men's misunderstanding of science and Christian faith after all.

That many conflicts have been generated on the basis of mistaken concepts and faulty interpretations cannot be denied. Yet it is necessary to remember that science and Christian faith do interact, do have something to say about each other, and must both be considered in the formation of a unified world view. To seek to escape from the apparent conflicts that constantly arise between them by retreating to a position in which these two perspectives are permanently kept apart is not the solution to whatever problems exist.

In this chapter we shall attempt in general terms to take a look at some of the ways in which science and Christian faith interact and overlap. The remainder of the book will then be devoted to tackling each of the major specific problems that presently exist.

Classical Arguments for the Existence of God

When science was born among men who at least formally had a religious perspective, it was natural that they should attempt to deduce either from logic or from their understanding of the world a proof for the existence of God. Such a proof would settle the question of faith once and for all—or so it might be thought.

Now the definition of proof must be considered carefully. Given the axioms and postulates of Euclidean geometry, it is possible to prove that the sum of the angles of a triangle is 180°. Such a proof has such a universal validity that no one except a mentally deficient person or a willfully and arbitrarily rejecting person could fail to accept. But most of the arguments advanced in either science or Christian faith are not of this type. They constitute what might be better called evidence than proof. The better and more compelling the evidence, the more assent can be obtained by members of the community; yet the intelligent dissenter or doubter cannot be categorically charged with imbecility or obstinacy. As we discussed in an earlier chapter, a rational faith in either science or Christian faith is based upon a careful assessment of the evidence available. To make the choice of faith is to accept for oneself the conclusiveness of the evidence.

In *God and Other Minds*, Alvin Plantinga argues that no logical proof can be given either for or against the existence of God. Logical proofs which have been proposed all have fatal flaws and constitute at best only evidence to be considered.

One proposed logical proof is credited to Thomas Aquinas and often referred to as the cosmological argument. Plantinga quotes it as follows.

There are at present contingent beings; whatever can fail to exist, does at some time fail to exist; so if all beings were contingent, then at one time there was nothing at all. But nothing could come into existence if there were nothing at all; so if all beings were contingent, there'd be nothing now; since there is something now, not all beings are contingent and there is at least one necessary being; this is God.

Another logical proof, credited to Anselm and often referred to as the ontological argument, is also quoted by Plantinga.

By the word "God" we mean to refer to the being than which it is not possible that there be a greater. Now suppose God does not exist. Things that exist are greater than things that do not. So if God does not exist, then there is something greater than God— that is, there is something greater than the being than which it is not possible that there exist a greater. But that's impossible. So it's false that God does not exist; hence God exists.[1]

We shall not belabor these classical "proofs" for the existence of God further here. Their very abstractness seems to divorce them from the personal framework of Christian faith, and their logical flaws can be learned about by reading God and Other Minds.

Arguments for the Existence of God from the Natural World

Scientific studies of the natural world have uncovered and heightened aspects of the world that may be cited as evidence for the existence of God.

Temporal nature of the universe. A variety of evidence indicates that the universe has not always existed but came into being at a specific time and is so constituted that at least life in the universe will come to an ultimate end. One theory of cosmological origins is the Big Bang theory. It postulates the beginning of the universe in one spot, from which all the matter of the universe has been subsequently expanding. The constant conversion of matter into energy, the finite amounts of radioactive material found, and the general experience that the disorder in the universe as a whole is increasing with time (increasing entropy in a closed system, ac-

---

[1] Alvin Plantinga, God and Other Minds (Ithaca, N.Y.: Cornell University Press, 1967), pp. 4, 5; pp. 27, 28.

cording to the Second Law of Thermodynamics), all argue for a universe that had a beginning and will have for all practical purposes an end.

The very mystery of existence evokes some sense of religious awe. Why should it be that I exist, rather than that I should not exist? How should it be that matter, and space, and time—and you and I—are here at all?

Order in the universe. Science presupposes order in the universe. The fact that science is possible means that order exists in the natural world and that such an order is compatible with the concepts possible in the human mind.

The Periodic Table of the elements is one great example of this order, which is objectively present in the world and cannot be ascribed to a particular perspective impressed on the world by the scientist. All the matter in the world is composed of the same set of slightly more than one hundred elements. These elements can be arranged in a periodic sequence indicating their constitution in terms of protons, neutrons, and electrons, each element differing from its neighbors by a difference of only one electron, one proton, and a small number of neutrons.

Order exists also among the variety of living plants and animals. In spite of the existence of millions of species of animals on earth, throughout nature there is a pervading similarity rather than a disorganized array of forms.

In *Man on a Spaceship*, W. Pollard quotes from the paper, "The Unreasonable Effectiveness of Mathematics in the Natural Sciences," by Eugene Wigner, Nobel laureate in physics. He points out the number of times in the history of science that a mathematical scheme, conceived originally as pure mathematical exercise in the mind of a mathematician, later turned out to apply exactly to a complex situation in the physical world. He writes,

> Since nature is certainly not itself a product of the human mind, the correspondence between the mathematical system and the structure of things in the natural world has a kind of miraculous quality about it.

And again,

> It is impossible to appreciate the force of these considerations without having personally experienced the amazing ways in which

the theories of mathematical physics apply to the natural world. I have a feeling that most physicists have become, through too much familiarity, insensitive to the really amazing and miraculous character of the correspondence which they live with and practice every day.[2]

Purpose and design in the universe. The universe is not only found to be ordered; it is found to be dynamically ordered in such a way that design appears apparent and purpose seems inherent. Arguments along this line have often been called teleological arguments. A modern exponent of the teleological argument is Teilhard de Chardin, who seeks to combine his Christian faith with the theory of evolution by seeing in the evolutionary process the outworking of the purpose and design of God.

The teleological argument is based on such observations as the unique properties of the earth to sustain human life, the extraordinary properties of water that also contribute to human life and civilization, the marvels of human and animal physiology, and many examples drawn from the plant and animal world where the existence of each of two participants is completely dependent on the existence of the other.

Man and his nature. The unique characteristics of human life call for the existence of a source. Can it be believed that the application of random chance processes over long periods of time to inanimate and impersonal matter could give rise to such human qualities as insight, rational thought, courage, duty, faith, love, conscience, hope, awe, reverence, God-consciousness, appreciation of beauty, self-consciousness, the desire for understanding—in brief, to personality?

Now it must be recognized that all of these evidences for the existence of God from the natural world are indeed just that: evidences. They can all be accepted as meaningless statements of the way things are. One grand meaningless product of chance, a long shot with all the odds against it, just happened to lead to us and our world. The mystery of existence, indications of order and design, and even the apparently unique characteristics of man himself can all be dismissed with one mighty exercise of existential faith

[2] William G. Pollard, *Man on a Spaceship* (Claremont, Calif.: The Claremont Colleges, 1967), pp. 44; 49.

in the attitude that such things must simply be accepted. Beyond that they have no meaning.

The rejection of these evidences does not argue for the mental incapacity of the rejecter. As to what is implied concerning the willful and arbitrary motives behind his rejection, only he can judge. This is a point at which Christian faith does have a comment to make. In the words of Paul,

> For what can be known about God is plain to them, because God has shown it to them. Ever since the creation of the world His invisible nature, namely, His eternal power and deity, has been clearly perceived in the things that have been made. So they are without excuse; for although they knew God they did not honor Him as God or give thanks to Him, but they became futile in their thinking and their senseless minds were darkened. Claiming to be wise, they became fools... (Rom. 1:19–22).

Here the perspective of Christian faith questions the mask of detached objectivity and inquires, "Did you reject these evidences because you had to—or because you wanted to?"

One other deficiency of these kinds of evidence must also be mentioned. They point to only a very few of the attributes of God. If a natural theology is constructed on their basis alone, the result is likely to resemble deism more than Christian faith. The quotation from Paul's letter to the Romans above indicates that natural theology can reveal only the power and existence of God. Natural theology alone suggests as models for God such concepts as the Great Mathematician, Machinist, Lawgiver or Designer. That God is love, that he cares for you and me, that he is righteous and holy— these attributes of him are not revealed by the natural universe. Only his own special revelation through the words of the Bible is able to convey them to us.

Arguments from Science against the Christian Position

Outside of the Christian community the above arguments for the existence of God seem to carry little weight today. Rather, the contrary mood seems to prevail, that the development of a scientific description of the world has made the whole religious perspective including the existence of God untenable. We have seen in

chapter 2 how the prevalent world view that developed with the
advent of science challenged traditional views of God, man, and
the world. The personal character of God, the unique position of
man, the importance of this earth in the totality of the universe—
all these were questioned and cast into a new light. On every hand
traditional views associated with the Christian position were in
full retreat or at least on the defensive. It is most important to
realize that what has happened is not the invalidation of the Christian doctrines, concepts, and values: what has happened is the
scientific invalidation of those caricatures of Christian faith which
masqueraded as true Christian faith as long as they could get away
with it.

Science has made God unnecessary. Once God was necessary in
order to explain how the physical world worked. Astronomers
needed God to keep the planets in order; even Newton invoked
God as necessary to correct perturbations intermittently in the
heavens. God was needed to bring the rain, to heal the sick, to
create life, and to provide a necessary mechanism in thousands of
other activities where man was ignorant of the physical events
occurring. Now science has filled in many of these gaps in man's
knowledge and is in the process of filling in many more. We don't
need God today, the argument goes, to keep the planets in place,
or to bring the rain, or to heal the sick. We know that gravity,
meteorological conditions, and the doctor are able to handle these
problems. Wherever God was equated with a mechanism on the
level of the natural world, he is no longer needed.

The argument is sound as far as it goes. Whatever "god" was
historically invoked to provide a supernatural mechanism where
man's knowledge of the natural mechanism was lacking was a god
of man's own invention. That god is indeed dying as science advances. Nor is it of any advantage to retreat a step from the world of
the physical and set up new bastions for the defense of this God-of-
the-gaps in the biological and psychological realms. We can expect
a biological and a psychological explanation eventually for biological and psychological phenomena.

What we are being forced to realize is that God is not an alter-
nate to physical, biological, or psychological explanations for phenomena which we do not yet properly understand. Rather we need
to invoke the two theses of chapter 1, a theme to be expanded in

later chapters. We must see God as primarily active in those phenomena that we normally think of as natural, active moment by moment in expressing himself freely in the natural course of events; these phenomena depend for their very existence on the power of God. We must also recognize the validity of more than one level of description for a given phenomenon. The ultimate meaning and interpretation of any natural event derives not from the event and its own natural mechanisms but from the place and interpretation of the event in relationship to God.

In the words of M. Jeeves, *"God, to the theist, while being the cause of everything, is in the scientific sense the explanation of nothing."*[3]

The argument is frequently advanced that because something can be described in mechanistic terms, or even because something "works" mechanistically, it is inappropriate to associate the phenomenon with God and his activity. This argument has a strange history.

Before the rise of science, God was seen fulfilling several capacities. He was (1) God the Creator, (2) God the Sustainer and Preserver, (3) God the Redeemer, Source of love and personal meaning in life, and (4) God the Mechanician, working out his will in nature.

Before the recognition of the general principles of gravity, God the Mechanician was credited with the direct maintaining of the planets in their proper orbits. The answer to the question "What holds the planets in space?" was properly and completely, "God does." When it came to be realized that the general gravitational interaction between material bodies could be described in terms of a basic physical phenomenon, it became evident that the view of God the Mechanician, directly holding the planets in space through a nonphysical process, was not satisfactory. The remarkable thing is that the recognition of a law of nature, an illustration of the efficacy of natural phenomena, should thereby lead to the conclusion that it was *not* God who was holding the planets in place. Even more remarkable is the conclusion that because the previous view of God the Mechanician needs to be reinterpreted, it follows that the place of God as Creator, Sustainer and Redeemer can all be summarily dismissed!

[3] Jeeves, *The Scientific Enterprise and Christian Faith*, p. 103.

Isn't it strange that the recognition that God works well and in an orderly way (rather than in a chaotic and disorderly way) should lead to the conclusion that it is not God working?

For thousands of years, the word of God has proclaimed to men, "Thou shalt not steal." To some extent men refrained from stealing because they believed that God would be displeased with them if they stole. Then sociologists recognized the fact that actually "not stealing" was a beneficial characteristic of society. A society in which stealing took place was a worse place to live than a society in which stealing was prohibited. Men recognized that the commandment of God was not an arbitrary dictum of an oriental potentate-in-the-sky, but that the commandment of God really worked. It described the structure of life best fitted for improving the quality of life in human society. The remarkably strange aspect of this development is this: When men believed that the commandment "Thou shalt not steal" had only arbitrary authority, they freely attributed it to God. But when men realized that the commandment "Thou shalt not steal" actually described the conditions required for the good social life, they concluded that God was *not* responsible!

Underlying all such conclusions is the following curious principle: if affairs cannot be understood, if they appear to be random and chaotic, then God is behind it; but if affairs demonstrate such order that they can be reasonably described in orderly fashion, and in particular if they are clearly effective descriptions of the human condition, then God can be dispensed with.

Science has made belief in the supernatural impossible. Once it was possible to believe in the supernatural. As little children are able to believe in fairies and Santa Claus, so in the infancy of the human race it was possible to see evidence of God and the supernatural everywhere, simply because so little was understood in natural terms. But now we ascertain truth according to the scientific method, and this guide to truth never tells us about the existence of God at all. Like the Soviet astronaut who returned from his space trip with his atheism confirmed because he didn't see God out there, modern man is likely to give up his belief in God because God cannot be scientifically detected.

Again there is some truth to the argument. It is curious, however, that though science has been effective in preventing belief in the traditional supernatural, it has been remarkably ineffective in preventing belief in the avant-garde supernatural. People are always prone to believe all kinds of things. Even in our modern age, their gullibility is a constant marvel. It is as though this propensity of human nature were not to be denied. Convinced that science has made belief in the traditional supernatural impossible, men today manufacture their own new supernatural. In astrology, scientology, drugs, Zen, Satan worship, and a hundred other ways, they make perverted human attempts to inject a supernatural element in life. Any element of objectivity is welcome in such a morass of self-delusion. Science can and should play the role of keeping people from believing nonsense; actually Christian faith plays the same role.

To take the position that science has made belief in the supernatural impossible is to misunderstand completely the purpose and potentialities of science. It makes the faith assumption that the scientific method is the only way to obtain truth in spite of all the evidence to the contrary. The steps in the argument go something like this:

1. Science apprehends the truth by a method involving only sense contacts.
2. Anything that can be apprehended by sense contacts is natural.
3. There is no truth except scientific truth.
4. There is no truth except natural truth.
5. Therefore, there is no supernatural.

The argument should go as follows, however:

1. Science apprehends the truth by a method involving only sense contacts.
2. Anything that can be apprehended by sense contacts is natural but may well have a supernatural interpretation.
3. The manifestation of the supernatural in the natural can be apprehended by science.
4. Any manifestation of the supernatural in a manner not apprehendable through sense contacts will be out of the domain of science.

5. Science is only one way of obtaining truth; the whole truth always requires more than the scientific perspective.

It is generally true that a scientific description is a natural description. What we need to realize, however, is that a natural description does not preclude a supernatural description. That brings us back once again to thesis 2 of chapter 1—that there are many levels at which a given situation can be described. It should be kept in mind that a scientific description is only one part of the comprehensive description.

Science has shown that Christian faith is only . . . . This sentence can be finished in half a dozen different ways. Statements claiming that science says something is *only* . . . are too numerous to count. The claim is made that science has shown that man is only a complex machine. That science has shown that Christian conversion is only a psychological experience. That science has shown that the development of the Christian faith is not historically unique and that hence Christian‧faith is only another human religion. That science has shown that Christian faith is only a sociological phenomenon, retained by those in power in order to mollify the poor and downtrodden.

We will be saying more about many of these topics in later chapters. The point of significance here is that science can *never* say that anything is *only* . . . . "Man *is* a complex machine." That is a scientific statement. "Man is *only* a complex machine." That is a subjective philosophical speculation not derivable from science. It is simply another repetition of the old fallacy: if science shows us that man is a complex machine, and if we can know nothing except what science tells us, then man is only a complex machine. Christian conversion *is* a psychological experience; it is also a work of supernatural regeneration. The Christian faith *is* another human religion; but it is based on the supernatural revelation of the One who made heaven and earth, who became a man who lived and died—and then rose from the dead! The Christian faith *has* been colored by sociological influences and it has been misused by people who never knew what the name Christian meant; but its content and its Lord are unique.

Every *only* is a subjective judgment of men. Science knows no *onlys*.

Miracles

One of the points at which science and Christian faith seem most obviously to be at odds is the subject of miracles. In order to be called a miracle, an event must have the following characteristics: (1) it must either appear to violate the laws of nature as they are currently known, or it must appear as an extremely improbable coincidence of diverse elements, and (2) it must have a deeper significance than simply being a rare and unusual event for the persons involved, usually related to their religious perspective.

The claim is made that science has shown that miracles are impossible. What is really meant is that because the structure of a miracle does not fit the structure of scientific truth, it cannot therefore be true. Actually, since miracles are unique historical events, science can say nothing about them at all, one way or the other. The only judgment that science can bring fairly is to say, "I wouldn't expect one." But that, after all, is the very nature of a miracle and hardly constitutes an argument against their reality.

One of the most troublesome aspects of miracles is that they seem to call for God to intervene in a normally orderly and well-behaved world in order to produce something special. Thesis 1 of chapter 1 is directed against this perspective. We must not think of the world as having been outfitted by God at some time in the past with the various physical laws that govern the behavior of matter, and of its having continued since that time on the basis of God's initial momentum without his specific activity in the whole system. In this framework a miracle becomes an oddity, an affront to the work of creation, a meddling with a self-sufficient world that is operating well. On the contrary, when it is realized that the very existence of the world from moment to moment depends upon the creative and sustaining power of God, that no natural law has any power of its own to continue, that no "expected" circumstance has any ability to bring itself into being, we come to the conclusion that God's activity in a miracle is not qualitatively different from God's activity in natural phenomena. In bringing to pass the law of gravity or the law of electromagnetic radiation, God acts freely and continuously. He is not constrained by these laws, as if he had to meddle with them to produce a different result. At rare times and in accordance with his specific purpose, he acts freely to produce what the world interprets as a miracle. For corn to grow does not require a different *kind* of activity by God than for the dead to rise. It is just that in the pattern of reality set by God, it is common and expected that the corn will grow. No particular surprise or deeper significance need be read into the growth of corn (although it is clear that a genuine reaction to the growth of corn produces both wonder and awe). But the resurrection of the dead is a unique and special kind of event, occurring in the present state of the world only at those rare times when the people of God were enabled to display the love and power of God in an unusual and striking way.

Let us return for a moment to the judgment of a scientist on miracles—"I wouldn't expect one." Why wouldn't he expect one? Because in the ordinary course of events his experience is that miracles do not happen. But no discussion of miracles ever suggests that they happen in the "ordinary course of events." As Jeeves says,

> It is sometimes not realized how relatively scarce the miracles are within the biblical narrative as a whole. . . . We find that they tend to concentrate around three major eras in the total biblical record, namely around the events of the Exodus of the people of Israel from Egypt, around the time of the proclamation of the prophets of the ninth century B.C., and lastly around the apostolic era recorded in the New Testament.[4]

On the other hand, as it would be totally unexpected that John Smith, a man, would have miraculous powers, so it would be equally unexpected if Jesus Christ, God incarnate, did not.

When miracles are recognized as a particular form in the outworking of God's purpose in the world, when they are associated with the preaching of God's Word, the spreading of the gospel of Jesus Christ, and the manifestation of God's witness in the world, they become clearly distinguished from the world of magic and sorcery. Then it becomes clear that miracles are not arbitrary violations of natural law to impress the people involved, but that they are appropriate evidences of God's free activity in making himself known.

---

[4] Jeeves, *The Scientific Enterprise and Christian Faith*, p. 31.

Is the Bible a Scientific Book?

The question as to whether the Bible is a scientific book has many possible interpretations. We might inquire first as to the criteria by which one would declare a book to be scientific. If we are consistent, we would say that it must report only the interpretations of sense data. Much of the Bible meets this criterion. The authors record events that they witnessed or established through careful consultation with eyewitnesses. But clearly the Bible is also partially not a scientific book, since it contains hearsay evidence— even if this evidence is the word of God.

But whether or not the Bible is a scientific book according to some generally accepted criterion is really not the primary consideration. The more important question is: does the Bible set forth a *true* description of reality? Christian faith presents a clear affirmation, "Yes, that is exactly what the Bible does."

Unfortunately, what constitutes a true description of reality is something that people have long debated. Some people argue that in order to be true a description must be literally correct. And others argue that in order to be true a description must be completely accurate no matter what criterion of accuracy is used to judge it. When these viewpoints are applied indiscriminately to the Bible, we obtain the conclusion that in order for the Bible to be called a true description of reality, it must be literally true in every place and exhaustively accurate. No book of interest meets these criteria. Perhaps a book in mathematics or formal logic might satisfy them, but no book that attempts to treat the matters of deep significance for personal existence can consistently be literally true and exhaustively accurate; this is prohibited by the very use of human language and by the problems of communication.

What then do we mean when we affirm that the Bible presents a true description of reality? We mean that we may have complete confidence in the truth of the insight given to us by the Bible, provided that we derive our insight in the right way. It must come from a contextual interpretation in the light of the purpose for which the Bible was written: to make known God as Creator and Redeemer and His Son Jesus Christ as Savior and Lord. This question has been treated at some length in *The Encounter Between Christianity and Science*.

If we want to know what the Biblical revelation says to us today, we must be guided by what the Biblical author was trying to say when he wrote, and by why he was trying to say it. In order to obtain a real understanding of the Biblical revelation, we must go beyond the face value of the words in our English translation, back to the words of the best text in the original language, back to the significance of these words in the days in which the originals were written, back to the concepts and customs of the people for whom the originals were written, back to the underlying purpose for which the originals were inspired by God.[5]

These principles for interpretation will lead us to view some portions of the Bible as literal statements of fact, and some as symbolic presentations of truth in a universally understandable form. They will lead us to view some statements in the Bible as scientifically true today, and to view others as no longer accurate though they stated truths in terms of scientific models of their own day. Bernard Ramm expresses much the same view in an article written for the *Journal of the American Scientific Affiliation*.

I think it is possible to teach the doctrine of creation from the point of view of the cosmological systems of Ptolemy, Newton or Einstein. I think the kinds of things Scripture wants to say can be said in the context of any of these three theories without dignifying the theories as such as revealed truth. . . . A revelation couched in terms of perfected science as of the year 3000 A.D. would have been a meaningless and confusing revelation. Therefore it is valid to make a distinction between the structural or literary forms in which a revelation comes and what the revelation itself teaches.[6]

Specifically what is meant by these claims will become clearer as we apply them to a variety of situations in later chapters. The view presented here is not based on a "low view of inspiration." It is based on a "high view of inspiration" that is faithful to the kind of book the Bible is intended to be.

One extreme viewpoint on what constitutes a true description has led to two great misunderstandings. The hyperconservative Christian and the non-Christian with a scientific background agree with one another that the Bible must be literally and completely

[5] Richard H. Bube, ed., *The Encounter Between Christianity and Science* (Grand Rapids, Mich.: Wm. B. Eerdmans, 1968), pp. 90, 91.

[6] Bernard Ramm, "The Relationship of Science, Factual Statements and the Doctrine of Biblical Inerrancy," *Journal ASA* 21 (1969): 98–104.

true whenever a scientific matter is mentioned in the text. The hyperconservative Christian finds that scientific views appear to conflict with a literal interpretation of some portions of the Bible; on the basis of his conviction, he attacks and misinterprets science. The non-Christian with a scientific background agrees that certain scientific views appear to conflict with a literal interpretation of some portions of the Bible; on the basis of his conviction, he rejects the Christian position. It is ironic that these two groups of people should agree on the wrong attitude toward the Bible, and then use their agreement to attempt to invalidate the other's position!

But Which Has the Priority?

When we deal with a question in which both science and the biblical revelation are involved, which has the priority?

In a real sense it must always be the biblical revelation—but not in every conceivable way. Insofar as our interpretation of the biblical revelation is faithful to its purpose, we have an authoritative and wholly reliable insight into the nature of the world. We do not place ourselves in a ridiculous position if we maintain, "Only a Christian knows what a cow is." (The word *cow* in this sentence is an irrelevance; it can be replaced by any other noun in the English language without affecting the truth of the statement.) When we maintain that only a Christian knows what a cow is, we do not mean that only a Christian knows about bovine biology, physiology, and psychology; we mean that only a Christian knows that a cow is a creature made by God, placed in the world to supply a variety of roles and needs, not the least of which is to be a source of food and drink for man. If a man thinks that a cow is *only* the end product of a long series of meaningless chance events, he does not really know what a cow is. If a man thinks that a cow is *only* a structure of complex organic matter which he is free to treat in any way that pleases him, he does not really know what a cow is. Because knowledge of the identity of the cow can come only from the biblical revelation, we must affirm the priority of that revelation.

No interpretation of ultimate significance can be made without the biblical revelation. Lacking the perspective it gives us, the things of the world are disconnected objects only, the events of the world are mere unrelated coincidences, and life is only a frustrating attempt to derive ultimate significance from insignificant trivialities.

The biblical revelation alone has the ability to let man see himself as he is. Science is done by men; men are judged and informed by the biblical revelation.

The biblical revelation alone has the ability to guide and judge the directions and motives of science. Science is helpless to define its own "ought." What scientists ought to be doing, and what scientists are forbidden to do because of the very properties of human nature, can be prescribed only on the basis of a personal judgment. In the biblical revelation we have the key to God's own judgment and evaluation.

The biblical revelation has the priority because it informs us of God's activity in history. That is something we cannot deduce from scientific procedures alone. The escape of the people of Israel from slavery in Egypt under Moses may be seen as the great Old Testament foretelling of the deliverance of the world from the slavery of sin by Jesus Christ. Archaeology consistently confirms the historical accuracy of the biblical revelation as a historical document; the interpretation of these historical events informs us of the constant outworking of God's purpose in history. The biblical revelation gives to us the eyewitness accounts of men who experienced the mighty acts of God in the world, of men who lived with Jesus Christ, saw him die, and then were overwhelmed with surprise and joy when he rose from the dead. Whether I can believe that Jesus Christ rose from the dead or not does not depend on my ability to rationalize the resurrection scientifically. I do not cease to believe in the risen Lord because resurrection is not a scientifically explainable phenomenon. The biblical revelation with its testimonies of eyewitnesses and with its accounts of events in the lives of those men who were transformed by the power of Christ's resurrection is confirmed in the present by its effects in the lives of those who commit themselves to God in Christ.

There are portions of the biblical revelation, however, which deal with subjects for which the authors could not be eyewitnesses. In these, insight had to be given in a general and basic way. This is particularly true of the final chapter of Revelation and the early portion of the first chapter of Genesis. Many of the symbols that appear in the beginning of Genesis reappear at the end of Revelation. Revelation is essentially a prophecy of the future, summarizing in apocalyptic style the final victory of the people of God in spite of present suffering and hardship. Although many attempts have been made to give specific literal interpretation to the events described there, attempts to press such interpretation have not been fruitful. Most commentators agree that much of the material must be taken as symbolic, the description being more reacted to than analyzed in detail, much as one would react to the total impact of a massive tapestry rather than becoming concerned about the details of the weaving. The early portions of Genesis take on a similar quality, and might be referred to as presenting a prophecy of the past. Genesis, presenting the great basic truths of man's origin and sin in a manner comprehensible by all its readers, becomes a counterpart to Revelation, presenting the great basic truths of man's destiny and judgment. The manner in which foundational truths are conveyed under these conditions deserves some attention.

Ultimately truth alone has the priority. And the truth is not a single-faceted thing. What, for example, is the true answer to the question, "Where did I come from?"

Answer 1. God made me.
Answer 2. The dust of the earth.
Answer 3. My mother's womb.
Answer 4. The union of my father's sperm and my mother's ovum.
Answer 5. A middle-class family.
Answer 6. A Christian home.
Answer 7. Ancestors from Germany.
Answer 8. The hospital where I was born.
Answer 9. Providence, Rhode Island.

We could go on listing *true* answers to the question, "Where did I come from?" Our answers would depend on our interpretation of the various words in the question and on the purpose for which we thought the question was asked. If I apply for a job and am asked this question, to reply, "God made me," would be both irrelevant and impertinent—just as irrelevant and impertinent as to remind my questioner of the biological origin of life. If the same question were asked in the midst of a profound discussion of matters of ultimate significance, to reply, "Providence, Rhode Island," would be equally irrelevant and impertinent.

Now if the scientific question of my origin is most appropriately answered in terms of the merger of sperm and ovum, and if the theological question of my origin is most appropriately answered in terms of the creative activity of God, is there any contradiction? Does one have priority over the other? Because the scientific answer does not mention God, do I condemn it as false? Because the theological answer does not deal with the physiological mechanisms of conception, do I regard it as insignificant and of no relevance? The theological answer does have much more ultimate content than the scientific answer; it is far more important to know that God made me than it is to know that I am the product of merger between sperm and ovum. If you could tell a person only one of these two answers and it had to last him for a lifetime, there is little question as to which answer would be the most significant for him to know. And if you had to write an account to answer the question of origins that would be useful and understandable by all ages and all cultures, I suspect that there would be little question as to which of these two possible types of answer you would give.

In a way, the situation to which some portions of the biblical revelation address themselves may be like the situation of answering questions about the "facts of life" from a child. When a little girl comes to her mother and asks about the *real* facts of life, but still is unprepared and uninterested in knowing all the clinical details, her mother might reply something like this: "When you grow up and become a woman like Mommy, you will meet a man like Daddy, whom you will love very much. He will love you very much, and one day—because you love each other so much—a baby that is part him and part you will start to grow in your tummy. When the baby is big enough to live by himself, he will come out of a special place made just for that—and be born!"

When the same girl is older, this kind of answer would not be the kind she would then be seeking, but it would hardly be any less important or significant for her mature life. Then it would be important for her to know about menstruation, intercourse, orgasm, and venereal disease. But which is the most important thing to know about sex, the mechanics of intercourse only, or the relationship between physical sex and interpersonal love relationships? One of the complaints against public school sex education is that only the mechanics of the act are stressed without due appreciation for love and for the spiritual attributes of the relationship between mutually committed lovers. On the other hand, good intentions based on love may meet with severe obstacles on the road to fulfillment without some knowledge of sexual mechanics. Which has the priority? Why make a choice? The account given by the mother to her little girl is no less true for its simplicity and omitting of the mechanical details. Nor does the realization that orgasm can be achieved by physical manipulation invalidate the central role of love in sexual fulfillment.

It may seem strange to have entered upon this digression into sex in the middle of a discussion of biblical revelation. I am convinced, however, that the interpersonal relationships between man and woman committed one to the other in love are among the clearest examples we have in human life of basic spiritual reality. This is the reason that Paul in his letter to the Ephesians (5:21–33) interweaves his discussion of the man–wife relationship and the Christ–church relationship.

Sometimes the presentation of truth given in the biblical revelation is like that of the mother to her little girl. It takes into account the kind of knowledge the listener possesses and the concepts that will make sense for him. It starts where he is and works with him. It meets him where he stands and sets forth the truth about God, the world, and the nature of man in terms that are understandable and acceptable by men of all ages, all cultures, all degrees of scientific understanding. To accomplish this, the biblical revelation uses thought models and patterns common to the authors and their listeners and sets forth through them the timeless truths that we need to know. As the truths about sexual relationship told by the mother to her little girl far transcend in importance and significance any of the later mechanistic details she was to learn, so the truths about origins and destinies revealed in the Bible far transcend in importance and significance any of the scientific mechanisms which may be discovered in the course of time. And yet this does not diminish the proper significance of the mechanisms nor the desirability of knowing and understanding them for a complete appreciation of the whole truth.

Science and the Bible: Mutual Aids in Interpretation

An important interaction exists between the scientific interpretation of the natural world and the theological interpretation of the biblical revelation in that each serves as an aid to interpretation of the other.

Science can be a useful guide in deciding what degree of literalness is appropriate in interpreting certain biblical portions where scientific knowledge is applicable. Since the scientific view is never permanently established, such an aid must be considered as subject to change and not the basis for dogmatic assertions. Nevertheless, it is evident that science has made valuable contributions to biblical understanding. Scientific developments in astronomical understanding have drastically altered earlier accepted interpretations placing the earth at the center of the solar system. Scientific estimates of the age of the universe and of man have affected the interpretation of the early chapters of Genesis and other portions of the Bible as well. Enhanced scientific understanding of the biological and psychological aspects of man have informed the biblical view of man. Increased appreciation for scientific mechanisms has emphasized the fact that God's activity is commonly encountered in natural phenomena rather than openly supernatural "violations of natural law."

The biblical revelation in turn provides insight into the nature of man. It raises the much needed warning against the supposedly unprejudiced objective conclusions of scientists. It provides the basis for human dignity and worth essential for determining how man is to be treated scientifically. And it forms the foundation for the great number of ethical problems that modern science is encountering with ever greater frequency.

As scientific investigations may provide data and insights that are evidence for the activity of God, though such insights are not the immediate purpose of the data, so the biblical revelation may provide statements of scientific mechanisms, though such statements are not the immediate purpose of the revelation.

Within the scientific framework, theological interpretations are secondary. The scientific answer to the question as to what holds the solar system together is gravity. Within the theological framework, scientific interpretations are secondary. The theological answer as to what holds the solar system together is God. Within the scientific discipline it is more important for the scientist to understand the role of gravity; within the theological discipline it is more important for a theologian to understand the role of God. Since theology deals with the ultimate meanings of life, it is always more important for *a man* to know that God holds the solar system together than to know that gravity does it. But to say that it is *more* important to know that God holds the solar system together in no sense minimizes the importance of knowing that gravity does. This is simply another way of saying that the biblical revelation has priority.

Scientific understanding also guides in the application of biblical revelation to everyday life. It acts as a bridge between the principle enunciated in the biblical revelation and the living out of that principle in contemporary society. This is true even in the work of world evangelization where a scientific basis for decisions is as necessary as a complete faith commitment to God. In a recent article, Edward R. Dayton says,

> Few people are asking "Why?" and even those with normally scientific approaches to problems are willing to "leave it in the hands of the Holy Spirit." . . . It is almost as though it said somewhere in the Bible that when one considers the task of evangelizing a lost world, one should switch to a completely nonrational approach to the problem.[7]

Again science and biblical revelation are allies and complementary approaches, each aiding and purifying the interpretations of the other.

Can Science Demonstrate the Reality of Christian Faith?

There is general agreement that science cannot demonstrate the existence of God. Evidences of God's creative activity in the world

---

[7] Edward R. Dayton, "Research: A Key to Renewal," *Journal ASA* 21 (1969): 15.

are uncovered by scientific investigation, but they remain evidences which must be interpreted in the light of an independent faith commitment. On the other hand, if Christian faith really produces changes in the individual, if the "new birth" of Christian theology is a reality, then there ought to be scientific tests that can be done with Christian men and women that would show them quite different from other non-Christian control groups. We ought to be able to show scientifically that the Christian group are on the average more loving, more compassionate, more humble—in brief more thoroughly pleasant and friendly individuals than their non-Christian counterparts.

There are a number of profound scientific difficulties in carrying out such an objective. Because no adequate interpretation of the Christian position argues that Christian conversion makes men perfect and sinless, it is not possible to look for a completely sharp dichotomy. All of us know non-Christians who are really more friendly and pleasant people than some Christians we know. The Christian position affirms that the friendly and pleasant non-Christian would become more loving and vital if he committed himself to Jesus Christ and that the negative and critical Christian would become even more unpleasant and self-centered if he did not commit·himself to Christ. In other words, Christian faith makes a real difference in the kind of person a man is and in the kind of life he leads, but this is to be measured against the kind of person he might or would have been. It is difficult to carry out the scientific test, therefore, because it is difficult to arrive at a meaningful sample group and at a meaningful control group.

Still, unless an objective change in a man's life, personality, and values follows from his becoming a Christian, the Christian claim that accepting Jesus Christ as Lord and Savior is accompanied by a new creative work of God is unsubstantiated. It still seems that on the average some kind of scientific testing ought to be possible to indicate that the Christian regeneration is objective reality and not simply subjective theology.

Some tests along this line, designed to measure the degree of racial prejudice and bias, have yielded fairly consistent indications. Curiously, they have shown that the greater the degree of orthodoxy and conservatism in a group's theology, the more likely members of the group were to exhibit racial prejudice. Such tests have led some psychologists to argue that a religious commitment naturally leads to racial and ethnic intolerance. More recent studies, however, warn of the care with which such scientific research must be done and the even greater care with which it must be interpreted. A close correlation was announced by Robert C. L. Brannon in *Psychology Today* between the religious *style* of a man and his probability of having racial prejudice. He distinguished between two such religious styles: (1) religion regarded instrumentally, as a means of selfish advantage, and (2) religion regarded devotionally, as a part of everyday life and central to the meaning of life. In most general surveys of church members these two groups would not be distinguished. Frequently the first group far outnumbers the second. Very strong correlation was found between those with an instrumental religious view and those with racial prejudice. Brannon concludes,

> More research must be done before we can understand this relationship clearly, but it is not too early to consider some of its implications. We cannot rely on organized religion in and of itself to apply the social doctrine of the New Testament. Only a small minority of churchgoers, those with a strong devotional commitment to religion, have heeded the parable of the Good Samaritan.[8]

We have cited this example in some detail, not because it represents a clear case of objective proof or a final conclusion, but because it shows the care that must be exercised in attempting to establish the effects of Christian conversion by a scientific method, and because it does indicate that such demonstrations may be possible and fruitful if sufficient precautions are taken in data gathering and interpretation.

Is There a Christian Philosophy of Science?

It is sometimes complained that there is no consistent Christian philosophy of science which takes account of the fact that Christians and non-Christians as well can be equally successful in the

---

[8] Robert C. L. Brannon, "Gimme That Old-Time Racism," *Psychology Today* 3, no. 11 (April 1970): 42. See also H. Newton Malony, "The Contribution of Gordon Allport (1897–1967) to the Psychology of Religion," *Journal ASA* 23 (1971): 97.

pursuit of science. The working out of a complete Christian philos-ophy of science is of course a monumental task, still very much in the formative stages because of the relatively short time since science has become a major influence on men's thought. Still, it is possible to make a few general comments to indicate the trend that such a philosophy must take.

A Christian philosophy of science must start with the reality of the created structure of the universe, both a created physical struc-ture and a created spiritual structure. This created structure is the work of God which he gives to us. If a description is in conformity with this created structure, it is a true description. Thus it is pos-sible for a non-Christian to know partial truth, but never total truth. Even the Christian indeed cannot lay claim to knowing total truth, but he has a greater breadth of created structure with which he can knowingly come into contact.

Christian science is *good* science, and good science is science that it faithful to this structure of created reality. Science that is honest, open, seeking to capture and to reflect the structure of the world that is really there—that is good science, and that is Chris-tian science. The non-Christian is successful in science, successful in apprehending partial truths of the universe, when and only when he appropriates for himself the Christian approach to the world without recognizing that he is doing it, and without acknowledg-ing the ground of reality that makes it possible for him to do it successfully. Thus the success of the non-Christian in science can be attributed to his use of Christian principles of scientific investi-gation, principles which seek above all else to be faithful to the created structure of the world.

Summary

Although historically science and Christian faith have not been separated but have been viewed as in conflict on a number of oc-casions, an attempted contemporary solution to the problem is to compartmentalize these two areas and keep them out of contact. This false solution does an injustice to both science and Chris-tian faith. The interactions between science and Christian faith must be faced fairly and without fear so that we do not lose a precious insight into the nature of reality.

The investigations of science have uncovered a variety of evidences that support the basic Christian contention of the origin of the world as the creative work of God. Although classical logical arguments seem to have little more than a scholastic appeal, the temporal nature of the universe, the existence of order in the universe, the existence of purpose and design in the universe, and the characteristics of man and human personality, all lend themselves to an interpretation that is wholly consistent with the Christian view of God as Creator and Designer. A man may reject these evidences, but he should carefully examine himself as to his reasons in the light of Rom. 1:19–22. Of course, these evidences from nature —this natural theology—can reveal only the existence and power of God; other knowledge of his character and relationship to the world, as well as insights into the nature of man and his problems, must come from the special revelation given by God in the Bible.

It cannot be repeated too often that the critical trouble in our present day is men's conviction that science has made belief in the traditional supernatural impossible. The popular argument goes something like the following:

1. Rational truth is obtained only by the scientific method.
2. The scientific method has shown that we are only objects, that life has no ultimate meaning or purpose, that God is dead, and that therefore in a real sense man is dead also.
3. The end of rational truth is despair.
4. Traditional religious faith is impossible.
5. We refuse to believe that we are only objects and that life has no meaning. We will make ourselves men and we will give life our own meaning.
6. Since we cannot use rational processes to accomplish this, we cannot use traditional religious faith.
7. We will use nonrational or irrational processes to accomplish this.
8. We will create our own supernatural.

And so we find ourselves today with men hysterically seeking to establish their own humanity, desperately seeking for the God whom they think science has destroyed, frantically trying to raise up a god of their own to take his place. What we have tried to say is simply this: modern man is right in refusing to accept his conclusion about the implications of science; he is wrong only in misunderstanding what these implications of science are. Points 1 and 2 above are both false as stated; what follows from them is necessarily false. Science has not destroyed the traditional values of Christian faith. It has rather destroyed those impostors, caricatures, and wooden idols of Christian faith which men had made for themselves and substituted for the real thing. Once it is realized that the essence of the Christian position is as vitally alive as it ever was, the need for the attempts to create modern substitutes vanishes.

Miracles pose no problem in the modern encounter between science and Christian faith when it is realized that God is always acting freely in both the natural occurrences of everyday life and in those special and unique occurrences of particular religious significance that we recognize as miracles. Thus, miracles are not some kind of interference by God in the normal course of events, as though events would go on in their own way without him if he didn't intervene, but a particular way in which God's unlimited free activity manifests itself.

Christian faith sees in the special revelation of the Bible a wholly authoritative and reliable insight into the nature of reality. The biblical revelation adds to the knowledge of the existence and power of God revealed in his created universe. It makes known his love and personal activity in the world, man's rebellion, and God's redemption. The great truths of the biblical revelation are given in terms suitable for comprehension by the men for whom they were originally written, and for all men who come after them, regardless of the particular state of the civilization or scientific knowledge. Eyewitness accounts of historical events and descriptions of the concurrent experience of God and his activity in the lives of men are reliable and trustworthy evidence of his work in the world both then and now. In those particular areas that deal with the vast patterns of the past or the future, we must expect to find true insight into reality set forth with a minimum of specific scientific mechanisms so as to maintain the purpose for which it was written and its universal application. To insist that every passage of the biblical revelation that seems to deal with a scientific mechanism must do so with absolute authority and finality, that the Bible must be literally and completely true whenever a scientific matter is mentioned in the text, is to miss the point of the kind of book the Bible is. In a misguided effort to preserve and defend a "high view of inspiration," the very spirit of the book and its purpose may be misrepresented.

Science can provide secondary interpretive aids to the biblical revelation, and the biblical revelation in turn can supply secondary interpretive aids to the scientific approach. Because the biblical perspective is far deeper and more inclusive than the scientific viewpoint, reaching to the area of ultimate meaning, the biblical revelation always has the final priority. This does not mean that the biblical revelation provides all the answers; it does mean that the answers that the biblical revelation provides are more important than any others for the overall meaning of life, and for the overall spiritual and physical wholeness of man.

If Christian faith produces the objective changes in the life of a man that the biblical revelation ascribes to a living faith, then these changes ought to be scientifically discernible. Difficulties in the experimental procedure involve problems of sampling and control, but further careful research should be productive.

Topics for Discussion

1. How do you react to the logical "proofs" advanced by Aquinas and Anselm for the existence of God? Can you find flaws in the argument? Do you think that such proofs should be possible even if these particular ones are not satisfactory? Why, or why not?

2. It is sometimes argued that order exists in the world because man thinks in terms of order and therefore superposes his own concepts of it on his view of the world. If the whole picture were looked at there would be even more evidence of disorder, chance, coincidence, etc. What do you think?

3. Is it fair to suggest to someone that his reason for rejecting the evidence for God from natural revelation is his own rebellion against God and his innate unwillingness to acknowledge God as his Lord?

4. Compare what you can find out about a painter by studying

his paintings, or a composer by listening to his compositions, with what you can learn about the same man by having lunch with him in a quiet spot where it is possible to talk. Is there a correlation with natural and biblical revelation?

5. Expound on the quotation from Jeeves on p. 111 in your own language. Why isn't God the explanation for anything?

6. Do you think that UFO (unidentified flying objects), ESP (extra-sensory perception), and LSD are manifestations of modern man's attempt to create a supernatural to fill the vacuum he believes science has caused in traditional supernatural expressions?

7. To what would you attribute the suddenly increasing and expanding interest in witchcraft in our highly sophisticated society?

8. Comment on the claim that science has shown that prayer is only self-hypnosis.

9. Have you ever experienced what you would call a miracle? Would it fit the definition of a miracle in this chapter? How do you tell a miracle from an unexplained natural occurrence? Could an unexplained natural occurrence be a miracle?

10. Paul Seely argues that the biblical writers assumed that the universe consisted of three stories: a top story consisting of a hard firmament; a middle story, the earth; and a bottom story, Sheol or Hades.[9] Can this description be accepted as a possibility without destroying the authority and reliability of the Bible? Why would the biblical writers use this picture?

11. Experiment with the claim, "Only a Christian knows what ———— is," by filling in the blank with various nouns. Do you have any trouble justifying the claim?

12. Choose a fairly complex and technical aspect of the field of work in which you are personally engaged. Then describe this aspect of your work as you would to a five-year-old who asked you about it; as you would to a college graduate specializing in your field. Is one description truer than the other? Did you tell the two questioners different kinds of things about your work?

13. Psalm 93:1 says in part, "Yea, the world is established; it shall never be moved." How would you have been likely to interpret this before the motion of the earth around the sun was known? How after? Do you think now that this line ever contained astro-

---

[9] Paul H. Seely, "The Three-Storied Universe," *Journal* ASA 21 (1969): 18.

nomical information? Has the change in scientific interpretation affected the revelation given by this line?

14. Suggest a short program of research investigation that your church or group might do to check on the effectiveness of the present evangelical style. Have you ever done such an investigation? If so, what was the result; or, if not, why not? Do you think that people might be afraid of such research?

15. Show how a scientific understanding helps a Christian to know how to go about "feeding the hungry."

16. Devise some kind of experiment that would unambiguously distinguish between a person in whom the Holy Spirit is dwelling and one in whom he is not. Do you think such an experiment will work? Why, or why not?

Chapter Seven

The Structure
of the World

Does a religious understanding of the structure of the world, specifically a Christian understanding, require for its validity that other modes of understanding be obviously incomplete within their own frames of reference? Or is it possible that there may be a whole series of levels on each of which it is possible in principle to give an exhaustive and complete description of the world without invalidating or violating descriptions on other levels? The first position has been advanced by Christians to argue that gaps in our knowledge prove the existence of God who fills that gap. And non-Christians have advanced that same position to argue that the existence of exhaustive natural descriptions has proven that a supernatural description in religious terms is both irrelevant and illusionary.

No single statement so vividly characterizes the essence of modern thought as the statement, "Man is only a complex machine." Complete acceptance of the notion that science has rendered untenable the faith, traditions, and morals of the past is part of the cultural heritage of our time. Seldom is it questioned that the process of rational scientific investigation has and does daily confirm that man is only a machine—that God is dead, and that therefore inevitably man, as *man,* is also dead.

Having accepted this conclusion as foregone and incontrovertible, modern man is still faced with the dilemma of achieving correspondence with his own experience. Francis Schaeffer emphasizes this idea.[1] Man, he says, is driven to attempt to overcome the inexorable restrictions of being "only a machine" by a variety of ingenious irrational existential experiments that have no basis in objective history or the universe, that cannot be verified or communicated, and that may ultimately leave him in greater despair than when he started. The irrational trend in modern philosophy, art, music, culture, politics, and theology is based on the assumption that a scientific understanding of the structure of the world is at hand and that this understanding vitiates a Christian understanding of it. If this premise, or at least the latter part of it, could be demonstrated to be false, or even if it could be demonstrated to be an open question, a significant contribution to current thought would have been made. And if such a demonstration could be made known with the force and conviction that its counterargument has enjoyed for the last twenty years or more, a radical change in the thrust of philosophical and ultimately practical thought might be effected.

Does a scientific understanding of the structure of the world make unnecessary and meaningless a Christian understanding? We must be careful to stay clear of oversimplifying approaches when we try to answer this question. To deny that there *is* a scientifically understandable structure of the world in order to defend the Christian perspective would be disastrous. Rather we must first recognize that there is such a structure, and *then* we must ask what it means. It is essential to point out that a scientific understanding is possible and to establish its limits; then it can be indicated why a Christian understanding is not simply redundant and a matter of personal subjective taste.

What Is This Structure?

There is a structure in the world that we can outline fairly simply. This concept was introduced in chapter 1, where in pages 29–35 we discussed the implications of thesis 2: *There are many levels at*

---

[1] Francis A. Schaeffer, *Escape from Reason* (Chicago: Inter-Varsity Press, 1968); *The God Who Is There* (Chicago: Inter-Varsity Press, 1968). See also "Is Man Only a Complex Machine?" A Symposium, *Journal ASA* 22 (December 1970).

which a given situation can be described. An exhaustive description on one level does not preclude meaningful descriptions on other levels. Now we must consider this thesis in more detail and explore its implications for the topics we wish to consider in later chapters. We will refer to the contents of figure 3 in much of the following discussion. Related models of a set of description or structure levels may be found in the writings of a wide diversity of authors, including non-Christian social scientist Michael Polanyi, Catholic priest-paleontologist Pierre Teilhard de Chardin, and Dutch Reformed philosopher-theologian Herman Dooyeweerd.[2]

The structure of the world can be viewed as something static, that is, simply a description of the way things *are*, or as something dynamic, that is, a description of the way things *developed*. Since the second view naturally includes the concept of evolution, it is necessary to emphasize that the problem of the structure of the world and its meaning does not originate uniquely with an evolutionary view. Even a person who is satisfied in his own mind that evolutionary theory is defective must still face the problem of the meaning of the structure of the world. If, after all, man as he exists today is only a complex machine, it really doesn't matter how he arrived at that state. The same question prevails—"Does a scientific explanation of this structure invalidate or make unnecessary a religious interpretation?"

At the most basic level of the scientific structure of the world is energy. This may be viewed in terms of the primeval *ylem*, the concentration of all the matter of the universe into the original primordial fireball of the Big Bang picture of the beginning of the universe. Or it may be viewed simply as another statement of the relationship between mass and energy stated by Einstein, $E = mc^2$, which expresses the equivalent energy E corresponding to a mass m in terms of the square of the velocity of light, c^2. Without energy, nothing exists. The scientist also finds as perhaps one of the most basic principles underlying the world that energy is always con-

---

[2] Herman Dooyeweerd, *New Critique of Theoretical Thought* (Philadelphia: Presbyterian and Reformed Publishing Co., 1953); *In the Twilight of Western Thought* (Philadelphia: Presbyterian and Reformed Publishing Co., 1960); Michael Polanyi, "Life Transcending Physics and Chemistry," *Chemical and Engineering News*, August 21, 1967; "Life's Irreducible Structure," *Science* 160 (1968): 1308; Pierre Teilhard de Chardin, *The Phenomenon of Man* (New York: Harper & Row, Torchbooks, 1959).

served; whatever energy is now present in the total universe must, if this principle is indeed valid, have been present at all times. The origin of this energy is a question to which the scientist cannot ultimately address himself. It is equivalent to the question, "Why is there such a thing as finite existence at all?"

Out of this primordial energy, according to the Big Bang theory, began to form what we might call the "elementary particles"— electrons, protons, neutrons—as well as the more recent finds of nuclear science—anti-particles, neutrinos, mesons, etc. An interaction developed in the primordial energy pool that gave rise to these elements of primeval matter. Or we could alternatively simply recognize that the building blocks of the chemical elements are the simplest forms we know of the transformation of energy into mass.

In figure 3 a dashed line separates the nonmaterial level of energy and the first of the material levels labeled elementary particles. The use of a dashed line indicates that a profound qualitative difference has taken place in passing from the lower (inner) level to the next higher (outer) level. In this case the profound qualitative difference occurs between nonmaterial energy and materialized energy in the form of elementary particles. A double dash line separates the uppermost (outermost) level referring to God from the other lower (inner) levels; the use of the double dash indicates a different kind of relationship between the God-level and other levels, as we shall point out more fully further on.

The formation of elementary particles from energy cannot occur without patterns of interaction that define the state known as particle and differentiate it from that known simply as energy. Similarly, as we proceed, it will be seen that a new degree of patterned interaction enters the structure of the world each time we proceed from lower (inner) to higher (outer) levels. The patterned interaction that bridges the gap between energy and particle is one of the main concerns of modern nuclear science.

What happens if we have patterned interactions between various elementary particles? We have atoms. One proton interacting in a specific stable way with one electron produces one hydrogen atom. Two protons interacting with two neutrons and two electrons produces one helium atom. Thirty-five protons interacting with forty-five neutrons and thirty-five electrons produces one bromine atom.

When atoms form patterned interactions with one another, we

have molecules. Two hydrogen atoms in interaction form one hydrogen molecule. One hydrogen atom interacting with one bromine atom produces one hydrogen bromide molecule. All the varieties of nonliving matter result from the patterned interaction between molecules. We have grouped elementary particles, atoms, molecules and nonliving matter together, not because there are no obvious differences between the different levels, but because all fall in the category of "material but nonliving" and are all rather clearly within the domain of the physical sciences.

When nonliving matter is brought together in the appropriate patterned interaction, living matter, the cell, results. Now it is certainly true that "life" may be difficult to define precisely. In fact, we may expect a certain fuzziness of definition at all of the dashed-line borderline cases where a qualitative change is in progress. As we proceed away from the borderline situations, however, the case becomes rapidly clearer. We have in everyday experience little difficulty in distinguishing betwen living and nonliving matter. What is there that differentiates a living system from the nonliving matter which forms its constituents? It is apparently nothing more than a beautiful and complex *pattern* of interaction by which nonliving matter is organized and organizes itself to produce the manifestations of life. We have placed a dashed-line separation between nonliving and living matter because here again we have passed another qualitative boundary; we have passed from the realm of the physical sciences into the realm of biology.

The patterned interaction of living cells produces a vast variety of plants and animals. Whether a dashed line should separate the cell from plants and animals may be debatable, but we have included it to indicate the qualitative difference between less complex and more complex life forms, and to mark off the purely biological features from the botanical and zoological features.

When the patterned interaction of cells exceeds a certain degree of complexity, we customarily distinguish the product of this complex pattern from the product of less complex patterns. The *most* complex pattern of cell interactions we call a human being, distinguishing him from the animals of the world, with which he shares many similarities. Our dashed line in figure 3 marks this qualitative difference between the human animal and nonhuman animals; it marks the boundary between zoology and anthropology. What is

THE STRUCTURE OF THE WORLD

there that differentiates a human being from the nonhuman cells from which it is formed? As life appears to result from a particular patterned interaction of nonliving matter, so humanness—or human soul if you will—appears to result from a particular patterned interaction of nonhuman cells. As nonliving matter is organized or organizes itself to manifest life, so it appears that nonhuman matter is organized or organizes itself to manifest human soul.

The patterned interaction between men produces what we immediately recognize as social structures. Interactions between social structures represent the most complex form of interaction that exists in the human sphere. This fact has led some, such as Teilhard de Chardin, to propose that the next great step in the evolution of man—a step that will make man one with God—will be initiated with heightened interpersonal interactions.

This then is a brief description of the scientific structure of the world. Starting (either chronologically or ontologically) with energy as the basic source of all matter and motion, we proceed through a series of steps involving patterned interaction to electrons, protons, and neutrons; to atoms and molecules; to many types of nonliving matter and then to living matter; to the cell and its manifestation with increasing complexity in plant, animal and human being; to the human social system and its internal interactions. In this pattern of increasingly complex interactions, several qualitatively different groupings appear to be indicated. The most striking of these represent changes from energy to matter, from nonliving to living matter, and from nonhuman to human character. At the borderlines between these areas there are bound to be fuzzy areas where clear and dogmatic definition is not always easy to make. Is the tobacco mosaic virus alive or not? When its core and sheath are separated, neither exhibits any signs of life; when they are put together, the ensemble has the ability to infect other living matter. A similar difficulty comes in attempting to decide at which stage of the "fossil man" record human soul is to be considered present.

At the highest (outermost) level in figure 3, God has been included in this description of the structure of the world. This level has been separated from other levels by a double dashed line to indicate a profound difference between the God-level and all other levels. (1) A God-description is not a scientific description in the

same sense as this term can be applied to all other levels in figure 3.
(2) The God-level is not reached as a result of a complex pattern
of interaction of lower levels, something that is true of every other
level in figure 3. (3) If any mention of God is to be included in
such a description, it must be everywhere, in every level, in every
line, in every concept. If it is inappropriate to omit God completely
from the structure of the world on the grounds that our understanding of natural mechanisms does away with our need for him, it is
equally inappropriate to insert God's activity only at the beginning
or only at those times of qualitative change pictured as dashed lines
in figure 3. We have placed the God-level at the top (outer edge),
therefore, to emphasize the necessity of knowing God in order to
understand the ultimate meanings of this world, and we have used
a double-dash separation to emphasize that the whole structure is
everywhere completely dependent upon God for its very existence.

Does a scientific description of the world invalidate a religious
description? It doesn't matter at all in answering this question what
approach we take to the structure of the world. We can start with
society and delineate the structure by analysis, or we can start with
energy and delineate the structure by synthesis. If it is possible
reliably to describe the world in terms of this natural structure, have
we made a religious interpretation unimportant or impossible?
What does this very real structure mean? It does not provide its
own interpretation to us; like all other facts, it is not self-interpreting. Does it mean that man is no more than matter? That nonliving
matter is no more than a collection of elementary particles? That
man is only one of the many forms of energy with no intrinsic characteristics that transcend the impersonal materiality of the physical
world? When we describe the structure of man in this way, have
we said after all that man is only the product of natural forces and
is therefore only a very complex organic computer?

The Parts and the Whole

One way to approach an answer to these questions is to take
another look at the constituents of this structure. It can be seen
that the various levels of the structure are each a *whole* composed
of parts on lower (inner) levels, and a *part* for a whole on higher

(outer) levels. For example, a cell is a whole composed of parts that can be categorized as elementary particles, atoms, molecules, and more complex forms of nonliving matter. At the same time the cell is a part in the more complex wholes describable as plants, animals, man, and human society. The structure we have described consists of a series of increasingly complex parts which form wholes. These in turn are parts for a more complex whole. In view of this basic relationship between the various levels of the scientific structure of the world, it is important that we have an appreciation for the relationship between parts and wholes.

In geometry it is usually concluded that the whole is the sum of the parts. And yet, although this is done mathematically, in a real sense it is not even strictly true in geometry. Consider, for exemple, three lines of equal length; what is the whole of which they are the parts? If they are laid end to end, the whole is a line three times as long as any of the parts. The properties of the whole are identical with the properties of the parts, except for the fact that the whole is three times as long as one of the parts. It appears that this is a case where it makes real sense to speak of the whole as being the sum of its parts. But, suppose that we arrange these three lines in the form of an equilateral triangle. Can we really say that the whole, the triangle, is only the sum of its parts? Can we derive the concept of triangle from a single line? Can we derive the concept of angle from a single line? In a real sense the triangle is more than the sum of three lines. Why is it more? Because a triangle represents three lines in a specific patterned interaction. *It is the pattern which gives to the whole that which is not present in the parts.*

Now there are two major fallacies about parts and wholes. The *reductionistic fallacy* claims that there is nothing in the whole which is not basically describable in terms of properties of the parts. Since the properties of the most elementary parts in the structure of the world can in principle be described in terms of the physical sciences, then every aspect of the world can be treated in terms of the physical sciences. Going one step further, the reductionistic fallacy argues that it is therefore established that there is nothing except physics and chemistry in the totality of existence, including of course the life of man.

The other fallacy is what I will call the *additive fallacy*. This position agrees that indeed the whole is more than the sum of its parts, but that this "more" is something that has been added from outside of the system. Consider the following illustration. A piece of wood is allowed to combine with oxygen to burn and produce a flame. Let us now (in a somewhat exaggerated fashion to be sure) consider the possible reactions of the reductionist and the additivist to this situation. How is one to understand the nature of the flame? In our illustration, the flame represents the whole, and the wood and oxygen represent the parts, which in a patterned interaction produce the flame. The reductionist would say that we should get at the physics and chemistry of the parts and in order to do so would therefore separate the wood and the oxygen. When the wood and the oxygen are separated, the flame goes out. So the reductionist might conclude that flame is only an illusion, that there really isn't any such thing as flame because it just disappears when we separate the wood and oxygen. On the other hand, the additivist might conclude that when the wood and oxygen are separated, the flame returns to "flameland" until the next time that wood and oxygen are brought together in combustion. Actually, of course, the flame is the product of the patterned interaction between the carbon of the wood and the oxygen to produce carbon dioxide with an accompanying release of energy. The flame is real, but it depends completely for its existence upon a specific interaction in a particular pattern.

From this consideration we arrive at the following conclusion: when parts interact after a pattern to form a whole, the whole frequently has a set of properties which are characteristic of this patterned interaction but are not deducible directly from the parts that make up the whole, and which require a description on a higher level. Sometimes this difference between the whole and the sum of its parts may appear as only a small change among quite similar entities. But sometimes this difference between whole and parts is so great that the whole seems to belong to a qualitatively different realm than any one of the parts. When two atoms form a molecule, the property of vibration comes into being. A single atom cannot vibrate; vibration is a property of the interaction between atoms forming a molecule. When many atoms interact to form a solid crystal, the property of color comes into being along with many other products of this interaction. When nonliving matter interacts to form living matter, that living matter has properties qualitatively different from those of nonliving matter. Properties such as perception and will require at least a description on the biological level as well as the chemical level. When cells interact to form human beings, these human beings have characteristics qualitatively different from those of other animals. Properties such as self-awareness and God-consciousness require at least a description on the psychological as well as the biological level. When human beings interact to form social groups, new properties again come into existence: politics, language, and crime, to name but a few.

The Systems Concept

Another way of looking at the relationship between parts and whole, that is, between the different levels of the structure of the world, is in terms of a *systems concept*. As scientific developments have increased in complexity, and as the technologist has attempted to do more and more with materials at his disposal, a whole new field called *systems theory* has grown up. This development is in response to the need to regard the properties of very complex assemblages of constituent interacting parts in terms of the properties of the total system, as well as in terms of the properties of the isolated parts. The total system represents the whole.

As an example, consider the system that we recognize as an automobile. This system has various subsystems: fuel pump, spark plugs, carburetor, brake linings, transmission, wheels, etc. Each of these subsystems has smaller sub-subsystems and basic parts. Put them all together in a particular patterned interaction and the automobile emerges. When one sits behind the wheel of a well-designed and attractive car and experiences the exhilaration of being in control of a swiftly-moving powerful vehicle, one recognizes the systems properties of an automobile. Being a deadly missile on the highway in the hands of a careless driver is also a systems property of the automobile. When the system is broadened to include all the subsystems necessary for a properly functioning automobile in motion, it is clear that the human driver is also a very complicated subsystem of the total "moving automobile under control" system.

In a system, influences can be directed either to the system as a whole through interaction with a systems property, or to the system through a part by interaction with the property of a part. Thus the system of a moving automobile can be brought to a stop either by the automobile running into a wall (interacting with the total system) or by a failure of the fuel pump (interacting with a part). In either case the parts and the total system are closely interrelated. Very little that affects the total system leaves the parts unchanged, and very little that affects a part leaves the total system unchanged.

One of the principal mechanisms in the development and operation of systems is the *feedback mechanism*. To speak of feedback is simply to indicate some means by which the performance of the system at one time may be used to guide its performance at a later time. If the human driver is considered a subsystem, then the speedometer, the gas gauge, and the warning light for high beam are all feedback mechanisms. It is the feedback mechanism which plays a large role in the operation of the human system; hunger and pain are illustrations of feedback in action. In the construction of machines with simulated intelligence (for example, automatic dishwashers, self-tuning TV sets), feedback mechanisms play an important role.

In the language of the systems concept, such properties as life and spirit are systems properties. They are not properties of the isolated parts nor are they unreal illusions. They do not result from the addition to the subsystems of something from outside the system when they interact. As it is possible to interact directly with a system by interacting with a systems property, so it is possible for life to interact directly with life and for spirit to interact directly with spirit. Likewise, as it is possible to interact with a system by interacting with a part of the system, thus affecting in some way the whole system, so it is possible to affect life by interacting with some nonliving or living subsystem or to affect soul by interacting with some nonspiritual subsystem.

Questioning Some Popular Discontinuities

In popular discourse we usually assume that a sharp discontinuity exists between such pairs of concepts as living and nonliving, spiritual and nonspiritual (in the sense of having a soul or not hav-

ing a soul), and material and mental. Although it may seem obvious
from common experience that under ordinary circumstances a practical discontinuity exists between these pairs of concepts, we need
to question whether this discontinuity is necessarily intrinsic to the
structure of the world or whether it may be only apparent in our
common experience. We will argue instead that each pair is intimately related and that a continuous progression from each member of the pair to the other probably characterizes the actual structure of the world.

Living and nonliving. It is extremely difficult to arrive at a satisfactory definition of life. Self-preservation and propagation through
interaction with the environment appears to be one of the most
basic criteria by which living things are distinguished from nonliving. The popular notion of being alive usually involves participation in some kind of motion. According to the picture that we have
been developing here, it appears that life should be considered as a
systems property in a system where the parts interact according to
an appropriate pattern. The pattern does not arise wholly from the
parts; the pattern orders the parts in the configuration of their
interaction. We would therefore not be surprised to find that there
was a fairly continuous range of possibilities between nonliving and
living, depending on the complexity and efficacy of various patterned interactions. By our definition of life, we should not be surprised to find that it may be appropriate to speak of some things
having more life than others, or to speak of different degrees of life.
It is therefore inappropriate to suppose that all the objects in the
world can be separated into two mutually exclusive groups, those
that have life and those that do not.

I know of no scientist today who believes that living matter
comes about by the addition of some "vital force" from the outside
to nonliving matter. I know of no biologist or biochemist who believes that life in matter arises from any other process than as a
manifestation of the interaction of nonliving matter according to a
specific pattern. But neither do I know of anyone who considers life
only an illusion, something *totally* reducible in all its aspects to
physical science alone. In fact, if indeed there is nothing more
about a living body than there is about a rock, human beings have
always valued life far above its merits.

Soul-full and soul-less. It is difficult to arrive at a satisfactory definition of life. It is also difficult to establish firm criteria that will distinguish between a living body with a soul and a living body without a soul. We argue that this is for the same reason; the discontinuity between the soul-full body and the soul-less body does not correspond to the actual structure of the world.

The issue of soul-full versus soul-less is heightened when we consider another question: When does this unique spiritual quality of man (soul) come into being? If we adopt the evolutionary view of the development of man, we are then faced with a new question. What period of time or what transformation corresponded to the introduction of soul into the soul-less body? If we reject the evolutionary view completely, we are still faced with the comparable question when we attempt to decide at what point in the development of a human fetus in the womb the soul appears. It should be clear from all of our discussion of these questions that *no answers are possible*. No advance in scientific understanding will enable us more accurately to pinpoint the appearance of soul. The question "When does a man's soul come into being?" has no answers because it is essentially a meaningless question. It incorrectly assumes that a time can be set for the event under inquiry and that a man's soul has a certain timeless identity independent of his body.

To make it possible to set a time for the coming into existence of soul, it would be necessary that there be two well-defined states: the soul-less and the soul-full. But this use of the word *soul* cannot be related to the world as it is. Every living creature possesses aspects of those attributes we associate with the concept of soul. A cat has soul: specifically it has a cat's soul. A dog has soul: specifically it has a dog's soul. By this we mean simply that the characteristics associated with soul in terms of a description of life on the "spiritual" level are at least partially present also in cats and dogs. They remember pleasant and unpleasant circumstances, they respond to love, they make their wants known vocally, and they develop attachments to persons and places. Such animal souls are by no means identical with human souls, however, for the entire being (physical, biological, psychological, and other aspects) of a cat or dog falls short of the capabilities and potentialities of the entire being of a man. The soul of any creature is commensurate with the total development of that creature. The soul of the cat is manifested as the systems property of the totality of all the cat's subsystems. The soul of a man is manifested as the systems property of the totality of all the man's subsystems.

Whether we are dealing with the evolutionary form or the fetal-development form of the question of the origin of the soul, we can maintain that soul is present over a very wide range of time and conditions, and that what we define as human soul—capable of insight, rational thinking, self-consciousness, conscience, hope, God-consciousness, awe, reverence, appreciation for beauty, and the desire for understanding—comes into being as the result of a gradual process of development. If man evolved from lower animals then soul was present in the animals, and soul was present in the sub-human life forms, and soul is present in *Homo sapiens*. But in every case and at every time the word *soul* refers to the particular systems property of the totality of the life-system then active. When conception is started by the union of sperm and ovum, the resulting life-system has a soul at every time in its life span commensurate with the then existing life-system. The two-week-old fetus has the soul of a two-week-old fetus; it is less human than the soul of a two-month-old fetus, which in turn is less human than the soul of an eight-month-old fetus.

Another question may be asked which is quite relevant to the above discussion. When does the unique spiritual quality of man (soul) pass out of existence (either end or undergo transformation)? What shall we say of the man who suffers such grave brain damage that he becomes a living vegetable with no trace of human qualities? What has become of his soul? Or what shall we say of the hopelessly senile person whose human soul can be seen tragically to disintegrate through the years until he becomes almost sub-human in experience? Can we ask where his soul has gone? The point is that we cannot meaningfully assume some changeless identity that exists partially or completely independently of the physical, biological, and psychological body of this life and then passes away from the body upon death. Nor can we try to answer such questions by assuming the possibility of soul-full and soul-less states as two mutually exclusive categories. Any concept of a soul-identity that transcends the specific physical embodiment at a given time and condition must be attributed to a creative act of God beyond the experiences of life in this world. If a soul is to exist after the death of the body, it must be a soul newly created by God for a new mode of existence, for the soul that we see, experience, and deal with in this life is intimately and indissolubly related to the health and life of the body.

The psychosomatic unity of man is attested to both by the biblical revelation and by the increased findings of modern scientific research. When certain subsystems of the total human system are altered either physically or chemically, attributes of the total system are also altered. The taking of drugs is an example of chemical alteration of a particular subsystem of the human being that results in the alteration of the total personality of the person. Unless the soul of a person is to be totally separated from any observable or measurable property of that person, evidence abounds that the soul is a very changeable and unstable entity indeed.

Consider, for example, what is meant when we speak of "I" as though the "I" of today were the same as the "I" of a decade ago or of a decade in the future. The "I" of today is bound to the "I" of yesterday by only a single influence, only by memory. What is there in common between the child of five and the man of fifty? Take away the tie of memory, and what identity is left between the man and the boy? Does a victim of amnesia respond to a movie of himself in childhood in any other way than indifferent non-recognition? There is only one common link between the boy and the man: they are each the embodiment of a specific life-system at two different times during its life. Any other criterion we attempt to develop to establish continuity fails. Every atom in the body of the person has changed. Total changes in personality, outlook, philosophy, and perspective are not uncommon. But if we had watched that particular embodied life-system with a hidden camera through the years, we would have been able to trace a continuity from boy to man.

Whether the boy and the man are necessarily each the embodiment of the same psychological or spiritual life-system is not so easily demonstrated. If the man develops from the boy in the normal course of events, memory affirms the common root. But suppose that something happened to that boy in the course of his life: a severe accident that affected the working of his brain and altered his personality. In what sense is the link of continuous personality present? Is the "I" before the accident the same as the "I" after the accident? Or shall we say that the "I" before the accident died, and that the "I" after the accident was born at that time? But then we would have two personalities, two "I"'s, evidenced by embodiment in a single life-system, and even our definition given above to link a person at two stages of life would prove deficient.

The body, the soul, and the "I" of a person are fragile and changeable things. The Christian faith in the power of God is essential for the preservation of a form of personal identity. It is only by his creative work in restoring new life to a dying and decaying life-system that preservation of the personal soul is possible. This is the reason that the Christian hope is in God's work of resurrection, in which he will create a new life-system for each life-system that has existed in this world. This biblical emphasis is at least a little surprising if the existence of a man's "I" is really concentrated in a soul that is independent of his body. Helmut Thielicke expressed himself emphatically on this point a number of years ago.

> Faith in the so-called immortality of the soul is no faith at all. It is rather a highly questionable assumption, which can be made even by a complete heathen and worldling. One can make it without caring two pins for God. One can still make it, even if one considers the resurrection of the Lord a highly superfluous spectacle of pious fantasy. . . . There *is* no such thing as immortality; God *gives* immortality.[3]

In some sense the experience of Christian conversion can be related to these considerations. The event of regeneration is pictured as a creative act of God, a second birth, whereby a new element to the "I" is brought into being (for example, in Rom. 7:15–32). The "I" after conversion is not the same as the "I" before conversion; the latter has been and is being in some sense put to death, while the former is newly born. Conversion not only "saves" a man's soul, it also changes it.

Material-less mind and mindless matter. The mind versus matter controversy has raged as long as the living versus nonliving, and the soul-full versus soul-less controversies, with as little resolution. It is no surprise, in view of all that we have said above, that the consensus appears quite reasonably to be that there can be no human mind

---

[3] Helmut Thielicke, *How the World Began* (Philadelphia: Fortress Press, 1961), pp. 248–49.

where there is no human matter, but that the functions of mind transcend the properties of matter alone.

The human brain is composed of matter, but it represents the most highly complex patterned interaction of matter known to man. It is instructive to compare in a purely quantitative way the complexity of the brain to other areas of scientific investigation. In the field of physics there are about 1000 (10^3) properties that form the basis for investigation and description. The number of questions treated by chemistry is about ten thousand times greater (10^7). The number of bits of information in the DNA chain in biological studies is some one hundred times greater yet (10^9). Finally, if we consider the number of synapses in the human brain, we find that it is one hundred thousand times greater still (10^{14})! Simply as a computer, the human brain is the most complex and compact instrument known to man.

The property of mind is a systems property of the totality of the subsystems that make up the thinking creature, the most significant subsystem being the brain. Without the subsystems there would be no mind. Yet the properties of mind transcend the properties of the subsystems as the properties of the whole transcend the properties of the parts.

Is This Only Baptized Materialism?

Some may object that after all this is nothing but a case of attempting to Christianize a materialistic view of life. I do not believe such an objection is justified.

First of all the discussion given deals only with what may be called *created* spirit. It proposes that the Eternal Spirit, God, brought into being by an act of creation a system composed of matter but so organized as to manifest the attributes of real spiritual quality. The spiritual personality of the whole man finds its causative and relational source in the Spirit of God, who brought man into being in his own image. To say that God created man in his own image is not to argue that God made man out of God-stuff; the Christian position has always been that God created man out of nothing, bringing into being a creature capable of spiritual relationship to himself. That God should bring real personality into being in the creature through a particular patterned interaction of impersonal matter is certainly a fit thought for reverence and awe.

Second, the view advanced here does not argue for some absolute principle that *all* spirit must be the result of material interactions. The biblical revelation of the nature of God gives no room for the belief that God himself is the product of material interactions. It argues instead for a view of God as intrinsic Spirit, a completely different mode of existence than anything that we can really apprehend on the models of our common materialistic experience. Our point once again is that all created spirit appears to be the result of a patterned interaction in matter; this created spirit reflects in part the spiritual nature of God himself and permits communication and fellowship between man and God. But this created spirit is not divine; it is sinful, in need of regeneration, and in need of divine healing.

Is Man Only a Complex Machine?

The best way to answer this question is to recognize immediately that whatever else needs to be said, man *is* indeed a complex machine. The sense detection system of man is the envy of many attempts to reproduce it in simpler machine form. Machine-like functions of man can be described in terms of the scientific disciplines. The point of debate hangs on the word *only* in the above question.

We should expect that every event in which a human being participates *can* be described on each of the levels of figure 4, and *must* be described on each of the levels if a comprehensive description is desired. Every event in which a human being participates can be described in terms of the physical sciences, in terms of the biological sciences, in terms of the psychological and social sciences, and ultimately in terms of that theology which relates the event and the man to God. There is never a question of something happening on this level but not on another; the question is always one of something happening on every level simultaneously.

We may expect, therefore, to be able to produce a physical description of every activity of a human being. Although we cannot in fact produce an exhaustive physical description at the present time, there is in principle no reason to believe that something *on the physical level* must of necessity elude us in setting forth a physical description. It is not, for example, necessary for the perspective of Christian faith that God be invoked to supply the physical mechanism at some point where human understanding of the natural physical mechanisms breaks down. Even if a complete and exhaustive description on the physical level were at hand (or on any other of the lower, inner levels), it would be a false interpretation to conclude that no other description was valid or necessary for a complete understanding. It is at this point that the common fallacy enters; it is at this point that the true statement "Man is a complex machine" becomes the false statement "Man is only a complex machine."

One of the most outspoken advocates of the reductionistic position with respect to man is Dean E. Wooldridge, author of *Mechanical Man*. Because he is able to provide (or to suppose that provision is possible) a physical description of phenomena occurring in the human body, he concludes that man is only a complex kind of machine. The remarkable feature of his work is that, having proved to his own satisfaction that he himself is only a kind of machine, he then ventures to offer philosophical and even ethical pronouncements. In a final chapter, "Social Attitudes," he concludes that there is no place for a personal God, that moral attitudes are genetically determined and hence inevitably evolutionarily developed, that man's ambition and drive can survive the knowledge that he is only a machine, and that the world is thereby delivered from the trouble-causing concepts of absolute right and wrong. The last words of the book are:

> Society profits when its members behave more intelligently. And men who know they are machines should be able to bring a higher degree of objectivity to bear on their problems than machines that think they are Men.[4]

This conclusion appears to be a tragic misreading of history.

The basic issue, of course, is whether the principle of physical reductionism can be supported. Granted that the structure of the parts (subsystems) that compose a man can be described in prin-

---

[4] Dean E. Wooldridge, *Mechanical Man* (New York: McGraw-Hill, 1968), p. 204.

ciple in terms of physics, does this mean that man, the whole (the system), can be *completely* described in terms of physics as he engages in interpersonal relationships? The issue is not whether there are unique human experiences that have no counterpart in any physical or chemical process; every human experience—conversion, love, courage—*must* have some physical and chemical counterpart in the body, especially the brain. The issue, rather, is whether *everything* about man is *explained* by a physical and chemical *description*. Once these physical and chemical processes have been discovered, is there nothing else meaningful that can be said about the phenomena involved?

In *The Identity of Man*, Jacob Bronowski offers a rebuttal to the reductionistic point of view. Speaking from a humanistic framework, he answers in the affirmative the question "Can man be both a machine and a self?"[5] In accord with the discussion we have developed, he argues that the distinction between a self and a machine is not to be found by analyzing the activities inside the body, but instead by seeing the body within its total interacting environment. Within any given subsystem of reality, there may be the appearance of machinery. The realities that transcend this machinery are to be encountered in interactions on the level of the total systems (wholes) involved and not on the level of the subsystems (parts).

Take any event in the life of a human being. For example, let us take the great experience of Christian conversion, in which a man recognizes the relationship between himself and his Creator, and commits himself to God and to Jesus Christ as Savior and the Lord of his life. How shall we describe this event, and how shall we interpret the description? Conversion will bring with it activity and changes on the level detectable by the physical sciences. Conversion is a physical event. Conversion will bring with it activity and changes on the level of the biological cell. Conversion is a biological event. Conversion will bring with it activity and changes on the level of the psychological perspective. Conversion is a psychological event. Conversion will bring with it activity and changes on the level of social interactions. Conversion is a social phenomenon. Conversion will bring with it activity and changes on the level of

---

[5] Jacob Bronowski, *The Identity of Man* (Garden City, N.Y.: Natural History Press, 1965).

spiritual meaning and personal commitment. Conversion is a religious event, involving interaction with God in a particular person-to-person mode.

Conversion is not *only* a physical event, not *only* a biological event, not *only* a psychological event, not *only* a social event, not *only* a theological event. Which of these descriptions can be left out without depleting the total understanding of what has happened in conversion? To be sure, the focus of the conversion experience is the relationship on the theological level between a man and God, but it could be no experience at all if it did not have its effects on the subsystems of man, on his sociology, psychology, biology, and physical processes. Clearly it is a false argument that the possibility of exhaustive description on a single level excludes the meaningfulness, validity, or necessity of descriptions on all other levels. Any attempt to understand the human being in terms only of subsystem descriptions will inevitably lead to an impoverishment of life and a dehumanization of man.

Systems properties are not illusions, or meaningless, or neglectable because the operation of subsystems can be exhaustively described without reference to the systems property. Life is a systems property of nonliving matter; but life is no illusion. Personality—soul, if you will—is a systems property of impersonal, soul-less matter; but personality or soul is no illusion. The dilemma of how it is possible for the living to arise from the nonliving or of how it is possible for the personal to arise from the impersonal can be answered in a way that preserves the correlation and the reality of the systems property at the same time. It is the *pattern* of the interaction that supplies the organizing and enabling basis for these developments. And the pattern is not wholly derived from the parts, but somehow is given to them in the same way that the shape of a triangle is not derived from three straight lines of equal length but must be imposed on the three lines in order for a triangle to result. Chance may be invoked for the establishment of these favored patterns of interaction, but the difference between chance and Providence is only the difference in perspective of the viewer.

We can have, and we will have, an increasingly complete scientific understanding of the structure of the world in terms of the mechanisms of interaction. But if we attempt to deal with human beings as though they were machines or animals, or if we attempt to deal with living creatures as though they were not living, we will find ourselves in great difficulty. We will be violating the principle that the whole must be treated on the level of wholes, not on the level of the parts which make it up.

Summary

The world has a structure that can be described in scientific terms. Whether the structure is detected by assuming the validity of evolutionary theory as a description of the development of more complex from less complex forms or by analyzing the structure presently observable by starting with society and breaking down into successively smaller components, the result is essentially the same. And the question that must be faced is the same: When we have at our disposal a scientific description of the structure of the world, do we have any need or any room for a religious description?

Once energy has manifested itself as matter, the structure of the world can be broken down into three main categories: material but not living, living but not human, and human. The two thresholds for qualitative change evidenced in this structure occur between living and nonliving and between human and nonhuman. All the available evidence indicates that the manifestation of life results from a particular pattern of interaction among entities which are themselves nonliving. We have suggested the analogical conclusion that the manifestation of humanity results from a particular pattern of interaction between entities which are themselves nonhuman. Thus there is expected a continuum on the scale of life between nonliving and living, depending on the particular pattern of a given situation. So also it is expected that there will be a continuum on the scale of soul between nonhuman soul and human soul, depending on the particular pattern of a given situation.

Such qualities as life and soul are best understood from the scientific perspective as systems properties characteristic of a whole composed of subsystem parts. Such wholes or total systems have properties not inherent in the parts themselves when those parts are not engaged in patterned interaction. Two commonly held views fall short of accounting for both the mutual dependence of whole and parts and the transcendence of whole over parts. The reductionistic view tends to argue that life and soul are only illusions because they are not inherent in the parts or subsystems themselves, and the additive view tends to argue that life and soul must be added from outside to nonliving and soul-less matter respectively.

In order to have an adequate description of an event or an experience, it is necessary to have a description on all the levels possible: physical, biological, psychological, sociological, and theological. When—or if—the description on the physical level is completely known, for example, this in no sense makes descriptions on other levels unnecessary or invalid. It is not possible to collapse the levels one upon the other, to view theological events as only sociologically caused, to view sociological events as only psychologically caused, and so on, without sacrificing an appreciation for the properties of the whole which characterize each level uniquely. A physical description of the world is incomplete without a psychological description, and a psychological description is incomplete without a theological description. So also a theological description is incomplete without descriptions on other levels.

The unity of man is supported by both science and the biblical revelation. The intimate relationship between the personality or soul and the body of a man is attested by a wide variety of evidence. In accord also is the biblical emphasis on the importance of resurrection, a work of God in which a new creature—a new body-soul— is raised up to life after the old body-soul has passed into death.

Man is a complex machine. But to assert that man is *only* a complex machine is to equate the whole with the sum of its parts and to fail to recognize the necessity for a multilevel description in order to do full justice to what kind of creature man is. Even if it should be possible for us to describe in detail the physical mechanisms associated with every action, every thought, every impulse of a man, we would still not have a clue to what it all meant without the recognition that the man is a child of God, made by him for love and communication.

Topics for Discussion

1. Consider the following remarks by Bertrand Russell in *A Free Man's Worship in Mysticism and Logic, and Other Essays,*

That Man is the product of causes which had no prevision of the end they were achieving; that his origin, his growth, his hopes and fears, his loves and his beliefs, are but the outcome of accidental collocations of atoms; that no fire, no heroism, no intensity of thought and feeling, can preserve an individual life beyond the grave; that all the labors of the ages, all the devotion; all the inspiration; all the noonday brightness of human genius are destined to extinction in the vast death of the solar system, and that the whole temple of Man's achievement must inevitably be buried beneath the debris of a universe in ruins . . . all these things, if not quite beyond dispute, are yet so nearly certain, that no philosophy which rejects them can hope to stand. Only within the scaffolding of these truths, only on the firm foundation of unyielding despair, can the soul's habitation henceforth be safely built.[6]

How would you reply to Dr. Russell?

2. Are you satisfied that it really makes little difference whether the structure of the world is considered to have arisen by evolutionary processes or is simply a statement of the way things are? Do the philosophical backgrounds that usually go with these two ways of looking at the problem make a difference?

3. Why is there so little evidence for forms of existence that are on the borderline of living–nonliving or human–nonhuman? Does this lack of evidence argue against the case presented in this chapter?

4. Discuss the relationship between parts and whole for the cases of musical notes and a symphony, or brush strokes and a masterpiece of painting. Describe the various subsystems in each case, and also the uniquely systems properties.

5. Describe the way a reductionist or an additivist would treat the effect of death on the soul of a man. Can you think of additional evidence for or against these two positions?

6. Describe the role of feedback mechanisms in the operation of an automatic record player. Now include yourself as a subsystem of the whole record player and listener system, and describe additional feedback mechanisms.

7. How do you decide in practice whether a dog is alive or dead? An ant? A rosebush? A cactus?

---

[6] Bertrand Russell, "A Free Man's Worship," in *Mysticism and Logic and Other Essays* (New York: Norton, 1929).

8. Consider the systems properties of a watch and the nature of the patterned interactions involved.

9. The quickening of a fetus has historically often been taken as the evidence that human life and soul were thereafter present. Is this a good criterion? What kind of criterion would you propose for permitting abortions? (See chapter 10 for further discussion.)

10. Which is more nearly human: a one-year-old healthy chimpanzee or a man with such severe brain damage that there is no evidence of consciousness? Why?

11. What happens to a person's soul when he is sleeping?

12. In some cases of mental illness, two or more personalities are exhibited by the same embodied life-system (patient) at different times. How are these related to his soul, or souls?

13. You are serving on a jury. The man under trial is convicted by a wealth of evidence and eyewitnesses as being guilty of premeditated murder. Between the murder and the trial, however, the man has suffered an accident to his brain which has *permanently* removed all memory of events preceding the accident, including of course the murder. The defense argues that the man on trial is not the same man who was guilty of murder. What do you vote for as a member of the jury?

14. It would frequently be a convenient way out of difficulties to hold that a man's soul had no direct correspondence to any physical, biological, or psychological phenomena that could be tested. Do you think this is an acceptable position?

15. How do you understand the Christian teaching on resurrection in the light of 1 Cor. 15?

16. If I were able to construct an artificial man by using *exactly* the same processes and mechanisms found in a real man, would I have only a machine or a real man?

17. If the brain is likened to a switchboard, is there a switchboard operator? Who or what is it?

18. Describe the experience of eating a tasteful meal in the company of good friends on each of the levels of figure 4. Do you lose anything from the description by omitting one or more levels?

19. If the biochemical reactions involved in every thought process were describable in terms of the appropriate equations, would this pose a threat to the reality of human personality or to the existence of God? Why, or why not?

20. What do you reply to a person who affirms that his conversion to Christ was a supernatural, not a psychological, phenomenon?

21. The heart is "only" a pump, but reports are heard that marked psychological changes frequently occur in recipients of heart-transplant operations. Speculate as to possible reasons.

22. Describe the difficulties a man can get into if he believes that he is *not* a machine.

Chapter Eight

Determinism and Indeterminism

The practice of the scientific discipline makes two inherent assumptions. It proceeds on the premise that the phenomena under investigation are to a large or complete extent determined—that reproducible experiments under the same initial conditions will yield identical results—and that predictions of future situations can be reliably made on the basis of present knowledge. Growth in scientific understanding usually follows from a better description of the factors active in determining events and actions. But this response is not limited to the pursuit of science; it is also part of our common everyday experience. We expect the laws of cause and effect we have experienced in the past to be reliable guides for the future. The throwing of a light switch is expected to produce a light; if it does not, we look for the break in the cause-and-effect chain.

We do not believe that there should be freedom of choice for the light when we throw the switch, but we do believe that there should be freedom of choice as to whether or not we turn it on. It is at this point that the issue of determinism has become a major stumbling block for modern philosophy and theology. The progress of scientific understanding of the human individual has been interpreted as removing all differences between him and that electric light circuit which responds deterministically to the throw of the switch. It is argued that all of the psychological, moral, ethical, and religious choices that men believe they are called upon to make, and which they believe themselves responsible for making, are actually no choices at all. The appearance of choice is only an illusion; the decision is completely determined by a combination of physical, biochemical, psychological, and sociological factors over which the individual has little or no control. In this context, for a Christian to invite a man to accept Jesus Christ as Lord and Savior is a meaningless gesture. To quote, "Whosoever will may come," is to attempt to base reality on fantasy.

There are at least three contexts in which the question of determinism versus indeterminism needs to be considered. The first is the context of the physical world itself: are the laws of physics and chemistry deterministic or not? The second is the context of the psychological and sociological: are a man's psychological and sociological responses completely determined by his physical and biological constituents or by his social environment? The third is the context of the theological: how can the sovereignty of God, with its implication of divine determination of all events in the world, be reconciled with human freedom and responsibility? In this chapter we shall examine different aspects of this problem in each of these contexts.

Determinism in Classical Physics

The achievements of classical physics appeared in the late nineteenth century to be so outstanding that nothing was beyond its power. Indeed it was commonly felt that the era of scientific discovery was drawing to a close and that only refinements and sophisticated improvements in detail lay ahead.

This success of classical physics rested upon a mechanistic view of the world. Matter in motion was the key, and all the complexities of the world could be reduced to the movement of bodies under the impulse of forces after the pattern of a mechanical machine. Matter in motion obeyed well-defined and known deterministic laws which controlled in principle both the past and the future. The scientist Laplace is famous for his comment that

> An intellect which at a given instant knew all the forces acting in nature, and the position of all things of which the world consists —supposing the said intellect were vast enough to subject these data to analysis—would embrace in the same formula the motions

of the greatest bodies in the universe and those of the slightest atoms; nothing would be uncertain for it, and the future, like the past, would be present to its eyes. (*Introduction à la théorie analytique des probabilities*, Paris: Oeuvres Complètes, 1886)

There is no wonder that this confidence of physics exerted a profound influence on philosophy which persists to the present day.

Contemporary thinkers interpreted this state of affairs in two quite opposite ways, depending on their own presuppositional position. Some saw in this all-encompassing mechanistic determinism a final argument against the existence of God. As long as God was considered to be in evidence only when he provided a mechanism not understood by men, the belief in an all-sufficient mechanistic view effectively did away with the need for God. On the other hand, there were some who interpreted the determinism of classical physics as being exactly what one should expect on the basis of the biblical teaching of the sovereignty of God, who predetermines and predestines everything according to his will. When the determinism of classical physics was shattered in the developments of the early years of the twentieth century, both of these positions lost the support they had sought in the deterministic view.

Modern physics has moved quite a way from the matter-in-motion perspective of classical determinism. The concept of a field of force has grown as a way of describing interactions not depending on matter in motion. The gravitational field describes the interaction between two masses; the electromagnetic field describes the interaction between charged bodies and electric or magnetic fields. The force on a mass in a gravitational field, or on a charge in an electric or magnetic field, can be described as a direct interaction between the mass or charge and the active field present. When a positively charged body attracts a negatively charged body, no matter is in motion between them. The repulsion between two like magnetic poles, as an example of action at a distance typical of a field, is a common wonder that delights children of all ages. In the general theory of relativity the very nature of matter is reinterpreted in a dramatic way, the existence of matter being viewed simply as a local property of the four-dimensional space–time continuum. But in spite of these drastic changes in the way in which the world was viewed, the deterministic aspect continued. Fields can be as deterministic as matter in motion.

Then new effects began to be observed that didn't fit the pattern of classical physics at all, or, even worse, seemed to be in direct violation of predictions from classical physics. The existence of a stable atom consisting of a positively charged nucleus and a negatively charged electron in motion about the nucleus cannot be explained in terms of classical physics. There the prediction is that the electron will spiral into the nucleus and the atom will collapse. Light, which was commonly supposed to be a wave phenomenon, began to exhibit particlelike behavior. Electrons, which were commonly supposed to be particles, began to exhibit wavelike behavior. Allowed energies for electrons inside atoms, which were commonly believed to be continuous, were found to be markedly discontinuous, only a few discrete values of energy being allowed. Protons in radioactive atoms were found to be emitted from these atoms even though, according to classical physics, they didn't have enough energy to get out of the atom. It was evident that a radically different type of approach was needed.

Quantum Mechanics and Indeterminacy

To meet the need to describe these new kinds of effect, three new concepts seemed indicated: (1) when an atomic particle is confined to a certain region of space, like an electron in an atom, the values of energy allowed for this particle do not include all possible positive values as would be the case for a classical particle, but instead are limited to a relatively small number of specific values (it is said that the energy is *quantized* rather than continuous); (2) matter exhibits both a particlelike and a wavelike behavior, depending on the particular experimental conditions dominating; and (3) the basic description of natural phenomena must be in terms of a statistical analysis giving probabilities rather than certainties, not on a mechanical model yielding values of absolute exactness. The scientific discipline developed in the 1920s to incorporate these features into physics is known as *quantum mechanics* or *wave mechanics*.

Statistical analysis was used in physics for a long time before quantum mechanics but assumed new importance and immediacy in the new perspective. In classical physics, statistical approaches giving the probability for a given action were commonly used to deal with situations where a very large number of particles were involved. In principle it was believed that the exact behavior of all these particles could be calculated, but the labor involved and the difficulty of determining the position, velocity, and forces for each particle were so great that it was more convenient to describe what happened on the average by a statistical process. Laws that relate the pressure, volume, and temperature of a gas, for example, are this kind of statistical classical law; each of these quantities is an average value over innumerable individual gas molecules, which can be calculated and measured with a high degree of precision. Statistics in classical physics, therefore, helped out as a convenience in cases where ignorance was a practical matter only.

The situation is quite different in quantum mechanics. Here the theoretical framework that has successfully coped with the problems showing the inadequacy of classical physics at the atomic level leads directly to the conclusion that a statistical description is at least a practical necessity, and at most an actual representation of physical reality. In other words, a statistical description in the quantum mechanical view is not only a convenience; it is a necessity. One of the best known formulations of this basic indeterminacy is the Heisenberg indeterminacy principle, which in one form states that the location of a particle and the momentum of that particle cannot both be known with complete accuracy at the same time.[1] If we let $\triangle x$ represent the uncertainty in the position of the particle and let $\triangle p$ represent the uncertainty in the momentum of the particle (its mass multiplied by its velocity), then quantitatively

$$(\triangle x)\,(\triangle p) \geq h/4\pi$$

where h is a fundamental constant, known as Planck's constant, with a value of 6.6×10^{-27} erg sec. If the mass entering the momentum p is large, e.g., the mass of a baseball, then because of the very small value of h, it is evident that the uncertainty in position $\triangle x$ will be so very small as to be completely undetectable. On the other hand, if the mass entering the momentum p is a typical atomic particle mass (the mass of an electron is about 10^{-27} gram),

---

[1] Werner Heisenberg, *Quantum Theory* (New York: Dover Publications, Inc., 1930), p. 20.

it is also clear that the uncertainty in position $\triangle x$ can become sizable.

Such quantities as position and momentum, related by the Heisenberg indeterminacy principle, are called *complementary* quantities. Quantum mechanics asserts that it is not possible to know the exact values of two complementary quantities at the same time. In a practical way this limitation can be viewed as imposed by the fact that an experimenter changes the properties of an atomic system in the very process of measurement. For example, the momentum is not the same after a measurement of position as it was when the position was being measured. The limitation cannot be considered as only an experimental limitation, however, because the theoretical structure of quantum mechanics as presently constituted leads to the same conclusion without reference to experimental limitations.

What this interpretation of quantum mechanics means about the structure of reality and how ultimate the interpretation is are questions not yet completely resolved in the scientific community. The majority position today is that these limitations are intrinsic and will not later be shown to be merely temporary. This view, advanced and defended by Niels Bohr and his followers, has been consistently opposed by a few major physicists, most notably Albert Einstein. For a variety of philosophical reasons these opponents of ultimate indeterminacy argue that the indeterminacy is only apparent as a result of present inability to penetrate to the hidden variables that underly the present apparent structure of the world.

Within the framework of quantum mechanics with its indeterminacy principle, the probability of experimentally measuring a certain position or a certain momentum still obeys wholly deterministic equations and laws. It is true that the position and momentum themselves no longer obey deterministic equations, but the probability of experimental measurements giving an actual value does obey such deterministic equations. This fact suggests another possible interpretation, namely, that the appearance of indeterminacy is introduced by our determination to continue the description in terms of such classical quantities as position and momentum. What if the property of position is just as inappropriate for an electron as would be the properties of color or temperature? To be sure, all the large objects we know have a position—or so it seems. But

166

how do we know that the concept of position is applicable to a 10^{-27} gram glob of electrical charge? Maybe the probabilities that we introduce are a much more accurate representation of the actual electronic state than are such quantities as position or momentum. And these probabilities do obey deterministic laws. Perhaps the indeterminacy is a property of our experimental techniques *and* our conceptual framework, whereas the quantities that really describe the particles obey laws that are just as deterministic as the laws obeyed by position and momentum in classical physics.

As classical determinism had a profound philosophical effect, so also quantum indeterminacy has had its effect on philosophical thinking, although by no means to the same extent. Again the interpretation of this new possibility is affected primarily by previously accepted presuppositions. There are those who accept it as evidence that there is room for freedom after all, even in a world that appears to be highly deterministic. They argue that the evidence of indeterminacy shows that there is a realm in which Divine Providence can work and a realm in which personal choice can affect decisions. On the other hand, there are those who see indeterminacy as evidence that at its most ultimate level the world is governed by chance; hence they interpret it as one more argument against the existence of a God who cares for the world and works daily in it. In his book *Chance and Providence*, William G. Pollard attempts to combine these two aspects of indeterminacy into a common whole.[2] He argues that apparent chance in a scientific sense is completely compatible with divine providence in a theological sense. Although we cannot prove God's providential activity by noting the existence of chance, we can recognize the presence of chance as the physical means underlying the biblically revealed activity of God's providential care.

Complementarity

In the previous section we pointed out what it means to consider position and momentum as a pair of complementary quantities. This

---

[2] William G. Pollard, *Chance and Providence* (New York: Charles Scribner's Sons, 1958).

particular complementary pair is really an expression of a more fundamental complementary pair, particle and wave. Light, as well as atomic particles, exhibits both particlelike and wavelike properties. To be completely characterized as a particle, the position must be exactly known; but if the position is exactly known, no wavelike properties can be detected, for wavelike properties imply extension in space. The wavelike properties are related to the momentum, because the momentum is related to the wavelength of the corresponding waves. Therefore to characterize completely an electron as a particle means to make $\triangle x$ negligibly small, which means to make $\triangle p$ very large. On the other hand, to be characterized completely as a wave, the wavelength must be exactly known; but if the wavelength is exactly known, no particlelike properties can be detected, for the measurement of wavelength requires an extension in space. This is equivalent to making $\triangle p$ negligibly small and $\triangle x$ very large. Such an atomic particle is not both a particle and a wave; it is *neither* a particle *nor* a wave but simply exhibits particlelike and wavelike properties under the appropriate circumstances.

Our previous distinction between giving a physical description in terms of position and momentum with the necessity of incorporating the indeterminacy principle, or in terms of probability obeying deterministic laws, is another kind of complementary set. In quantum mechanics we cannot have both a description in terms of position and momentum *and* a deterministic form to this description.

Niels Bohr proposed a complementarity principle to encompass and explain these experiences.[3] He argued that our understanding of nature has arrived at such depths of nature's complexity that we cannot expect to be able to formulate picture-concepts that will describe nature adequately. At one time one concept (for example, particle) will be the most useful, at others another (for example, wave) will be the most useful; neither concept, however, has intrinsic or general relevance. We have no way from our common

---

[3] Niels Bohr, *Atomic Theory and the Description of Nature* (New York: Cambridge University Press, 1933), p. 28; chapter in *Albert Einstein: Philosopher-Scientist*, ed. P. A. Schilpp, Library of Living Philosophers (Evanston, Ill.: n.p., 1949), p. 199; *Physical Review* 48 (1935): 702; *Nature* 121 (1928): 580; 131 (1933): 422; see also J. A. Wheeler, *American Scientist* 44 (1956): 360.

experience of arriving at a picture-concept—a model—of the electron, for example, which is able to correspond with the actual properties of the electron. The best that we can do is to combine two or more models drawn from our common experience, applying them under the conditions in which they are the most appropriate.

How general a concept is that of complementarity? Does it have applications beyond the area of physics? Those who follow Bohr generally argue that it does, while others feel that indeterminacy in quantum mechanics is only a temporary limitation. They are likely to argue that to stop at a complementarity principle is to abdicate scientific responsibility and to "drop out" of an investigation that should be pushed harder.

It is hard to deny, however, that there are many concepts outside the area of physics to which the complementarity principle seems to give useful insights. Such concept-pairs as the use of a word to communicate information and the analysis of the meaning of the word, justice and mercy, and free will and determinism, all demonstrate complementary characteristics. Consider in detail the complementary set free will and determinism, and attempt to prescribe what experiments would have to be done in order to prove the reality of either free will or determinism. To demonstrate determinism, one would have to prove that the future of a person is determined by the past; to accomplish the proof, one would have to carry out detailed experiments on the potentials of various portions of the brain and the attendant biochemical functions of the body. Such an approach, however, would sever the natural course of existence for the person and make exercise of free will impossible. Similarly, if the person is put in such a situation that the exercise of free will can be demonstrated, it is impossible to make the measurement that would judge determinism.

Psychological Determinism

If it is believed that human psychological behavior is only a manifestation of physical and chemical processes going on in the body, and if physical and chemical processes are believed to be governed by a deterministic set of laws, then for many the conclusion follows that a person's psychological behavior (the manifestation of his personality) is also determined. The discovery of indeterminacy in physics might be expected to have a profound influence in contradicting this conclusion.

Three mitigating considerations must be taken into account, however. (1) In our previous discussion of physical indeterminacy, we pointed out that even in that area itself we cannot be sure whether the apparent indeterminacy results only from limited experimental and conceptual resources or whether it really represents the structure of reality. (2) The physical indeterminacy principle is important only for atomic particles. The mass of a nerve cell, such as might be expected to play a key role in psychological processes in the brain, is some 10^{18} times greater than that of an electron. The direct effects of physical indeterminacy on the nerve cell, therefore, should be negligible. (3) As proposed in our discussion in chapter 7, the psychological behavior of a human being should be considered as a systems property. Now, it does not follow that because the subsystems obey deterministic laws, the total system must also obey the same or similar deterministic laws.

In a sense, our argument for a multilevel description of reality in accordance with thesis 2 is an argument for a number of complementary descriptions. We can cast the conclusions of chapter 7 into the terminology of our present discussion by pointing out that a description on each of the levels of figure 3 is complementary to descriptions on all other levels. A description on one level may be deterministic; the description on another level may be indeterministic. Because the lowest level of description in accordance with the physical sciences might be cast in a deterministic frame does not mean a priori that a description on any other level must be also in a deterministic frame. Many examples could be cited of physically indeterministic subsystems giving rise to a deterministic systems property. Consider, for example, a collection of a large number of radioactive atoms. If the systems property is the time that it will take one-half of these atoms to decay radioactively, then this time can be predicted quite accurately, that is, it is a determined property. On the other hand, the time at which a given atom will decay is completely indetermined, not only practically but theoretically as well; that is, the theoretical model describing the radioactive decay gives only a probability for decaying in a given time interval. Similarly, there appears to be no a priori reason why deterministic subsystems cannot give rise to an indetermined systems property.

A number of sources of indeterminism could be cited for the psychological behavior systems property of a human being without invoking the indeterminism of quantum physics. Sources of indeterminism affecting the systems property might arise from random fluctuations in the thermodynamic properties of the surround: from random fluctuations in the temperature of the brain or from random variations in blood supply to the brain. Whether or not such random sources of indeterminism have anything at all to do with free choice and personal responsibility of the individual is another question. In fact, it would seem that purely random influences on the brain would diminish personal responsibility rather than establish it (by personal responsibility we mean a deliberate choice of the will, not an uncontrolled fluctuation in thinking.) It appears very difficult, if not impossible, to establish a criterion by which measurement of brain processes could distinguish a mechanically determined and a "free will" personal decision.

An interesting approach to personal freedom (we might say, a complementary approach!) has been developed by Donald M. MacKay in *Freedom of Action in a Mechanistic Universe* and in *Christianity in a Mechanistic Universe*.[4] Without specifying any particular model for mental processes, he simply grants that these processes per se may obey deterministic laws. Then he asks whether or not it can still be maintained that a person has freedom of choice. The crux of the argument hangs on a distinction between two different ways that the words *freedom of choice* can be used. One way maintains that in order for a choice to be free, it must be in principle unpredictable by anyone. MacKay rejects this definition as not corresponding to what we normally mean by responsible free choice. He argues instead that a choice is free and consistent with human responsibility if there is no "determinate specification that is binding on (valid and definitive for) everyone, *including the agent*, before he makes up his mind."[5] In order to illustrate this position, he imagines a superscientist who by his great knowledge of the workings of a man's brain predicts what that man's course of

[4] Donald M. MacKay, *Christianity in a Mechanistic Universe* (Chicago: Inter-Varsity Press, 1965); *Freedom of Action in a Mechanistic Universe* (New York: Cambridge University Press, 1967).

[5] MacKay, *Freedom of Action in a Mechanistic Universe*, p. 17.

action will be in a given situation and writes this prediction down on a piece of paper. If he keeps his prediction a secret, and if he is indeed a superscientist, he can wait to see his prediction infallibly fulfilled. But does this prove anything about the man's freedom of choice? MacKay argues that if this prediction had the same kind of inevitability as, say the prediction of the next lunar eclipse, then it ought to be true whether the man sees the prediction or not, whether he believes it or not, and whether he likes it or not. It is precisely this characteristic that such a prediction does not have. For if the man sees the prediction and believes it, then the state of his brain is changed and no longer corresponds to that upon which the prediction was based. For the man himself, the prediction has no inevitable binding force; it does not compel him to believe it or to disbelieve it. He remains free in spite of it. In *The Scientific Enterprise and Christian Faith* Malcolm Jeeves points out that this is a special case of a problem worked out by Karl Popper some years ago

> when he showed that even with a determinate computing machine no such machine could produce a convergence onto a specification of its own future state which would still be valid if it was embodied into itself, because the actual embodying of that specification in its information system would make the specification out of date.[6]

This is another instructive way of looking at the interaction between parts and whole, or between subsystems and total system. If the subsystems are used to predict the systems property, interaction with the total system alters the subsystems so that the prediction no longer holds.

Cultural or Social Determinism

It is evident that many of our customs and choices derive from the culture and social structure in which we live. David Moberg points out that

> the language of any man and all his basic habits of eating, sleeping, eliminating, working, worshipping, playing, communicating, med-

---

[6] Jeeves, p. 151.

icating, and interacting are unquestionably shaped and modified
by his cultural environment.[7]

This is no less true of Christians than of non-Christians. A large
factor is provided by contemporary culture in the way any given
Christian, for example, responds to issues of segregation versus
integration, women's liberation versus female subjection, pacifism
versus interventionism, or capitalism versus socialism; or in the way
he feels about diet, clothing, bodily ornaments, tobacco, alcohol,
lotteries, recreation, and birth control. The church group a Christian affiliates with will strongly reflect both his position on the
intellect-emotion continuum and his place in the economic
structure.

Pitfalls associated with these ideas are to be found, as usual, at
both extremes. The person who maintains that his choices and
preferences are wholly matters of his individual freedom and not
largely determined by the context of his society is frequently unable to distinguish relative tradition from absolute prescription. He
is unwilling to change in little things to which he attributes major
significance; he tends to ascribe moral value to purely traditional
customs.

On the other hand, the man who argues that all of our choices
are inexorably determined by our social environment so that any
manifestation of free choice at all is only an illusion, contributes
the sociologist's version of the man-is-only-a-machine syndrome.
Such a man may argue that because it is possible to see sociological
causes for historical events, and because it is possible within limits
even to offer reliable sociological predictions about the behavior and
response of societies, there is no necessity for any other kind of description on other levels. When he does, he is falling victim to the
attempt to describe without a multilevel view of reality.

David Moberg summarizes the situation: "Both free will and
social determinism validly apply to human behavior when each is
properly understood to operate within realistic bounds of factual
limitations."[8] He points out that not all children born in the crime-
infested ghetto become juvenile delinquents and not all children

---

[7] David O. Moberg, "Social Science," in *The Encounter Between Christianity and Science*, p. 266.

[8] Moberg, "Social Science," p. 268.

born in the mansion become ideal citizens. The concepts of social determinism are useful in estimating the *probability* that a given course of social action will follow from a given set of social constraints.

Theological Determinism

The theme of theological determinism with its focus in the sovereignty of God runs throughout the biblical revelation. The prophet Isaiah (14:24), for example, says,

The Lord of hosts has sworn:

> "As I have planned,
> so shall it be,
> and as I have purposed,
> so shall it stand."

The doctrine that God's purposes in the world are always accomplished is one of the most practical and universal of the biblical teachings. As soon as this is realized, however, it inevitably raises the question, "If God's will is infallibly performed, how can I be responsible?"

The biblical revelation does not stop with the doctrine of the sovereignty of God. It is equally clear on the doctrine of the responsibility of man, sometimes combining these two presentations in the same instance. It may be useful to consider a few examples which illustrate this point.

When God sent the king of Assyria against the Samaritans to carry out his sentence of judgment against them, the king of Assyria had no knowledge of being used in this way and acted out of his own motives. By one act the sovereign purpose of God was accomplished and the law of God was broken. The king of Assyria was held responsible for his actions (Isa. 10:5–13).

God announced to Solomon that he would take the kingdom from his descendants in judgment against him (1 Kings 11:11). This judgment came into effect when Rehoboam, Solomon's son, accepted the evil counsel of his young companions to threaten the people with worse hardship than before and ten of the tribes of Israel rebelled. God's purpose was achieved, and yet Rehoboam was fully responsible for his sin before God. We have here also an example of the need for complete sociological and theological descriptions of this event in order fully to understand what happened.

When Jesus was warning against the sin of leading little children astray, he said, "Woe to the world for temptations to sin! For it is necessary that temptations come, but woe to the man by whom the temptation comes!" (Matt. 18:7).

The coexistence of God's sovereignty and man's responsibility is clearly brought out in Matthew 26:24, where Jesus said of his betrayal by Judas Iscariot,

> "The Son of man goes as it is written of him, but woe to that man by whom the Son of man is betrayed! It would have been better for that man if he had not been born."

and in John 17:12, where he spoke of the same event,

> "While I was with them, I kept them in thy name, which thou hast given me; I have guarded them, and none of them is lost but the son of perdition, that the scripture might be fulfilled."

Finally, the death of Jesus itself is a clear example of this kind of situation. If ever an event were part of God's purpose, it was that his son Jesus Christ should come to effect the reconciliation of the world through his death. "This Jesus, delivered up according to the definite plan and foreknowledge of God, you crucified and killed by the hands of lawless men" (Acts 2:23).

Interpreters of the biblical revelation have always been aware of this duality of the biblical revelation, maintaining the simultaneous meaningfulness of both the concepts of the sovereignty of God and the responsibility of man. In the area of personal faith in Jesus Christ, they have recognized that the Bible says both, " 'No one can come to me unless the Father who sent me draws him' " (John 6:44) and "Every one who calls upon the name of the Lord will be saved" (Rom. 10:13). It is difficult to maintain the balance between these two apparently contradictory biblical affirmations. Historically the pendulum has swung from those who emphasized the sovereign predestination of God at the apparent expense of human responsibility and freedom of choice to those who emphasized the human prerogative at the apparent expense of the trustworthiness and reliability of God's purpose.

This concept-pair—sovereignty of God and responsibility of man —has many of the attributes of a complementary pair. It is not unique in interpretations of the biblical revelation, and such pairs are commonly cited in theological circles as examples of *paradox*. Each of these pairs seems to involve two apparently contradictory concepts to describe reality fully, the cause of the contradictory appearance lying in our inability to pictorialize to an extent required by reality.

In an article in the *Bulletin of the Evangelical Theological Society*, Vernon C. Grounds has summarized the following set of seven such paradoxes in the biblical revelation: (1) the ontological paradox, or the paradox of the Tri-Unity of God; (2) the cosmological paradox, or the paradox of God's being wholly separate from his creation and yet completely involved in the creation; (3) the epistemological paradox, or the paradox resulting from the Christian claim that all knowledge comes ultimately through revelation; (4) the anthropological paradox, or the paradox described above in terms of man's complete freedom of God's complete foreordination; (5) the christological paradox, or the paradox of the divine-human personality of Jesus Christ; (6) the soteriological paradox, or the paradox of salvation that is simultaneously a manifestation of God's justice and God's mercy; and (7) the eschatological paradox, or the paradox of limitless love and eternal punishment.[9]

Perhaps it is helpful to consider these theological paradoxes in terms of the complementarity principle of the physical sciences. This is not to maintain that any direct connection exists but that a useful analogical perspective may be gained. The complementarity principle in physics also arises at the point of the determinism versus indeterminism conflict. There it is resolved by recognizing that the reality is, for example, an electron, which is neither exactly a particle nor exactly a wave. Yet, in order to describe reality fully, it is necessary, from one experimental viewpoint, to consider an electron to be like a particle; under another equally valid but different experimental viewpoint, it is necessary to consider an electron to be like a wave. So, in the case of the paradox of God's sovereignty and man's responsibility, we might argue that the actual situation so far transcends our normal experiential concepts of sovereignty and

---

[9] Vernon C. Grounds, *Bulletin of the Evangelical Theological Society* 7 (1964): 3.

responsibility that we do not have the conceptual pictures available for an adequate description in toto. We can be completely effective, nevertheless, by recognizing that from the perspective of cosmic significance the sovereignty of God is the best picture; from the perspective of man's activity and day-by-day response to God, however, the responsibility of man is the best picture. As the reality of the electron blends the particle and the wave pictures, ultimately removing apparent contradiction, so the reality of man–God relationships blends the sovereignty and responsibility pictures, ultimately removing the apparent paradox.

Sometimes Christian theology is called into question because it involves the postulation and the acceptance of doctrinal or philosophical statements of a paradoxical nature. First of all, it must be clearly understood that a paradox is not a logical contradiction. To maintain both that man is completely responsible for his action and that man is not responsible for his actions at all, would be a contradiction. On the other hand, to maintain that God is completely sovereign and that man is wholly responsible is not a contradiction but a paradox. If this invoking of two apparently conflicting models to describe reality more completely occurs frequently in theology, as indicated above, it occurs no less frequently in modern science. To pretend that the paradoxical nature of the deepest Christian doctrines makes them unacceptable in a scientific world-view is to admit ignorance of modern science.

Summary

A strong drive in scientific research to establish deterministic connections and causes is sometimes interpreted to have philosophical or theological consequences. Because apparently deterministic laws govern the physical processes in man, or the biological, psychological, or sociological processes to some extent, it is sometimes concluded that all of man's activity—physical, mental, and spiritual —is determined beyond his control or choice. In this perspective, all of man's apparent freedom to choose, or all of man's responsibility to make meaningful choices, is reduced to only an illusion. Thus, such a perspective is closely correlated with the argument that man is only a complex machine.

Physics has undergone a major revolution in thinking in which the strong and absolute physical determinism of the previous century has been replaced by a view that stresses, at least, the experimental indeterminacy in the physical world and, at most, the intrinsic indeterminacy of the world. Whether or not such indeterminacy, even if intrinsic to the world, has any real or effective connection with such subjects as man's freedom of choice, however, is extremely doubtful. The change in thinking in physics has affected philosophical thinking to some extent, but it has done this more by analogy than by direct application.

One of the useful concepts to be emphasized in the attempt to make philosophical sense of the new quantum physics is the concept of complementarity. It was argued that whenever the area of our pursuit of knowledge becomes sufficiently far removed from the experience of common living, even when this is highly sophisticated with modern technology, we are no longer able to conceptualize appropriate models to describe reality. Instead, the best that we can do is to construct a number of different models out of our common experience, each of which will describe a different facet of reality and all of which must be brought to bear in order to have a reasonably complete description of reality. This principle of complementarity is not meant to serve as an excuse for accepting apparent contradictions or of terminating the search for a better understanding when it is possible to press on and achieve this understanding. But it suggests that there may be areas of knowledge—and this is true in physical science and in spiritual revelation alike—which are so profound or so complex or so removed from our ability to understand, that the very best we may be able to do is to use several different models, each from its own appropriate perspective. It teaches us that knowledge in the form of complementary pairs or in the form of theological paradox is not somehow a deficient, unacceptable kind of knowledge but may represent the very best and most realistic knowledge available to us. In fact, to attempt to describe reality in terms of only one member of a complementary pair or of only one aspect of a paradox may be destructive of effective action.

The arguments that physical, psychological, or sociological determinism invalidate the experience of responsible human choice all suffer from aspects of the same difficulty. They all assume that if a deterministic description is possible on one level, then it must necessarily follow that no other description is valid or necessary. We have argued once again the importance of a multilevel description for a complete picture of reality, with the possibility that some levels may correspond to deterministic law patterns while other levels may correspond to indeterministic law patterns.

In all of these kinds of discussion it is important to keep in mind that any fully rational and comprehensive view of human experience must take into account all of the data. Data come to us regularly that we not only do but must make responsible human choices; to neglect these data is to attempt a resolution of a difficulty without using all the pertinent information available. An appropriate closing thought is voiced by MacKay.

> Our question . . . is not: can we believe in our freedom on the basis of what we know of physiology; but quite the other way round: Do these facts of our experience create an embarrassment for theoretical physiology?[10]

Topics for Discussion

1. Define the conditions that make freedom of choice a thing to be valued. For example, is freedom of choice valued in a watchdog? A precision worker on an assembly line? A chess player? An opera singer? On the basis of the discussion, define what it means for an act to be free.

2. Discuss how life insurance tables enable a company to be profitably operated on a deterministic basis, even though the individual's life span is largely indeterminate.

3. How is it possible for computer estimates of election returns to predict so accurately the outcome of a national election on the basis of only a very small sample of voters? Does the prediction of the computer affect your freedom to vote as you please even though the outcome is virtually known before you vote?

4. Do you see any possible dangers in building a strong case for the reality of divine providential activity on the basis of the indeterminacy principle of quantum mechanics?

5. Find a complementary pair of quantities in a musical composition; in a painting.

---

[10] Donald M. MacKay, in *Brain and Conscious Experience*, ed. J. C. Eccles (Springer-Verlag, 1966).

6. Consider the pair justice and mercy; test for whether or not they are truly complementary.

7. Does an animal have freedom of choice? Would you say that your pet dog or cat was wholly determined, wholly indetermined, or partly determined and partly indetermined? Why? Is your pet only a complex machine? What reasons do you have for your conclusions?

8. Do you think that random variations in brain processes would add to or detract from the concept of personal responsibility and freedom of choice? What kinds of experiences would you expect to accompany such random variations?

9. Choose a person whom you believe you know very well. Attempt to predict what this person will do if you ask him a specific question or make a specific move toward him. Keep this prediction to yourself; test it. Now try again but let him know about your prediction. Does his knowledge of your prediction make a difference?

10. Look for evidence of cultural and social determinism in your personal ideas of human beauty, sexual attractiveness, proper worship, value of work, and materialism. Is it equally true that your personal ideas of honesty, love, and forgiveness are culturally and socially determined?

11. Explore the facets of one of the other theological paradoxes proposed by Dr. Grounds. Is the pair of concepts involved truly complementary? Is a resolution of the paradox conceivable, as distinguished from being possible for you to do?

Chapter Nine

The
Evolution Controversy

Few issues in the interaction between science and Christian faith have aroused the degree of emotional involvement brought forth by the evolution controversy. While debates about determinism have troubled scholars in the retreats of the intellectual world, the evolution controversy has tumbled into the open, in the schools, the churches, the courts, and the homes.

The intensity of the conflict can be appreciated only when it is realized that to many combatants there is simply no middle ground. D. Bolton Davidheiser charges in *Evolution and Christian Faith*, "Acceptance of a theory of evolution leads logically to a religious position which, if called Christian, is Christian in name only."[1] And in a letter published in *Moody Monthly* Micah Leo states, "Those who embrace 'theistic evolution' have intentionally or unintentionally placed a kiss of death on their Master."[2] On the other hand, there are Christian scientists who believe that this response is intrinsically destructive. Walter Hearn, for example, writes in *The Encounter Between Christianity and Science*, "Opposition on Biblical grounds to the theory of evolution by natural selection is unwarranted and actually harmful to Christianity."[3]

Why is there such intensity to the discussions on this subject? Is it possible to effect a resolution?

---

[1] D. Bolton Davidheiser, *Evolution and Christian Faith* (Philadelphia: Presbyterian and Reformed Publishing Co., 1969), p. 24.

[2] Micah Leo, letter in *Moody Monthly*, February 1970, p. 6.

[3] Walter R. Hearn, in *The Encounter Between Christianity and Science*, p. 220.

Why Is Evolution Considered Such a Threat?

The very term *evolution* has become identified in the minds of its religious opponents with an atheistic and anti-Christian view of life. This identification has been derived from the fact that some atheistic and anti-Christian writers have found *their concept* of the meaning of evolution to be an effective weapon to use against *their concept* of the meaning of Christian faith. No evaluation of evolution can even be started, however, without an appreciation for the fact that the term *evolution* is used by opponents and defenders alike in three quite different ways. A lot of the heat generated results from a confusion of these three different usages by proponents of both sides of the controversy.

The special theory of evolution, or micro-evolution. What may be called the special theory of evolution states simply that on the basis of empirical and scientific observations it is possible to conclude that living creatures undergo changes in physical and biological structures, particularly in response to changes in environmental conditions. This form of the theory of evolution is essentially incontrovertible as it can be observed in some form by virtually everyone. It is accepted by all workers in the field as scientifically established. The Christian biologist David Lack, for example, says,

> So let it be stated categorically that the evidence for the occurrence of animal evolution is overwhelming and that all serious students accept it. It may be added that this view is accepted by nearly all reputable religious writers, both Catholic and Protestant.[4]

Here then is an insight into the first cause of the intensity of the evolution controversy. Whenever evolution is attacked, the evolutionist immediately concludes that the special theory is being attacked, and he knows very well that there is excellent scientific support for the special theory; he concludes that his attacker is an ignoramus or religious fanatic. On the other hand, the one who opposes evolution is not even willing to grant that the special theory should be called evolution. Davidheiser states categorically, that "*micro-evolution* is a misnomer and use of the term should be

---

[4] David Lack, *Evolutionary Theory and Christian Belief* (London: Methuen, 1957), p. 23.

avoided by everyone who does not accept evolution."[5] Is there any
wonder, therefore, at the furor that is raised when parties of these
two persuasions attempt to communicate with one another? The
evolutionist thinks that science is being attacked because the scientific evidence for the special theory is in his mind the major body
of evidence for the whole evolutionary perspective. The antievolutionist will not even concede that the data supporting the special
theory have anything to do with more general evolutionary ideas
at all.

The general theory of evolution, or *macro-evolution.* The general theory of evolution is still in the field of biology, but it assigns
much more basic changes to the evolutionary process. Usually it
encompasses a view which presupposes the existence of nonliving
matter and then proposes the development of all living creatures
from a common origin resulting from the transformation of nonliving to living matter. In his book *Implications of Evolution,* G. A.
Kerkut summarizes what he sees as the seven basic assumptions
made in setting forth the general theory of evolution. They are
that (1) living matter arose from nonliving matter, (2) this process
occurred only once in history, (3) viruses, bacteria, plants, and animals are interrelated, (4) protozoa gave rise to metazoa, (5) various
invertebrate phyla are interrelated, (6) vertebrates arose from in-
vertebrates, and (7) within the vertebrates, amphibia arose from
fish, reptiles arose from amphibia, birds and mammals arose from
reptiles.

There is evidence to support this theoretical framework, but it
is inherent in the problem that actual scientific proof is almost impossible to come by. Kerkut himself says in the same book,

> May I here humbly state as part of my biological *credo* that I be-
> lieve that the theory of Evolution as presented by orthodox evolu-
> tionists is in many ways a satisfying explanation of some of the
> evidence. At the same time I think that the attempt to explain all
> living forms in terms of an evolution *from a unique source,* though
> a brave and valid attempt, is one that is premature and not satis-
> factorily supported by present-day evidence.[6]

[5] Davidheiser, *Evolution and Christian Faith.*

[6] G. A. Kerkut, *Implications of Evolution* (Oxford: Pergamon Press, 1965),
p. vii.

It is no negative reflection on the general theory to say that a person who affirms that he believes the general theory is making a statement which is primarily a faith commitment.

Again there is fuel for the conflict. The evolutionist believes that the solid scientific data involved in demonstrating the validity of the special theory, when coupled with the analogical and fossil evidence for the general theory, make belief in the general theory of evolution the only present solution with scientific integrity. Christian geologist Donald Eckelmann, for example, writes,

> At the present pace, it is not unreasonable to expect a rather complete documentation of man's prehistoric development by the close of the twentieth century. This is not to say that all gaps in the record will be filled and all refinements of the record complete. Gaps and areas of uncertainty will always exist, simply because we can never have a complete fossil record. The point here is that the evidence will become so strong that arguments against an evolutionary origin for modern man will be regarded (by informed people) in the same way that arguments against a heliocentric astronomy are regarded today.[7]

The evolutionist regards any attack on the general theory as first of all an attack on the special theory and, second, as an attempt to refute scientific data which form a recognizable pattern, even if all the pieces are not presently at hand. Once again, therefore, he interprets such an attack as an attack on science by one not scientifically informed. On the other hand, the antievolutionist believes that acceptance of the biological general theory of evolution must inevitably lead to certain philosophical conclusions inimical to Christian faith. Since the general theory cannot be scientifically proved, the antievolutionist feels himself confirmed in believing that people accept the general theory only out of antichristian motives.

Evolutionary philosophy or evolutionism. Evolutionary philosophy is no longer in the area of biology, and there is some question whether it deserves the name *scientific.* Assuming that biological evolution as involved in the special and the general theory represents an established law of nature, philosophical evolutionists extrapolate

---

[7] F. Donald Eckelmann, in *The Encounter Between Christianity and Science,* ed. R. H. Bube (Grand Rapids, Mich.: Eerdmans, 1968), pp. 160–61.

from these results in biology to draw conclusions about the evolutionary development of history, ethics, and religion. Philosophical evolutionists see all of life and history caught up in one grand development leading to higher and better forms of life. Such a position can be clearly antichristian, or it can attempt to be consistent with the Christian perspective on life.

In its antichristian form, such philosophical evolutionism may involve an exaltation of man, a denial of the reality of moral guilt in any religious sense, and hence an interpretation of the life and death of Jesus as nothing more than a good example. In this view, man's continued development and improvement are inevitably assured as man, now become conscious of evolution, completes for himself the process of the ages. Evolutionism of this type is a faith system which competes for the religious allegiance of men. Against it the Christian faith is called to stand.

Philosophical evolutionism, however, may also be cast into a Christian perspective. As God is seen to be the motivating power behind the evolutionary processes of the past, so he is seen as the power which will bring them to fruition in the future. When human soul evolved, moral choices became possible. Man's historical failure involves him in actual moral guilt, deliverance from which can be accomplished only by the life-bringing atonement of Jesus Christ. When a man commits himself to Christ, he returns to the path of evolutionary advancement and plays a role in his own time in the advancement of God's kingdom. The final fruition, when God will accomplish the ultimate purposes of the evolutionary process, corresponds to the millennial and eschatological hopes of the biblical revelation.

The biological evolutionist need not embrace philosophical evolutionism at all. The Christian biological evolutionist will certainly not embrace any antichristian perspective on this question. The evolutionist therefore, particularly the Christian evolutionist, sees no point in an attack on evolution in order to guard against evolutionism. In his own life he recognizes the potentialities and the problems of both the special and the general theory of biological evolution. He either sees no necessity for deriving philosophical conclusions from a biological theory or he derives conclusions consistent with his Christian and biblical perspective. Arguments made from a religious point of view and directed against the general theory in order to prevent extrapolation to antichristian evolution-ism he is likely to regard as irrelevant and totally misguided. On the other hand, the religiously motivated antievolutionist is con-vinced in his own mind that most of the ills of the modern world can be traced to the public acceptance of evolutionary thinking. Since there would obviously be no basis for evolutionism if the foundations of the biological general theory were discredited, he centers his attack upon them.

In every case, the evolutionist and the antievolutionist mis-understand each other so critically that any kind of intelligent com-munication is rendered essentially impossible. It is only when the special and the general theory are recognized for what they are that any kind of resolution of this tension can be achieved. Attempts to produce descriptions on the level of biology need have no conflict with biblically provided descriptions on the ultimate level of man–God relationships. The evolutionist must realize that he has vir-tually no scientific support for extrapolating biological evolution into a general principle of life, and the antievolutionist must realize that he has no justifiable religious grounds upon which to attack a scientific theory dealing with biological mechanisms.

Key Concepts in Evolutionary Thinking

Several general concepts play key roles in the development of pro- or antievolutionary thinking. We will consider three of them in this section: the second law of thermodynamics, uniformitarian-ism, and the Flood.

Second law of thermodynamics. Thermodynamics is a branch of science that attempts to "define the possible" in general terms, usually involving energy relations and comparisons. One of the quantities entering thermodynamic relationships, *entropy*, is not a common quantity of usual experience. Entropy can be interpreted physically as a measure of *disorder*. The second law of thermo-dynamics states that in a closed (taking into account all the energy inputs and outlets) system the entropy must increase with time. This does not mean that in specific processes entropy cannot be decreasing, but rather that if we take account of all the inputs and outlets, we will find that the total entropy is increasing. For example, when water freezes to form ice, the order in the system is increased. Now the atoms assume positions on a regular geometric lattice instead of being randomly distributed, thereby decreasing entropy in the water system. The second law of thermodynamics asserts, however, that when the decrease due to ordering in freezing is balanced against the increase associated with all other related possesses, the total entropy of the water and its environment, the world and the universe, has been increased.

Life itself is antientropic. Life exists by an ordering of material into the kind of complex patterns of interaction of which we spoke at some length in chapter 7. But life does not violate the second law of thermodynamics, for the production and maintenance of life on earth is costing the universe in entropy increases which exceed the entropy decrease associated with living systems.

Antievolutionists frequently assert that evolution violates the second law of thermodynamics. They argue that throughout the eons a decrease in entropy would have been associated with the transformation from nonliving matter to living matter, to the human being. The argument, however, is invalid. It is evident that any evolutionary process on this earth could not and cannot proceed without increasing the entropy in other portions of the universe. The most evident source of such entropy increase is in the power output of the sun, which continuously transforms matter into energy through the same hydrogen fusion reaction typical of the hydrogen bomb. Once this aspect of the closed system is realized, it follows that evolution is not a contradiction of the second law of thermodynamics. It follows also that any related argument, such as how, when it does not happen today, the energy of the sun could bring life into being from nonliving matter, has nothing to do with the second law of thermodynamics but represents quite a different attack that must be answered in a different way. Evolution may be an improbable process, but it does not violate thermodynamics.

Uniformitarianism. When scientists attempt to describe physical activities and events of the past in the history of the universe and our world, the most natural approach is to determine whether the physical laws in evidence now were also in evidence then. If such an approach produces consistent results, it may be concluded that the assumption of a uniform behavior of natural laws is justified. If such an approach produces inconsistent results, it becomes necessary to make further inquiry. We must then question the uniform behavior of natural laws or at least the environmental boundary conditions that determine the practical effect of behavior according to these laws. The general assumption giving rise to this kind of scientific approach has been called *uniformitarianism*. Results derived from such an approach support an evolutionary view of the development of living creatures and of man; hence they come under criticism by antievolutionists.

G. G. Simpson and W. S. Beck define uniformitarianism as follows,

> The doctrine of uniformitarianism is that the fundamental properties of the universe, the nature and the modes of interaction of matter and energy, have not changed. They are independent of the passage of time.[8]

Antievolutionists frequently attack this position by arguing that it leaves no room for catastrophes in the early history of the earth or for nonuniform variations in atmosphere, climate, temperature, and so on. The criticism is unjustified, at least for modern use of the principle of uniformitarianism. J. R. van de Fliert points out that

> Most present-day geologists . . . use it in the sense of a constancy of physical and biological laws, which does not at all exclude, for example, periods with climates differing from that which we know presently, or alternating longer quiet periods with shorter "catastrophic" or paroxysmal episodes.[9]

The principle of uniformitarianism does provide guidance that such exceptions from a uniform behavior will not be assumed unless the physical evidence demands it.

An example may be cited here to attempt to show the irrational prejudice of the scientific community against those who puncture the uniformitarianism principle. Consider the way in which the

---

[8] George G. Simpson and William S. Beck, *Life: An Introduction to Biology* (New York: Harcourt, Brace and World, 1965), p. 757.

[9] J. R. van de Fliert, "Fundamentalism and the Fundamentals of Geology," *Journal ASA* 21 (1969): 69.

writings of Immanuel Velikovsky were received.[10] In *Worlds in Collision*, Velikovsky described the last two in a series of cataclysmic events that he claims occurred thirty-four and twenty-seven centuries ago. According to his hypothesis, the earth, Venus, Mars, and the moon were involved in near encounters after Venus burst from the planet Jupiter and wandered through the heavens before stabilizing in its present orbit. Evidence for this position was derived from a study of literary references in the mythological and astro-mythological writings of the various peoples of the world, including the Old Testament among many others. Reception in scientific circles was cold, but primarily because of Velikovsky's methodology rather than his assault on uniformitarianism. In a later book, Velikovsky sought to provide archaeological, geological, and paleontological evidence for his hypothesis. Some of his predictions have proved to be remarkably accurate, but a wholly objective judgment has been difficult to make. It is interesting that it was not so much Velikovsky's threat to uniformitarianism as it was his approach and personal response that provided the context for his reception by the scientific community. Velikovsky is an interesting non-Christian advocate of cataclysm, and a reading of his works should be included in a study of this type of material. Whether or not his impact on the interaction of science and biblical revelation is helpful is a moot question. Does it help to speculate that the manna upon which the Israelites fed in the wilderness, to cite but one example, can be accounted for as carbohydrates derived from the carbon and hydrogen gases in the tail of a comet that brushed the earth with its tail?

The Flood. Antievolutionists sometimes suggest that a biblical answer can be given to the geological and paleontological evidence that seems to favor evolution. They argue that it is to be found in the Genesis Flood which covered the whole earth in the day of Noah. In *The Genesis Flood*, J. C. Whitcomb and H. M. Morris seize the opportunity to uphold the biblical account of Creation, as opposed to the scientific theories of evolution, and the biblical account of a universal flood, as opposed to the scientific views of local floods, at one and the same time. They conclude,

---

[10] Immanuel Velikovsky, *Worlds in Collision* (New York: Doubleday, 1950); *Earth in Upheaval* (New York: Doubleday, 1955).

The uniformitarian time-table of modern paleontology must be rejected as totally erroneous; and a Biblical catastrophism (centering in the year-long, universal Deluge) must be substituted for it as the only possible solution to the enigma of the fossil strata.[11]

As we have said before, there undoubtedly are many and serious problems with a uniformitarian and evolutionary interpretation of the geological and paleontological data. There appears, however, to be almost universal agreement between geologists and paleontologists, both Christian and non-Christian, that the physical data for a universal flood are simply not to be found. Christian geologist J. R. van de Fliert expresses the consensus of such opinion when he says,

> If I had been told a few years ago that an apparently serious attempt would be made to reintroduce the diluvialistic theory on Biblical grounds as the only acceptable working hypothesis for the major part of the geological sciences I would not have believed it. . . . It is almost incredible that such an effort, which must have cost an enormous amount of work and money, has been made for such a bad procedure as this.[12]

It does not appear likely that a panacea-like substitute for geological ages and evolutionary processes can be found in a universal flood.

Age of the Earth

One commodity that evolutionary processes require is time. The age of the earth becomes a critical factor, therefore, in pro- or antievolutionary arguments. At one time a traditional interpretation of the biblical record (not justified by the record) placed the creation of the world at 4004 B.C. Although antievolutionary advocates have allowed somewhat more uncertainty than this, they usually conclude that the earth cannot be more than a few tens of thousands of years old at most. Thus there is a marked contrast with the generally accepted scientific age of the earth of some five billion years.

----

[11] J. C. Whitcomb and H. M. Morris, *The Genesis Flood* (Philadelphia: Presbyterian and Reformed Publishing Co., 1961).

[12] van de Fliert, *loc. cit.*

The determination of the age of the earth puts uniformitarianism to the test. A variety of methods exists for estimating the age of the earth on the assumption that processes presently going on with a known rate proceeded at this same rate from some point of origin in the past. There is absolutely no denying that every such age determination rests upon some basic presupposition about the past which cannot be checked. But if a variety of different methods of age determination give about the same age, then either the uniformitarian assumption is essentially correct (who cares about a few tens of millions of years discrepancy in five billion years?), or all of these processes were affected by nonuniform changes in the past in the same way. G. K. Schweitzer[13] describes how the following techniques all give rise to about the same estimate for the age of the earth: (1) the time required for the crust of the earth to cool from a molten state to its present temperature, (2) an estimate derived from the salinity of the oceans, assuming a rate of salt transport to the ocean, (3) the rate of transformation of igneous to sedimentary rocks, (4) the recession of the moon from the earth, assuming it started very close to the earth, (5) the presence of radioactive potassium-40 and uranium-235 in the earth's crust, (6) isotope ratios, assuming equal ratios at the beginning of the earth and known radioactive decay rates, and (7) radioactive decay products assuming known decay rates. Radioactivity estimates of the age of meteorites are about the same as the above estimates for the age of the earth, and estimates of the age of the galaxy from star distributions and separations of binary stars or openness of star clusters again give about the same value. Finally, estimates of the age of the universe from the velocity of recession of galaxial clusters are also of the same order of magnitude.

Particularly striking age evidence was obtained from a study of radioactivity products and isotopic ratios on rocks and dust brought back from the moon by Apollo 11. The results of six investigations on different dust samples using five different atomic systems for analysis give the following ages: 4.66, 4.5, 4.60–4.63, 4.75, 4.76, and 4.7 billion years. These data represent an agreement to about 2 percent between different samples and measurement techniques. The

---

[13] G. K. Schweitzer, "The Origin of the Universe," in *Evolution and Christian Thought Today*, ed. R. L. Mixter (Grand Rapids, Mich.: Eerdmans, 1959).

THE EVOLUTION CONTROVERSY

experimental papers are published in the January 30, 1970, issue of
Science.

There *are* assumptions related to the determination of age by
various radioactive systems. Loss and contamination are constant
problems that can be guarded against only by care and repeated
sampling. In radioactive carbon dating for more recent events
within the last 50,000 years, for example, it is assumed that the
carbon reservoir in the atmosphere has remained constant over this
time. Attempts are being made to check the reliability of this assumption. Constant checks are made with other methods of dating
for determination of consistency. Experimental and interpretational errors of several percent and in gross cases even by factors of
two are quite conceivable; it does not appear, however, that factors
of ten thousand can be accounted for or justifiably defended in any
conceivable way.

Antievolutionists sometimes charge that evolution-supporting
dating is really the result of a circular reasoning. They argue that
fossils are dated by the layer in which they are found, and that the
layers are dated according to which fossils are in them, all controlled by the presupposition of the theory of evolution. Comment-
ing on the treatment given by van de Fliert to this objection, Roger
J. Cuffey remarks:

> He stresses quite nicely the fact that the use of fossils to indicate
> geologic time is a matter of repeatable, verifiable observation; such
> use is not a circular-reasoning device based on a preconceived bias
> for evolutionary explanations of life history.[14]

Faults can be found with any scientific theory. Progress is usually
made not by rejecting the totality of the hypothesis because of the
apparent isolated problems but by adapting and correcting the
major hypothesis to accommodate the special cases. If evolutionists
have been guilty of overlooking the basic shortcomings in evolutionary theory in their zeal to support evolutionary faith, antievolutionists have been guilty of ignoring the vast and complex
web of interagreement between theory and observation in order
to focus attention on a few apparently contradictory evidences.

As one looks at the question of the age of the earth, there are

---

[14] Roger J. Cuffey, *Journal* ASA 21 (1969): 71.

essentially two possible reactions that one can choose between. Either one can conclude that the earth really is some 5 billion years old because all the physical indications converge on such a date, or one can conclude that God has created the earth at some arbitrary date (20,000 years or 15 minutes ago makes no difference) with all the appearances of being 5 billion years old in every detail. (There is, I suppose, the third possibility that every indication we have about the age of the earth is meaningless because we simply do not understand the physical world well enough to make meaningful interpretations and guesses; if this antiscientific position should be true, it would practically eliminate the possibility of any discussion at all.)

As far as a scientist is concerned in his professional attempt to describe the physical world in the categories of the physical level, it does not matter at all whether the world is 5 billion years old or only appears in every detail to be 5 billion years old. In fact, if the world *appears* to be so, then scientifically it *is*. In his work and physical descriptions, the scientist must then go on from that assumption. Regardless of which option is correct, he will come up with an appropriate description.

And as far as man is concerned in his human attempt to understand the meaning of existence and the character of matter in terms of ultimate meaning and theological significance, it does not matter at all whether God created the earth 5 billion years ago or 15 minutes ago. The only significant thing for him to know is that God *did* create the earth.

Thus we come to the conclusion that, as a human being in search of meaning and ultimate understanding, it is intrinsically important for me to know only that God did create the world. As a scientist it is important for me to know only that the world is of the same character as if it had its origin 5 billion years ago.

Scientific Study of Origins

An origin, like a mathematical singularity, is a point or region where analysis blows up. The origin of the universe and hence the origin of finite existence is essentially outside of the domain of the scientific inquiry. Although science can trace processes into the past on the assumption that the laws of nature were obeyed then in the same form as now, it is rendered helpless when called upon to face the very beginning of these laws themselves.

The so-called Big Bang theory of the origin of the universe involves such an extrapolation. It goes back to what can only be described as a conceptual and mathematical singularity. If, at the beginning of the universe, all of the matter was condensed into an infinitesimally small geometric region, what happen five minutes earlier? This is the kind of question that scientists neither like to nor can face, and they are led to postulate some kind of model that will deliver them from the starkness of this beginning. One such model has been revived from time to time. Linked with cyclical philosophical views of life, the theory of the cyclical or oscillating universe proposes that what we seem to see as an expanding universe is only the expanding *phase* of an oscillating universe. Alternately expanding and contracting, it repeats the cycle over and over for eternity. The singularity of the origin in the Big Bang model is effectively removed therefore, for what happened five minutes before the origin of this expanding phase can now be identified with the last five minutes of the previous contracting phase. There is no scientific basis for such an oscillating universe.

Another cosmological theory that does away with the singularity of the Big Bang origin, but which has had some scientific support, is the steady-state model of the universe. This theory proposes that the universe is always expanding with ever greater velocity and that new material is "created" as the universe expands. In this model, if we extrapolate backwards in time, we never reach a beginning; the universe always appears the same throughout all time! How the new matter comes into being—at the rate of about one atom per century for a volume about the size of a skyscraper— is not known, but the Christian should not be misled into believing that the use of the technical term *create* makes this a theistic theory. This rather unorthodox scientific speculation has been reported dead on several different occasions, but new findings or interpretations have to date been able to keep the steady-state theory alive as a possible view.

It is probably only reasonable to conclude that no presently conceived cosmological theory for the origin of the universe on scientific grounds is completely adequate or acceptable. It is quite likely that our scientific ideas will undergo some radical changes in the future. For these reasons it is as usual very important not to associate the Christian doctrine of Divine Creation with any particular scientific cosmology.

Beginnings of Life and Spirit

The origins associated with life and spirit on earth are somewhat different from the kind of origin associated with the whole universe itself. Although it is beyond the domain of science to reach back to situations before natural law existed, it can consider the mechanisms involved in the production of life and spirit in creatures on the earth, provided that these origins occurred in the history of the earth and in the context of existing natural laws.

As pointed out in our previous discussions, there is no reason to believe that any other ingredients contribute to the wonder of life than a particular complex patterned interaction of nonliving matter. This patterned interaction could have been brought about supernaturally by the special working of God in a moment of time at a precise point in the history of the world. Or this patterned interaction could have been brought about by the normal activity of God which we recognize as natural law, including the proper environment and circumstances. It is the task of the scientist to answer the question: Could life have arisen on the earth as the result of a propitious coincidence of natural forces? He can attempt to answer this question in only one convincing way. Insofar as possible he must reconstruct the likely circumstances existing on the earth at the time he considers the origin of life to have occurred. If he can demonstrate in the laboratory that life can be produced by the appropriate coincidence of environmental and atmospheric conditions, then at least he knows what might have happened. And the *scientific* understanding of the nature of life then requires that he proceed *as if* life had started on earth this way.

Discussions of the origin of life very soon come around to a consideration of *spontaneous generation*. The antievolutionist claims that the evolutionist's arguments for the origin of life commit him to spontaneous generation, a process which has been scientifically shown not to occur. Now, to be sure, the research associated with

THE EVOLUTION CONTROVERSY   195

the name of Pasteur did show that spontaneous generation does not occur in the modern age, and this work forms the basis for modern methods of sterilization and modern theories of disease. On the other hand, spontaneous generation does appear as a central concept in the ideas both of creation and of evolution. If an observer were to watch an event of creation by divine fiat, he would conclude that he had witnessed an event of spontaneous generation. And if an observer had been present to witness the organization of nonliving matter to form living matter under the influence of unusual environmental and atmospheric conditions on the primeval earth, he would also conclude that he had witnessed an event of spontaneous generation. Common experience indicates both that God does not create by divine fiat and that living matter does not arise spontaneously from nonliving matter today. But such experience says absolutely nothing about what might have happened under different conditions in different times in the past. To argue that the evolutionist is inconsistent for maintaining that such generation of life occurred only in one period in the past is to advance a pseudo-uniformitarianism that outdoes the uniformitarianism relied on by evolutionists. And to say that spontaneous generation as the result of divine fiat deserves recognition as biblical Creation, whereas spontaneous generation as the result of divine activity in the world's development does not, appears to be an unwarranted distinction.

The problems raised by the origin of the human soul appear to be immensely greater than those raised by the origin of life. Actually, however, the two questions are completely analogical. Life results from a patterned interaction of nonliving matter; soul (or spirit) results from a patterned interaction of living matter. Matter, life, and soul are all products of God's creative activity. God may have created life by divine fiat, but investigation of the scientific mechanisms involved indicates that it is scientifically appropriate to consider the possibility of the development of life from the interaction of nonliving matter under the appropriate conditions of environment and atmosphere. God may have created human soul by divine fiat, but investigation of the scientific mechanisms (the relationship between the manifestations of human soul and the biological and psychological characteristics of the living organism) indicates that it is scientifically appropriate to consider the possibility of the development of soul from the interaction of living matter under the appropriate conditions. If God brought life into being by a process of physical interaction, does this make life any less wonderful or meaningful—or any less real—than if God had brought life into being by divine fiat? If God brought human soul into being by a process of biological interaction, does this make human soul any less wonderful or meaningful—or any less real— than if God had brought human soul into being by divine fiat?

We conclude that the argument for the uniqueness of human soul is not an argument against the evolutionary process. God called the whole universe into existence in the first place and maintains it moment by moment. There is no reason that his creative activity could not have brought human soul into being by an evolutionary process. If by the term *spiritual evolution*, therefore, we mean that process by which increasingly complex and appropriate patterns of interaction in a creature's body develop (and not a natural process by which less moral is inevitably brought to more moral) until they manifest themselves as human soul, no real objection can be brought against its use.

Human Evolution—The General Theory

What kind of evidence is there for the general theory of evolution, and in particular for the evolution of man from the animals? On this question there is considerable disagreement. John Moore, writing in the *Journal of the American Scientific Affiliation*, says, "The careful critic is able to assert quite accurately that there is no empirical evidence in existence to support the General Theory of Evolution."[15] At the same time, in *The Encounter Between Christianity and Science* Donald Eckelmann says, "The paleontological record clearly portrays an evolutionary origin for man and relates man unequivocally to the animal kingdom via primitive anthropoids."[16]

Both of these authors are scientists and both are Christians. Why

---

[15] John N. Moore, "Evolution: Required or Optional in a Science Course?," *Journal ASA* 22 (1970): 82.

[16] Eckelmann, *loc. cit.*, p. 166.

do they disagree so violently? The answer is at least partially that the evidence for the general theory is circumstantial and analogical, rather than direct and incontrovertible. Under these circumstances individual preferences and presuppositions permit a wide variety of interpretations.

The basic evidence lies in the fossil record and in the biological analogies that can be drawn between human beings and other animals. The fossil record indicates the following groupings of man-like creatures with the time ago given in parentheses: *Cro-Magnon* (50,000 years), *Neanderthal* (80,000 years), *Swanscombe* (300,-000 years), *Heidelberg* (500,000 years), *Java* (400,000 years), *Peking* (400,000 years), *Australopithecus* (1 million years), and *Zinjanthropus* (1.75 million years). Looking at this evidence, Donald Eckelmann concludes that

> man has a long, continuous history which can be traced back over several million years to primitive manlike animals. . . . Present-day modern man, older primitive men, and still older manlike animals existed in large numbers spread over large portions of continents. . . . Like it or not, the scientific record clearly points to man developing by successive evolutionary stages from early anthropoid stock.[17]

At the same time, authors like D. Bolton Davidheiser minimize the differences between these different fossils with statements like the following:

> Leakey's work is largely financed by the National Geographic Society, and they published in their magazine (September 1960) a picture of a restored *Zinjanthropus* which surely would not draw a second glance in the New York subway, provided he was wearing a cap that concealed the fact that he had no forehead.[18]

Nevertheless, the fossils are there. Their apparent age appears to correlate approximately with differences in their characteristics from those of modern man. Both their age and their existence must be correlated with the rest of an individual's view of the age and history of the earth. Scientific interpretation of the fossil record appears to be based most effectively on the general theory, with all of its admitted problems. In this kind of situation, the general the-

---

[17] Ibid.
[18] Davidheiser, p. 337.

ory of evolution plays the same role for the biologist as quantum theory plays for the physicist. In each case, the theory appears to be the best currently available. For guiding scientific research, it shows the most usefulness, but if it is applied or interpreted philosophically, it must be regarded with skepticism.

What is man? Different scientists will define a man differently. A physiologist will define a man as a primate with blood groupings like the apes. A paleontologist will define a man in terms of the conformation of his skeleton. An anthropologist will define a man in terms of tool-using or of conscious burying of the dead. A comparative psychologist will define a man in terms of ability for verbal expression. There is certainly something unique about a man even scientifically, otherwise there would be no need for a branch of science called anthropology. But it is evident that, biologically, man is very like the animals. Medical research aimed at the alleviation of human suffering is most successfully carried out first on animals. Surgical procedures are worked out with dogs and pigs, nutritional studies are carried out with rats, and various animals are used to test new chemicals or drugs before these are used or tested with human beings. Clearly there are many biological properties of man so similar to those of animals that it is possible to make this kind of research.

When these similarities both in skeletal construction and in biological function are considered still further, it is apparent that man is more like the primates than he is like the other animals. Vaccine to immunize against polio is cultured in monkey tissue; it will not grow in tissues of other animals. Growth hormone from the pituitary gland of rhesus monkeys is active in the human being; growth hormones from other animals are not. Psychological similarities can also be noted. Young chimpanzees can for a while be brought up by a human family almost as if they were human youngsters. The ability of such chimpanzees to perform humanlike mimicry is familiar to any devotee of the circus.

Antievolutionists frequently argue that the gaps in the fossil record are so common and so widespread, including in fact any evidence whatsoever of transitional forms between species, that one cannot hold to a development of all species from a common source. The objection cannot be answered in a wholly satisfactory way by evolutionists today. Two comments may be made, however. First, evidence seems to be developing within evolutionary circles that major transitions between species occurred within relatively short periods of time. If indeed the evolutionary process did proceed in fits and starts, so to speak, the relatively small number of transitional forms ever in existence might account for their scarcity among the fossils. The second comment really only extends the first. If the species represent the biologically stable life forms, then the transitions between species represent very special periods and conditions that again might well be difficult to substantiate in the fossil record.

Our position with regard to the question of evolution is very similar to that discussed above concerning the age of the earth. There are essentially two choices. Either one can conclude that the process of evolution really did give rise to the human being because the circumstantial and analogical data all point in this direction, or one can conclude that God created man by divine fiat (or any other process except evolution) with all the appearances of having been produced by a process of evolution.

As far as a scientist is concerned in his professional attempt to describe the biological structure of man, it does not matter at all whether man is *really* the result of an evolutionary process or whether he only *appears* to be the result of such a process. As far as the scientist is concerned in his work and biological descriptions, he must assume that effective research will be guided by the theory of evolution. Regardless of which option is correct, he will come up with an appropriate biological description.

As far as a man is concerned in his human attempt to understand the meaning of existence and the significance of human personality in terms of ultimate meaning and theological significance, it does not matter at all whether God created man in a process of evolutionary development or whether God created man in an act of divine fiat. The only significant thing for him to know is that God *did* create him.

Thus once again the conclusion is the same. As a human being in search of meaning and ultimate understanding, it is intrinsically important for me to know only that God did create me, regardless of how he did it; as a scientist it is important for me to know only that my biological constitution is of the same character as it would have been if produced by an evolutionary process.

Teilhard de Chardin

Perhaps no other writer has tried more completely to combine a Christian perspective with an evolutionary view than the French priest-paleontologist Pierre Teilhard de Chardin. In a number of books he poured out his faith that the evolutionary process was the evidence of the triumphant working of God in the world. No discussion of evolution and Christian faith would be complete without at least a brief summary of his thought.

Teilhard marked four great periods in the history of the world and the evolutionary process: (1) cosmogenesis—when the world of matter was formed, (2) biogenesis—when the world of life came into being, (3) noogenesis—when the world of spirit came into being, and (4) Christogenesis—when the superspirit of oneness with God in Christ comes into being. We are living today in the period between noogenesis and Christogenesis. Through all these periods Teilhard sees the irreversible process of evolution proceeding in a single unfailing direction, bringing more complex out of less complex.

In our day Teilhard is refreshing because he is so optimistic. The only question is whether or not he has grounds for his optimism. For example, he rejects the gloomy predictions of the pessimists and looks with expectation at the growing interaction between men. He sees this as the first step toward superhumanization, superpersonalization which will finally result in the onset of Christogenesis. Whereas in biological processes, evolution caused branches which diverged, Teilhard argues that in noological processes, evolution causes branches which converge. Their ultimate point of convergence he calls the Omega Point, to be identified with the God of Creation, the Father of the Lord Jesus Christ. Thus the convergence of mankind is not something to be resisted but to be rejoiced in.

Teilhard interprets love as the way in which we participate today in God's work of evolution. To hate is to resist the work of God in the evolutionary process. Because men are "evolution become aware of itself," we have the exciting challenge of direct participation in the evolutionary process. According to Teilhard, we must see the earth and all that it holds as a whole, exceeding the sum of the individual parts. And we must respond to the love of God—the energetic force driving the antientropic evolutionary process to completion—by opposing every effort leading to divergence between men and by supporting every effort leading to convergence.

In a study of Teilhard, D. Gareth Jones summarizes the criticism of Teilhard from a Christian perspective.[19] While recognizing Teilhard's contribution to an appreciation for God's work in Creation and in the Incarnation, he also points out the absence in Teilhard's thought of an appropriate response to sin and Christ's work of atonement. He argues that Teilhard's solution is at least as much a product of Teilhard's own deep personal psychological needs—to find a purpose for man, to reconcile love for God and love for the world, to be both truly Christian and fully a man—as it is of the objective data or evidence. In Teilhard's system, evil and sin are simply by-products of the process of evolution and have nothing to do with the central issues of life. Thus his view of evil must be metaphysical rather than moral and individual salvation becomes essentially irrelevant, for either all of mankind will arrive at Omega or none will.

The attempt of Teilhard de Chardin to unite evolutionary theory and Christian faith cannot be considered a scientific contribution to evolution. Rather, it must be classed almost wholly as an ingenious venture into Christian evolutionism. Although valuable insights can be gained by an understanding of Teilhard's perspective, perhaps in the long run it is his optimism which is the most destructive, since it cannot really find room for the reality of *moral* guilt and divine forgiveness.

An Interpretation of Genesis 1–3

If the early chapters of Genesis are not there to tell us about the age of the earth or the mechanisms underlying cosmology and biology, what function do they have? No treatment of these questions would be complete if we did not consider briefly the nature of the revelational content of these chapters. Our discussion will be similar to that provided in considerably greater detail by A. van der Ziel in *Genesis and Scientific Inquiry.*[20]

---

[19] D. Gareth Jones, *Teilhard de Chardin* (London: Tyndale Press, 1969).

[20] Aldert van der Ziel, *Genesis and Scientific Inquiry* (Minneapolis: Denison, 1965), pp. 11–82.

The first three chapters of Genesis can be divided into three sections: (1) a logical and systematic account of creation in Gen. 1:1 through Gen. 2:4a, (2) an imaginative and symbolic account of creation in Gen. 2:4b through Gen. 2:25, and (3) an imaginative and symbolic account of the human dilemma in Genesis 3.

Gen. 1:1 presents a summary of the creation account. The creation story that follows is cast into a seven-day pattern. The seven-day week, part of the religious experience of the people for whom the book was written, is superposed on the works of creation culminating in a seventh day of praise and glory to the God of Israel. The stated days are not always coincident with the completion of a given creative act.

The first creative act is the creation of light. Light is the prerequisite for any work to be done. God is the sovereign of both day and night; the light needed for work comes directly from his creative activity. No mention is made of the sun, the normal source of light, because the sun god is a common feature of pagan mythologies. To emphasize the priority of the God of Israel over other gods, in the Genesis creation story the sun is created on a later day with very little fanfare. The phrase, "and God saw," indicates the completion of an act of creation. In each case comes the judgment that the creation is good.

On the second day, God separates the water on earth from the waters in the sky by placing the firmament between them. Thus is emphasized the sovereignty of God over both heaven and earth. There is no need to apologize for the cosmological model used; it is the common view held by the people for whom Genesis 1 was written. The phrase, "and God saw," does not appear at the end of the second day.

The third day emphasizes the sovereignty of God over both land and sea. God rules over the waters introduced in Gen. 1:2. The pagan mythological view of a sea deity is ruled out. As the dry earth is separated from the seas, the land is ready for habitation just as, earlier, the skies were made ready for the heavenly bodies. The phrase "and God saw," appears at this point therefore. Note that on both the second and third days, the work of creation is described as a "separation."

In the remainder of the third day, the second part of creation begins. Now the earth, under the creative energy of God, brings forth grass, plants, and trees for food for the animals and man who are about to be created. God's provision for his creatures is stressed by this preparation of the world as a fit dwelling place for them. The phrase "each according to its kind" has nothing to do with the biological concept of species but simply expresses the common experience that each kind of living creature produces others of the same kind. Again a phase of creation is completed.

In the fourth day God's creative activity adorns the heavens with heavenly lights, again in preparation for the creation of man on earth. These heavenly lights were to serve those on earth by being signs and indicating seasons, days, and years. With devastating effect, the author does not even deign to mention the sun and moon by name. Speaking simply of a "greater light" and a "lesser light," he strikes directly at any pagan sun or moon god idolatry. To these lights is assigned the task of separating light from dark, a work that God had previously accomplished without their aid at all.

On the fifth day, the waters bring forth fish of all kinds, and birds appear above the earth in response to the creative activity of God. There was nothing in the sea or flying in the air that God did not create; even the sea monsters are his creatures. For the first time comes the blessing and command to be fruitful and multiply.

On the sixth day, the earth brings forth all the living creatures and animals that move across the face of the earth: all cattle, and creeping things and beasts of all kinds. The phrase, "and God saw," marks the completion of this creative work.

Finally the climax of the story is reached in the creation of man. For the first time God speaks personally, "Let us make." He designates a unique creature, man, made "in our image," to whom alone is given dominion over all the rest of God's creation. This creature, man, alone is conscious of his responsibility before God. Man's work is seen as part of God's good creation, including also the marriage relationship in the male–female created pair. To them and to the animals are given all the plants of the earth for food; this vegetarian diet symbolizes creation not yet marred by human sin. The work of creation was finished.

The seventh day of God's rest symbolizes the purpose of creation. As the weekly Sabbath in the religious life of the people for whom these words were written was a day set apart for the praise and worship of God, so the purpose of creation is to set up a world that will praise and glorify its Creator. Who is the God to be worshipped on the Sabbath? The God who delivered Israel out of Egypt, even the God who created heavens and earth.

As we read this account from Gen. 1:1 through Gen. 2:4, we are struck by the absence of those fantastic excesses that mark the mythological cosmogonies and creation accounts typical of the non-Judaic cultures living at the same time. And if we wanted to develop a chronological timetable for the development of life on earth, we could hardly come closer to that proposed in the general theory of evolution than the one given in the first chapter of Genesis.

A *second account*. A repeated account of creation starts in the last part of Gen. 2:4. The style of the writing is quite different, but there are no contradictions with the first account. Here the close connection between the created man and the soil of the earth is emphasized. The man is named, but it is not a normal name, for "Adam" means simply "the man." In Genesis 1, God is the commander, ordering creation into existence by the Word of his power. In Genesis 2, God is the sculptor, shaping, forming, and bringing to life.

The personalization of the man, not present in Genesis 1, involves the reader in the story that is being told. It is not only some Adam in the dim past of history that is being described, but one who is the representative of me also. I am involved in what Adam does—in his work, his creation, his marriage relationship, and his sin.

In Gen. 2:7, we are told that man became a living being. Note that the giving of life and spirit are simultaneous. By the creative act of God, man became a living (manifesting life) being (manifesting spirit). Man does not *have* a soul; he *is* a living soul.

The beautiful garden of Eden represents the whole of the created order in its freedom from the curse of sin. It appears again in Revelation 21 and 22, under conditions of a new creation free from sin. Man's work of agriculture and horticulture in this garden is part of the good creative plan.

The trees which appear here and in Revelation are clearly symbolic trees. The tree of life represents the concept of eternal life. The tree of the knowledge of good and evil represents the reality of this created order in which it is not good for the created man to have every conceivable experience. The experience of evil leads only to death. God's command not to eat of this tree flows from his love and understanding of the situation.

In Gen. 2:18–25, we have the search for a partner for man. The exercise of man naming the animals indicates his superiority over them. No animal satisfies man's need for a partner, for such a partner must be like the man but also uniquely different. The profound truth is revealed that man and woman are made to be together, that marriage is part of the good creation and is intended for partnership as well as procreation, and that sex is also part of the good creation. Since shame is the result of guilt, man and woman were unashamed to be naked.

The Fall. Genesis 3 follows in the same style as the second creation account. The chronological ordering of the good works of creation before the entrance of sin emphasizes that the creation is intrinsically good, that God is not the author of sin, and that sin is not part of but an aberration on the good creation. The creature is responsible for sin, not the Creator. And as we read of Adam's sin, we come to see that we also are sinners.

The temptation leading to the sin of Genesis 3 can be cast into a script dialogue, the principal features of which characterize every temptation that man ever encounters.

SERPENT: Is it really true that God told you that you couldn't eat of any tree in the garden? (*How outrageous!*)

WOMAN: No, the only tree we are forbidden to eat of is the tree of the knowledge of good and evil. But we aren't allowed even to *touch* that tree—or else we'll die! (*That does seem kind of unreasonable, doesn't it?*)

SERPENT: Don't be silly. You're not going to die. God just wants to keep you down so that you won't know as much as He does. Isn't it good to know everything?

The effects of their disobedient rebellion against God are immediately evident. (1) They know that they are naked; ashamed, they try to cover themselves. (2) They hide from God, realizing the break in their relationship with him. (3) The trust between man and woman is broken, as the man accuses the woman. (4) The woman tries to put the blame on God, since he was the one who made the serpent which tempted her. Their disobedience has given them the knowledge of good and evil, but it has severed their relationship with God and with each other. And so the effects of such rebellion are exhibited in the lives of each one of us.

The story emphasizes that sin entered into man's existence from the very beginning; it is at the very root of his nature. The curses of Gen. 3:14–19 are physical signs and symbols of the fall.

Finally, even under these circumstances, there is a note of hope. (1) God continues to communicate with man and does not simply cut him off forever. (2) God meets the shame that follows from their guilt by preparing coverings for them. (3) The man names his wife "mother of all living," indicating that he believes God and understands.

Gen. 3:22–24 closes on a note of finality about the loss of man's previous condition. There is no way for him to go back to the unspoiled creation on his own. If he is ever to make it back, it must be as the result of future acts of God on his behalf. It is these future acts of God, climaxed in the life, death, and resurrection of Jesus Christ, that make it possible for man—for you and me—once again to become residents of Paradise.

Valuable insights into the revelational content of the first eleven chapters of the book of Genesis may be obtained by a reading of *How the World Began* by Helmut Thielicke.[21]

Summary

The evolution controversy does involve some basic differences in presuppositions and convictions, but its emotional impact has been intensified by a series of misconceptions and misapplications on the part of both evolutionists and antievolutionists.

1. The evolutionist considers the empirical evidence of the special theory to be sufficient ground to support his acceptance of the general theory, and in many cases his acceptance of the philosophy of evolutionism. The antievolutionist refuses to admit that the empirical data have any relevance other than showing genetic variation and considers them of no importance in the evolution contro-

---

[21] Helmut Thielicke, *How the World Began* (Philadelphia: Fortress Press, 1961).

versy. If the evolutionist usually puts too much emphasis on these data, the antievolutionist usually puts too little.

2. The evolutionist frequently feels justified in making an extrapolation from the scientific data and theories of biological evolution into the realms of philosophy and religion. The antievolutionist frequently feels justified in making an intrusion into the biological theories on the basis of his religious convictions. If the evolutionist is misguided to attempt to develop a religion out of a scientific theory, the antievolutionist is misguided to attempt to attack a scientific theory on religious grounds. For the antievolutionist to attack the biological theory of evolution because he is opposed to the religious faith of evolutionism is similar to his attacking the quantum theory because he is opposed to the philosophical nuances associated with indeterminism and chance.

3. The evolutionist often argues as if the last word of scientific evidence were practically at hand for both the general theory and the special theory. The antievolutionist often argues as if there were no evidence at all to support the general theory. If the evolutionist is wrong to overemphasize confirmation of the general theory, the antievolutionist is wrong to find faults in the scientific support of the general theory without offering scientific interpretations of his own that are valid. It is always a difficult task to develop an adequate scientific description and a relatively simple task to find isolated instances that appear to contradict proposed scientific description. Evolutionists themselves realize the shortcomings of their theories, and antievolutionists never weary of using these quotations to argue that even the evolutionists admit they don't know anything. All too often, when put on the spot, antievolutionists retreat to a position like the following by Davidheiser with respect to explaining the distribution of animals on the earth.

> Since the scientific experts have problems in trying to explain the distribution of animals on the earth, it is hardly to be expected that Bible-believers should be expected to give all the answers. But since the evolutionists put animal distribution on a natural basis, it is required that they produce the answers to all the questions involved or keep looking for them. The creationist does not have this responsibility or obligation. The flood was an act of God and miracles were associated with it.[22]

---

[22] Davidheiser, *Evolution and Christian Faith*, pp. 281–82.

4. The evolutionist often argues that his understanding of evolution does away with the theological concept of creation. The antievolutionist curiously agrees with him and emphasizes that creation and evolution are antithetical. Davidheiser's use of the word *creationist* in the above quotation is in this context. If the evolutionist is wrong to believe that his biological description does away with the need for a theological description, the antievolutionist is wrong to believe that his theological description must make any biological description impossible.

The key to so much of the evolution controversy seems to lie in the recognition of the necessity and the propriety of descriptions of the same phenomena on different levels according to our thesis 2. Then a complete biological description does not do away with the need for a complete theological description, and a complete theological description does not do away with the possibility for a complete biological description. Evolution can be considered without denying creation; creation can be accepted without excluding evolution. The final resolution of the problems in the evolutionary description must come, if indeed they are ever to come, from improvements in scientific process and understanding. Evolution is a scientific question on the biological level; it would be unfortunate indeed if a scientific question were permitted to become the crucial point for Christian faith with its focus on the theological level.

The appropriate answers to the question of the age of the earth depend on the perspective of the questioner. From man's perspective it is most important to know that God created the earth, regardless of whether this was 15 minutes, 20,000 years, or 5 billion years ago. From the scientist's, it is most important to know that since the earth appears to be 5 billion years old, for all scientific purposes it is 5 billion years old. It would make no difference scientifically even if it were really true that God had created the earth 15 minutes ago with all the appearances of its being 5 billion years old.

We advanced a similar approach with respect to human evolution and the general theory. As a man it is most important to know that the human being is the result of the creative activity of God, regardless of whether this creative activity took the form of biological evolution or divine fiat. As a scientist it is important to know that since in many ways the human being appears to be the result of an evolutionary process, any scientific investigation of the human being must take into account at least the possibility of such an evolutionary process. Even if God created man by divine fiat with the appearance of man's having been developed by evolution, the only acceptable scientific position is to treat the biological phenomena involved in an evolutionary perspective.

The point at which evolutionary thinking must be opposed and attacked from a Christian perspective is when it ceases to be concerned with the biological development of living creatures and becomes instead a life-directing religious faith. Whenever any ethical or moral decision is made on the basis of a general evolutionary pattern to all of life, a purely subjective, nonscientific, and probably incorrect decision is being made. Evolutionism takes its place as one of the world's religions with cults and offshoots of various economic and political kinds. It affirms that there is no such thing as moral guilt, that man is risen from the animals and is destined to rise still further as he cooperates in and takes control of the evolutionary process. Evolutionism fails to understand both the wonder of man as a creature made in the image of God the Creator and the dilemma of man separated from his Creator by his willful choice of self-interest. Like all other attempts to derive an understanding of the theological and divine dimension by extrapolating from a scientific experience (that is, attempts to arrive at an understanding of the ultimate level of reality by extrapolating from descriptions on particular lower levels in terms of the nomenclature of figure 4), that extrapolation known as evolutionism is bound to fall far short of its goal. When men are treated as only evolved animals, when evil is treated as an inevitable by-product of a perfecting process, and when man's ability to solve all of his own problems is exalted over the basic inability of man to solve any of his ultimate problems by himself, only confusion and further suffering can result. If biological evolution is indeed true, biblical creation is also wholly true.

Topics for Discussion

1. Can the general theory of evolution be proved wrong? What kind of observation or experiment would be required? Can the

theory of creation by divine fiat be proved wrong? What kind of observation or experiment would be required? Can the point of view of theistic evolution, that is, that evolution is God's creative activity, be proved wrong? What kind of observation or experiment would be required? How do you make decisions in a situation like this?

2. Supporters of evolutionism often argue that there is clear evidence that on the average man is more moral today than several thousand years ago in the early days of written history. Do you think there is evidence for such moral evolution?

3. Do you think that a scientific theory, based on certain scientific data but not explaining everything, can be attacked justifiably on the basis of biblical revelation? If so, can you think of a case where the answer might be no? What would the criterion be?

4. Consider the marvelous self-organizing capabilities of living creatures. Is there anything else in the world with similar properties? Does the existence of such self-organizing capabilities demand a theological explanation?

5. You come home and find the bathtub half-full of water and a steady drop-by-drop leaking from the faucet. How would you estimate the length of time since the leaking started? How sure would you feel of your estimate? What kind of errors might be involved? Do you appeal to uniformitarianism in this case?

6. In spite of general scientific discreditation, books regularly continue to be written advancing the Genesis Flood as the basis for all the observed geological and fossil finds. Why is this in your opinion?

7. If God created you 15 minutes ago with the memory of a debt of $100 you owed to someone else, which of the following would be the proper action for you in the future: (a) accept the debt and repay the $100, or (b) refuse the debt because you never really borrowed the money at all.

8. Suppose that the steady state theory of the universe with its feature of matter being constantly "created" in outer space were to be accepted. Do you suppose that this would have a marked influence in leading people to a theistic view of the universe? Why or why not?

9. Do you agree that the origins of life and spirit are appropriate subjects for scientific investigation, provided that they occurred in historic time? Why or why not?

10. Distinguish between the possibility of spiritual evolution and evolutionism, showing how they can be directly opposed to one another.

11. Consider future paleontologists searching out the fossils of modes of transportation. They find many fossils of wagons designed to be drawn by horses. They find many fossils of cars designed to be driven by an engine. However, they find no trace of wagons with engines, or cars pulled by horses. With a little effort can you see any analogy to the problems of gaps in the fossil record of evolution?

12. Teilhard's optimism requires one to believe that as interpersonal interactions become more and more intense, a whole new and wonderful mode of existence will evolve. Do you feel there is any empirical evidence for this hope?

13. In his book *The Relevance of Teilhard*, Kraft suggests that one might look at sin as "moral entropy."[23] In view of the interpretation of entropy as a measure of disorder, how does this view strike you?

14. Consider the interpretation of Genesis 1–3 given in the last section of the chapter. What revelation, if any, in your opinion has been omitted by this kind of treatment?

15. Does it amuse you to realize that according to general relativity theory, whether we speak of the earth moving relative to the sun or the sun moving relative to the earth is almost only a matter of choice? Or that according to the Big Bang theory of the origin of the universe, light appeared before the sun?

---

[23] R. Wayne Kraft, *The Relevance of Teilhard* (Notre Dame, Ind.: Fides Publisher, 1968), p. 149.

Chapter Ten

Social Implications

A *person's views on science and Christian faith may* weather the storms of philosophical and theological conflict in the abstract. But whether or not they have real survival value is determined by what happens to them under fire in terms of actual social implications. It is my intention to offer some thoughts on a variety of issues in which both scientific and Christian concerns are involved; of necessity these must be my thoughts, and therefore they represent the approach taken by one Christian, not necessarily by all.

The question of why Christians can disagree completely with one another on matters of social application of their faith is constantly raised by non-Christians as an embarrassment to the Christian. Yet it is unquestionably true that two people can make opposite decisions with respect to a social application of their faith while at the same time both are being true to the principles of that faith. It is important to realize that this is not a weakness of guidance according to Christian faith. Any decision on social application involves two parts, not just one: (1) the basic data or presuppositions on which the decision is based, and (2) the principles that guide how the decision will depend on these data or presuppositions. The guidance provided by Christian faith involves only the second of these directly, and often provides no insight at all into the first.

Consider, for example, the Christian position with respect to the war in Indochina. If the data in hand were that Communist bandits from the north had invaded a peaceful South Vietnam in order to inflict suffering, bloodshed, and atheism on the helpless and peaceful residents, one decision of Christian faith might well be to go to the aid of these afflicted people in the south and do as much as possible to restrain the Communist bandits with whatever force and violence is necessary. The Christian decision in this case (as I amplify further in a later section of this chapter on violence and war) is to take part in military activity to restrain international evil. On the other hand, if the data at hand were that a civil war was going on in Vietnam in which poor and oppressed people were attempting to obtain some voice in their own destiny after decades of international deceit and betrayal by foreign nations, the Christian decision might well be to commit no armed forces to such an effort on behalf of the combatants but instead to attempt to bring about peace without military intervention. Both the decision to intervene and the decision not to intervene are Christian decisions. What makes them different is *not* the insight of Christian faith, which is rightly applied in one and wrongly in the other, but the data and presuppositions upon which this Christian faith is called to operate. This consideration emphasizes the Christian's responsibility to obtain all of the data available before committing himself to a course of action. But it also emphasizes that the fault in the situation where two Christians oppose one another does not necessarily lie in the inability of their faith to give appropriate guidance.

In recognition of the situation described above, I will attempt to provide some insight into the data and presuppositions that underlie the decisions discussed in the following sections. If then the reader disagrees with my conclusion, he must recognize it as a disagreement about these data and not about the authenticity of Christian faith.

The Crisis of Human Society

We live in a day when the pressures and tensions on human society seem to be greater than ever before. To be sure, it is likely that every generation has thought itself to be living in a day of extreme difficulty; still, it seems more unavoidable for ours to have apocalyptic thoughts. It now lies within the power of man to destroy the world by nuclear bombs if he enters into war, and it lies within the power of man to destroy the quality of life by population growth and environmental pollution even if he stays at peace. The choices that face us all seem equally difficult. We can choose to destroy the whole fabric of the modern system by whatever means are at our disposal in the hope that the subsequent world will be freed from present dilemmas. But do we have any empirical basis for optimism? We can choose to accept the present situation and do nothing about it, living either for the transient pleasure of the moment or in the hope that somehow God will act even though we are not willing to make the effort. Or we can choose to attempt to change the present system, knowing that there are tremendous odds opposing success and little real basis, humanly speaking, for the hope of a beneficial transformation.

The way in which we respond to the crisis in human society is determined to a large extent by our response to the basic question "What is wrong with the world?" We considered this question very briefly at the beginning of the first chapter of this book; now we wish to return to it again to look at it in a little more detail. There are four basic answers, and every man chooses at least one for himself whether he considers the question consciously or not.

The extreme advocate of scientism must conclude that there is nothing wrong with the world, simply because the concepts of right and wrong have no moral basis in scientific inquiry. If, in spite of this inapplicability of the scientific method, an attempt is made to derive ethical values from the scientific method, involvement in the "is-ought" fallacy, which we have previously discussed, is inevitable. The conclusion of scientism that nothing is wrong with the world is not acceptable today, if it ever was. Young people (and old people) are realizing with ever greater conviction that something *is* wrong with the world. The editor of *Physics Today* wrote in an editorial,

> Just what is wrong with our world we do not know, but we feel it is fundamental, basic, causal. . . . Perhaps the fundamental cause is a lack of new values to replace obsolete ones. Perhaps physics has contributed . . . by making old ways of thought look ridiculous.[1]

With the exception of the Christian position, almost every serious religious and philosophical answer to the question under consideration is that the trouble lies in the nature of the world

---

[1] R. Hobart Ellis, *Physics Today* 19, no. 12 (December 1966).

itself. The world is too big and complex, and I am too small and finite; I am at the mercy of the fates and forces far too great for me. The basic trouble with the world is a metaphysical one. I may work and strive, but if I do not temper my hope with realistic despair, I do not properly perceive the stark emptiness of reality. An eloquent exponent of this point of view was Bertrand Russell; his statement is quoted in the first discussion topic at the end of chapter 7. This is the only possible response for the sensitive and honest humanist. It is not enough. There *is* something wrong with the world; there *must be* something that can be done about it. This is what the young people today are saying.

A third answer to the question "What is wrong with the world?" is one that has been popular in all times. If something is wrong with the world, and if that something is not just the way that the world is put together, then what is wrong with the world is somehow related to the people in the world. The people in the world can be separated into two categories: you and me. Since I am concerned, the trouble must be you. This "you" may be a personal individual, but more often it is some institution or some system on which the blame for all evil can easily be laid. Now every human institution or system is imperfect and contributes to evil in the world to a greater or lesser degree; there is therefore no problem in identifying the general evil with the specific institution or system. Then the prescription is clear: get rid of that institution or system, and rid the world of evil. There *is* a need for a constant reformation of human institutions and systems, but it seems to be characteristic of this approach to the problem to identify all evil with a particular system. To destroy that single system is to free the world from all evil. Communists in the Kremlin argue that the imperialistic free enterprise system is the cause of all the world's troubles; destroy that imperialistic system in any way necessary and all the people of the world will benefit. Free enterprise advocates in Washington argue that Communistic totalitarianism is the cause of all the world's troubles; destroy that atheistic system in any way necessary and all the people of the world will benefit. What happens in identification of the world's evil with "you" is that the identifier believes himself to be right. Then because he is right, he becomes in his own eyes righteous. Now a man who believes himself righteous will appropriate for himself all kinds of prerogatives that he would not otherwise feel justified to assume; if it is necessary to destroy and even to kill in order to free the world from all evil, is this not worth it? The violent idealism of today's radicals cannot be understood except in this framework.

Let us take a look at the kind of issues that confront the world today.

—a population growth that threatens world-wide famine and deterioration of the quality of life
—increase in life-threatening pollution of air, land, and water
—war in Indochina with no end in sight
—a war in Africa ended only with terrible loss of life, and with new outbreaks likely
—war in the Middle East fed by centuries of ethnic hatred and becoming the focal point for the international giants
—most of the world's non-white population in dire poverty
—legalized racial oppression in Rhodesia and South Africa
—economic enormities caused by the alliance of the military with industry
—"security" in the knowledge that if the Soviet Union attacks us in nuclear warfare and wipes out 100 million Americans in a few hours, we can get even by wiping out 140 million Russians

There is *insanity* all over the world in high places! How does one relate to these issues? The idealistic radical—or the idealistic reactionary—knows how to relate to these issues. He is able to see every one of them as either an imperialistic or a Commie plot. He knows what to do—destroy and break down so that men may be free! This course of action is not open to the humanist, who believes that man has value and that violence only adds to evil. But what ground does he stand on?

There is finally the response of Christian faith which attributes personal evil in the world to a moral failure on the part of men. What is the matter with the world is first of all *me*. Behind each of the issues facing the world lies the self-centeredness of men, of whom I am one. Although I may believe myself to be right, in the Christian context I can never see myself as righteous except through the grace of God in Christ. There is something wrong; there is something that can be done about it; it is not only you who are wrong, but also I. The insanity all over the world in high places calls for a Christian plea for repentance. It calls for a Christian dedication to working without despair in spite of the odds and the difficulties, working in faith and hope, knowing that the God who created the earth and maintains it moment by moment by the word of his power will yet redeem it fully. This is the threefold strength of the Christian faith: (1) it permits the individual to view the existence of evil realistically and to recognize its basis in human nature separated from God, (2) it provides an effective attack by giving the means by which individuals and then societies can be given a new birth through faith in Jesus Christ, and (3) it makes it possible to live in hope and confidence in the power of God, both as it works through Christians here and now, and as it will work when God brings a new creation into being, in spite of the enormities of today's dilemmas.

Whatever Happened to Scientific Prestige?

For over a century the scientific method has been exalted as the only road to truth. It alone was seen as capable of providing all the answers to man's problems. When the need to catch up to the Soviet space program developed, science was exalted even further. Science was introduced into kindergarten, and funds for scientific research almost exceeded what could be reasonably spent. Today all this is radically changed. The scientist is no longer looked up to as the modern prophet or messiah. Funds for scientific research are difficult to obtain. Students choosing science as a career are decreasing in numbers. Scientific prestige that rose like a rocket a couple of decades ago seems to be headed for its nadir. What is the reason?

Once science was accepted without question as the only road to truth, it followed directly that anything unscientific was false. We smiled at the naïveté of the Soviet astronaut who reported the confirmation of his atheism by not finding God during his space trip, yet we agreed with him. The scientific investigation of the mechanisms of the human body provided a model of an organic computer or of a complex organic machine. Since science provided the whole truth, it followed that man was only an organic computer, only a complex machine. The scientific investigation of the universe revealed a fantastically immense and complex structure in both the physical world and in human history. Since science provided the whole truth, it followed that man was an insignificant object caught up in the vast turmoil of impersonal contingencies and fates.

A machine buffeted by fate is hardly a man. Not only did God die, man himself died. The baseless faith assumption that science provided the only road to truth led to the engulfment of modern society in meaninglessness and despair. But a man has to square his view of the world with his experience. Although he believes that science has shown by a rational process that he is only a complex machine, he cannot square this with his own experience in which he knows that he loves, decides, hates, responds, and takes part in meaningful human relationships. How is this possible? It cannot be possible, so he thinks, on the basis of a God who created the world and cares for the individuals in it—for hasn't science made these traditional religious views unacceptable? If it is going to be possible at all, he is going to have to provide the way himself. By an *irrational* process he is going to have to separate himself from the rational, physical, finite, material aspects of this life and construct a religious faith—a god, if you will—all by himself. The widespread interest that we see all around us, is astrology, witchcraft, drugs, and mystical religious experiences, bears witness to this almost hysterical attempt by man to resurrect his humanity in the modern world.

It is no surprise that when science is equated with the destruction of meaning and religious faith in life, when an irrational approach to life is equated with the only way to reestablish the humanity of man, that strong antiscience and anti-intellectual sentiments develop. We are living in a time when anti-intellectualism threatens to carry the day.

This reaction is strengthened still further by the increased awareness of the ethical impotence of science as a discipline. Scientists work away at increasing the store of knowledge, perhaps with the hope that some good may come of it but traditionally rather indifferent to anything other than the contribution to human knowledge. Men take the products of science and technology and use them for good, but perhaps even more commonly for evil. The application of the scientist's knowledge falls beyond his competence and frequently his interest. If he is faithful to his discipline alone, he can make no ethical judgment whatsoever. In a day when moral pronouncements are considered vital, again it is no surprise that an antiscience sentiment develops.

Furthermore, the scientific faith that promised deliverance for all men has proved, even when tampered with very little by human evil, to be a grand illusion. Technological advances have produced conveniences and delights, but they have also produced pollution and destruction of the environment. Improvements in medical treatment have enriched the lives of many, but they have also accentuated the population explosion. On every side, science's grand claim to be the modern savior is exploded. That antiscience sentiments should develop in such a context is inevitable.

How should the scientist, the engineer, the technologist respond to this basic pattern of disenchantment that characterizes so much of our modern perspective? Let me suggest a few possibilities.

1. Make it clear that science is one way of knowing, but not the only way.

2. Make it clear that science is not an impersonal exercise of unconcerned automata but the human enterprise of fallible men.

3. Show that scientists are human beings who care about other human beings.

4. Emphasize that scientific investigations cannot be expected to answer the most ultimate and basic human problems but that these answers must, even in the lives of scientists, be obtained through a religious encounter with the living God.

5. Challenge the postulates of modern popular philosophy which are based on the false premise that science has made all traditional moral, ethical, and religious bases unacceptable.

6. Defend the rational and scientific view of life as one of the important perspectives, but not the only one.

7. Work at the development of a rational faith as the only way to prevent irrational excesses.

8. Recognize that the pursuit of science calls for a personal commitment and that therefore only those with a real calling to this commitment should be encouraged to enter a career in science.

Misrepresentations and misconceptions of the purpose and power of the scientific method have come to full flower in our lifetimes. We cannot expect to overcome them unless we are willing to put our own understanding of science and life in order, and unless we are then willing to spend time and effort in communicating our humanity to others.

The Dilemma of the Church

The problems that characterize a society are also likely to be present within the church. The institutional church today is on the horns of a dilemma which would pull it in the opposing directions of ceremonial traditionalism and nonrational emotionalism. Sound biblical scholarship and teaching of biblical doctrines emphasize an intellectual approach to Christian faith which has all too often been subverted into a form of dead orthodoxy. Established churches feel that the beauty of their buildings with their lofty ceilings and stained-glass windows, the correctness of the liturgy, the quality of their trained choirs and musicians, and the established forms and practices are all an integral part of Christian worship, teaching, and fellowship. To many people, however, these symbols speak only of powerless faith and impotent traditionalism. Such individuals tend to jump to the other extreme, forsake formal church services, minimize the fellowship of the institutional church, and emphasize the free, emotional expression of a simple faith unencumbered by creed or doctrinal definition. The traditionalists are likely to regard the innovators as potentially blasphemous in their practices and destructive of the worthy practices established through many generations of use. The innovators are likely to regard the traditionalists as hopelessly out of touch with the times, tied inescapably to the establishment and hence unable to present a living witness to Christ, pedantic obscurantists infatuated with their own intellectual exercises.

All too often the traditionalist comes to identify the very reality of his religious faith with such ecclesiastical incidentals as windows, choirs, and liturgy. Any change in these incidentals is accordingly translated into a change in his faith. His religious faith ceases to be a spiritual reality and becomes instead a ceremonial observance. On the other hand, the innovator tends to lose all perspective of history and to regard himself as the first real Christian. Instead of seeing himself as part of the great family of Christians who have lived over the past two thousand years, he tends to reject historical insight and leaves himself open to the danger of repeating all the mistakes of the past.

The refusal of the traditionalist to recognize the changes in the times, the possibility for new modes of expression and worship, the need for new approaches in new circumstances, is certainly a barrier to cooperation and understanding. But no less destructive of the long-range witness of the church is the basically anti-intellectual position of the innovators. The relationship of spiritual understanding to spiritual life is not an incidental one; the biblical emphasis is consistently on the close and inseparable correlation between faith and life.

Man Come of Age

In his *Letters and Papers from Prison*, Dietrich Bonhoeffer introduced the phrase "man come of age."[2] Exactly what he meant by this phrase and how he would have developed the thought we will never know, since he was executed in a Nazi prison camp shortly before the end of the war. Probably Bonhoeffer meant primarily to explore the consequences of eliminating the "God-of-the-gaps" from other aspects of life in addition to physical science. Others have picked up his words and interpreted them to call for a radically different approach to Christian faith. If the assertion that man is come of age implies that he has arrived at the point in history where he is truly master of his fate and the captain of his soul and that he no longer experiences faith or knows spiritual needs, then it has very little support. The empirical evidence from history argues only too plainly that man's coming of age in a scientific and technological sense has done little to remove his intrinsic spiritual need. Frequently, indeed, it appears that technological maturity has aggravated the symptoms of spiritual sickness.

But if the phrase "man come of age" is used to describe the condition of modern man in which he now must make decisions that formerly could be left in the hands of God, it describes a situation of great importance for Christian understanding. There is growing evidence of a change in our whole mode of life. More and more, God is bringing man to the place where man must make decisions that previously he was not called upon to make. And the point is not just that man now can make certain decisions he was previously

---

[2] Dietrich Bonhoeffer, *Letters and Papers from Prison* (New York: Macmillan, 1967).

powerless to implement, but that it has become wrong for man to attempt to avoid making these decisions.

At one time in the past, there were certain illnesses for which a physician could do nothing except wait and see. The relatives were advised that the life of the ill person was now in the hands of God alone. Today there are life-saving drugs or treatment procedures for many of these same illnesses. The physician has the ability and the responsibility to make the decision which can prolong his patient's life. It now becomes wrong for him to do nothing and leave everything in the hands of God. He recognizes that God acts through him. The time may well be coming when the basic decisions of life and death will rest in the hands of men; when man must decide who will be born, who will live, and who will die; when man can no longer relax in the faith that God will take care of all these things without asking man to take up his responsibility and act.

Apparently the number of areas in which God works independently of man is constantly being decreased in proportion to those areas in which God works through men. In a real sense man has been brought to the age of responsibility where he must make those decisions from which his grandparents could safely absolve themselves. One of the most unfortunate attitudes sometimes found among Christian people today is that which seeks to evade opportunities and responsibilities for action. Grounds no longer exist for believing that these are areas men should not tamper with but are in the hands of God alone. It becomes more and more evident that God works out his will in the world through those men whom he chooses to serve him.

It is necessary to realize that the question is seldom "Should we use our ability to do this or that?" When man possesses the scientific knowledge to control birth, sex, intelligence, characteristics, and personality, he is going to exercise it. There is no point in debating the issue as to whether or not such knowledge should be sought or used. The issue to be debated, and as soon as possible, is *how* this new knowledge is going to be used and *who* is going to be responsible for the decisions.

Life as a citizen in a representative democracy or republic imposes responsibilities on the individual that do not exist for a citizen of a monarchy or a dictatorship. Much of the absence of specific social action advice in the New Testament can be traced to the fact that individuals in that day had essentially nothing to say about the operation of policies of their government. A participant in a representative form of government must always bear the responsibility for the actions and policies of that government. He must be involved in voting, policy-forming, and serving. He cannot leave the operation of that government in the hands of God alone, as though God did not act through the political activities of the citizens.

As man comes of age in the ways described above, two great and valued principles appear to be often at cross-purposes: freedom and human responsibility. On the one hand there is the ideal of freedom —not absolute freedom from all constraints or the license to do anything, of course, but freedom from man-made restrictions and regulations. On the other hand, there is the ideal of human responsibility, which calls for the care and protection of human beings. It must be realized that whenever freedom (as defined in this context) and human responsibility come into conflict, it is always freedom that must give way. Such conflicts are accentuated by the population growth. When men live at such distances from one another that they have little or no interaction, few man-made regulations are necessary. But when men start living together in large numbers and become more interdependent, all kinds of restrictions on freedom are essential. Freedom to drive without a license or at any speed or in an unsafe vehicle must be ended. Freedom to shoot guns must be ended. Freedom to own animals of all kinds and in large numbers must be ended in certain areas. Freedom to buy and freedom to sell must be regulated. Freedom to "live and let live" must be ended if it really results in meaning freedom to "live and let die." It has generally been concluded that even the freedom to "die and let live" must be abridged.

It is preferable, of course, when someone is in need, if others will voluntarily come to their aid and give out of genuine human concern. But what does one do if they will not come, or if they do not even know of the need? Is it better to preserve the freedom of the haves and let the have-nots suffer or to insure by legal regulations that the haves do share a little with the have-nots? Here is the whole puzzle of governmental welfare programs. They attempt to do by enforced measures what should flow spontaneously from human or certainly Christian love and concern. But when people will not give voluntarily, is it wrong to make sure that they at least produce the external fruits of Christian love, even if this means legal enforcement? Is the freedom of people to give or not to give more important than the desperate needs of other human beings?

Another pair of principles that sometimes appear to be in conflict as man comes of age are service to God and service to man. It would appear too shocking to state as a general principle that whenever a formal requirement for service to God comes into conflict with the need for service to man, it is always the service to God that must yield. And yet, if these phrases are understood properly, a statement very much like this is not only acceptable, but even biblical. What can be stated as a general principle is this: genuine service to God never requires one to cause injury to man. If a man's understanding of the requirements involved in service to God causes him to neglect the service of man, or to cause injury to man, he can be sure that his understanding is at fault.

A concrete example is the Christian's response to fair housing laws. Such laws severely restrict the freedom of a property owner to sell or rent his property; specifically they commonly prevent him from legally refusing to sell or rent on the grounds of his own personal prejudices about race, color, religion, national origin or ancestry. Many Christians have argued that such fair housing laws must be opposed because the free choice of the property owner is intrinsic to both their understanding of the Christian ethic of property rights and to a political and economic system based on Christian principles. In other words, such Christians argue that voting for a fair housing law is contrary to the service required of them by God. On the other hand, other Christians have argued that a full understanding of the Christian position on private property rights is first of all that it is not an absolute prescription, and second that it must at least include both the right to acquire property and the right to dispose of property, not only the latter. Furthermore the absence of a fair housing law fails in service to many human beings because it sanctions immoral discrimination by omission. It becomes clear, therefore, that real service to God requires the placing of other human rights above property rights in as equitable a manner as can be achieved.

Biblical guides to distinguishing what real service to God requires when it comes into apparent conflict with service to man can be found in Jesus' treatment of the sabbath regulations (Matt. 12:1–8) and of the Corban gift tradition (Matt. 15:1–5).

The Population Explosion and Birth Control

In *Man on a Spaceship*, William Pollard warns of the nature of the population explosion.

> Man had been fruitful through previous centuries, but disease and famine prevented him from multiplying. At the beginning of the Christian era there were only about 300 million human beings on the earth. It required seventeen centuries to double this number to 600 million. Then in 1820, for the first time, the world population of species *Homo sapiens* passed the one billion mark. By 1930 it had doubled to two billion. Just a few years ago, in the early sixties, it passed three billion. By 1977 it will have reached four billion, by 1990 five billion, and by the end of this century, in the year 2000, it will be well beyond six billion, and the world will be just twice as crowded as it is now.[3]

Other authorities feel that these latter figures will never be realized because the number will be drastically reduced by world-wide famines of devastating proportions beginning only fifteen or twenty years from now. What is the Christian response to these data? Is a deliberate course of action required, or is it sufficient to leave the matter in the hands of God, there being nothing else possible or proper for us to do?

Man's responsibility to have dominion over the earth extends to all areas that influence the well-being of the earth and the quality of life. If it appears that a continued uncontrolled growth of population threatens both the capability of the earth to provide and the quality of life for those alive, it becomes a Christian responsibility to limit the population. This is a revolutionary responsibility, for until now it has been the role of man to be fruitful and multiply to fill the earth. Now, in our time, that task is finally finished. The earth is full. We shall need a new program and a new perspective for the future.

---

[3] William G. Pollard, *Man on a Spaceship* (Claremont, Calif.: The Claremont Colleges, 1967), pp. 5–6.

We have never before had to face a future in which continued growth was not the touchstone of success. If in the past the continued growth in population of a city was the indication of prosperity and the good life, in the future such continued growth will be the mark of failure and disaster. Nothing can be exempt from this radical and revolutionary change in perspective. Our economics cannot be based on unlimited expansion and ever larger markets. Our politics cannot be based on greater influence through larger population. Our merchandising cannot be based on greater waste disposal sites. Our educational system cannot be based on providing ever larger numbers of graduates from ever larger numbers of entrants. Can we unlearn so much?

The essential in any plans for the future is a limitation on population. Every other aspect of the future's ecological problems demands that unlimited population growth be stopped and stopped soon. Obviously, population can be limited by only two devices: preventing birth or hastening death. In the first category comes birth control by a variety of methods including abortion; in the latter category comes euthanasia, together with all the traditional ways of hastening death such as starvation, disease, and war. In a Christian context I do not believe that we need to debate the control of population by facilitating famine, plague, and war; we can agree from the start that the Christian responsibility is to end these scourges of the human race, not to increase them. Euthanasia is a highly debatable practice and we shall say a little more about it below; by itself, however, it would not make a reasonable contribution to population control if used with any degree of human compassion and responsibility. The only effective means, therefore, are those that act to prevent the birth of a living child. Again, in a Christian context, I believe we can agree that attempts to terminate the life of a child after birth (infanticide) are unacceptable for a variety of reasons.

Various methods of birth control are grouped into three categories by Earl J. Reeves: abstention, prevention, and abortion. In view of the biblical emphasis that marriage exists both for companionship and procreation, abstention is an undesirable, as well as a relatively ineffective (because of intrinsic difficulties in practice), method of birth control.

The best technique to be used in birth control is that method of contraception best suited to the particular couple involved. As Reeves says,

> In general there would appear to be no Scriptural reason to deny a married couple the right to use any of the standard mechanical or chemical methods of preventing pregnancy. Even the question of the possibility of destroying life by destroying a fertilized egg through an IUD or a pill seems likely to be dismissed by most evangelicals as a highly theoretical and legalistic controversy.[4]

Christian couples have used various methods of birth control for many years according to their evaluation of health, financial, and family considerations. Now general population growth as a whole must be an additional consideration.

There remains the question of abortion, that is, induced removal of the fetus after conception and before birth. Is such ending of unborn life forbidden for the Christian? Some guiding principles relevant to both abortion and euthanasia can be set forth on the basis of our discussion in chapter 7 on the relationship between body and soul.

All life is a marvel; only human life is considered sacred. We do not hesitate to kill cows for food, although in other parts of the world this is unthinkable. Animals who are friends to man, such as dogs and cats, are afforded a position of greater value at least in our culture, presumably because of their association with human life. The Christian community has consistently upheld the sanctity of human life in a unique way. But the question is, what *is* human life? What is it toward which the commandment "Thou shalt not kill" is directed?

Webster's dictionary says that *human* means "characteristic of man." Of *man* the dictionary says, "an individual of the highest type of animal existing or known to have existed, differing from other high types of animals, especially in his extraordinary mental development." We have emphasized a number of times in past chapters the unique properties characteristic of the human personality: insight, rational thought, courage, duty, faith, love, conscience, hope, awe, reverence, God-consciousness, appreciation of

---

[4] Earl J. Reeves, "The Population Explosion and Christian Concern," in *Protest and Politics*, ed. R. G. Clouse, R. D. Linder and R. V. Pierard (Greenwood, S.C.: Attic Press, 1968), pp. 183–200.

beauty, self-consciousness, the desire for understanding. To be human then is to exercise the faculties made possible by the extraordinary mental development of man.

A chimpanzee is not human. Yet a one-year-old chimpanzee may display more humanlike characteristics than a one-year-old infant. It is recognized that the one-year-old infant has the potentiality to become human, whereas the chimpanzee does not. We give to the child the value placed upon an individual who will in the normal course of events exhibit the qualities of humanity; he is a *potential human*. We withhold from the chimpanzee the value placed upon a potential human because in the normal course of events it is impossible for him to exhibit the qualities of humanity fully at any time. The value we attribute to the life of the infant, or to the unborn fetus, is an imputed value, held in expectation of what the fetus or the infant can become.

A very old person or the victim of an accident may live in the condition of an unthinking creature often referred to pathetically as a "living vegetable." He exhibits none of the human qualities associated with extraordinary mental development. His mental faculties have ceased to function; in a real sense they have died. We also attribute to such a victim of senility or accident an imputed value, held in memory of what the elderly or injured person once was. He once *was* human; his humanity can be remembered and honored.

In an exact sense, neither the fetus nor the "vegetable" is human. If we are to contemplate ending the existence of the fetus, we must consistently consider ending the existence of the "vegetable." In fact, in such a comparison, the life of the fetus may be regarded as having the far greater value; it represents the potentiality for human development. The life of the senile or the brain-damaged is virtually at an end; only the memory of humanity remains.

These problems cannot be solved by trying to determine the conditions in which the living creature is soul-less as distinguished from others in which he is soul-full. Any time that a fetus is put to death, a life is being taken, but it is a *potential* human life, not an actual human life. Any time that a "living vegetable" is allowed to die, a life is being taken, but it is a *remembered* human life, not an actual human life. Shall we then indulge in abortion and euthanasia indiscriminately? Not at all. For the potentiality of human life and the memory of human life are very valuable indeed, second in value only to human life itself.

So we come to the conclusion that there are no easy rules which uniformly advocate or forbid abortion and euthanasia, but in every individual case, we must weigh the loss of potential or remembered human life against the loss of actual human life.

This is the criterion which apparently guided the statement of the American College of Obstetricians and Gynecologists on Therapeutic Abortion of May 1968. They suggest that therapeutic abortion may be performed (*only* upon request of the patient and after consultation with at least two other physicians) for three basic reasons: (1) when continued pregnancy will seriously damage the health of the mother, (2) when pregnancy results from rape or incest, and (3) when continued pregnancy is likely to result in the birth of a gravely deformed or retarded child. In each case the criterion is the value placed on actual human life as compared to the potential human life of the fetus. These are not situations where we can simply leave everything "in the hands of God," but situations to which God has called us to be his responsible servants. If we insist that a pregnancy be carried on to the death of the mother rather than resorting to abortion at an early stage of a known serious case, then we become guilty of violating the commandment not to put human life to death knowingly. If we insist that a pregnancy continue which will bring into the world a child who will not be loved but who will grow up in spiritual and physical deprivation, rather than resort to an early abortion, are we any less guilty of an inhumane act? If we use up resources needed to support human life in order to maintain the physical functions of a "living vegetable" year after year, are we not also guilty of inhumanity to the many actual human lives who suffer? These are not easy choices; but we cannot turn our backs on them.

As far as population and birth control are concerned, abortion is certainly not a desirable tactic about which to generalize. If practiced indiscriminantly it is dangerous both physically and morally to a society. George J. Jennings, in an article in the *Journal of the American Scientific Affiliation*, holds to this view.

It is not likely that abortion will become the dominant means for limiting human fertility even though it may be effective. . . . Western ideas of medical practice and health measures will un-

doubtedly advocate inexpensive contraceptives as the preferable
method rather than the more costly, and in some cases much more
dangerous, abortive method. It is possible that increased emanci-
pation of women and access to higher standards of living will
favor that most extreme method, sterilization, especially by
couples who have had several children.[5]

Certainly prevention of conception is the preferable course in birth
control, although there may be situations in the world where the
criteria set forth above may call for abortion to be used for a limited
period.

There is little question that the people of the world *could* limit
population through general use of birth control; the question is,
will they? The evidence is that only some rather traumatic and disastrous events occurring through unchecked population growth
will be sufficient to change the individual, social, cultural, and sexual drives for many children. These could be prevented if concerted
action were taken by the governments of the world, first to make
birth control financially attractive and many children financially
burdensome, and second, if necessary, to provide legal enforcements
for limiting the birth rate. In such a situation we would face another example of the conflict between freedom and responsibility
mentioned earlier in this chapter. The Christian must work for
those measures that favor responsibility.

Environmental Problems

A remarkable awakening has occurred in the last decade. After
thousands, and possibly millions of years of human life on earth,
man has reached the point where the earth's resources are being
stretched to the vanishing point, where man's attempts to provide
a better life for himself are threatening to pollute land, air, and
water to such an extent that the quality of life will be drastically
lowered, where man's waste alone seems on the verge of burying
him. People who give the advice just to forget these facts haven't
been out in the world lately.

In a recent book, William Pollard dramatizes present condi-

---

[5] George J. Jennings, "Cultural Factors Affecting Human Fertility," *Journal
ASA* 22 (1970): 53.

tions in the world by considering the earth as a spaceship. The realization that all the precautions which must be taken to send men to the moon must also be taken with respect to the earth—our only spaceship—spells out the nature of the problem.

> There are several fundamental requirements for a satisfactory spaceship. First it must have an adequate source of energy which will last throughout the trip. Next it must have an adequate food supply or means of producing food for the crew throughout the journey. The air and water reserves in the ship must be kept pure and adequate for all needs. Wastes must be reprocessed or disposed of in ways which will not contaminate the ship. And, finally, the crew must not be allowed to increase in numbers, and it must remain unified throughout the journey.[6]

Dr. Pollard believes that if population growth is limited, it will be possible to meet these requirements through the use of nuclear power sources.

One way of looking at the environmental problem is set forth by Garrett Hardin in an article in *Science*.[7] Consider one hundred farmers who each use the same meadow to feed their cows, each farmer having just one cow. With one hundred cows in residence, these common feeding grounds are being used to full capacity. But any one farmer may reason as follows: "If I put a second cow on the meadow, I will receive a 100% increase in my holdings, whereas it will only increase the overcrowding of the meadow by 1%." His logic is impeccable, and so he adds his second cow. So does each of his neighbors. The tragedy of the commons is the inevitable result. Environmental pollution is the sum of many small pollutions, each of which profits the polluter much more than it seems to him he could benefit the environment by stopping only his small contribution to the pollution. Think of this next time you light up the charcoal fire on your patio.

Curiously enough there have been some eloquent speakers who have thought that the blame for environmental difficulties is somehow to be associated with the Christian faith. In a paper in *Science*, Lynn White has proposed that the historical roots of the ecological crisis are to be found in the Judeo-Christian tradition of man as the

---

[6] Pollard, *Man on a Spaceship*, p. 11.

[7] Garrett Hardin, "The Tragedy of the Commons," *Science* 162 (1968): 1243.

ruler of the earth. By exalting man at the expense of nature, Dr. White argues, Christianity has separated man from nature, has argued against the oneness of man and nature, and has given divine approval to the unlimited exploitation of nature by man.[8] There is perhaps no doubt historically that men and institutions who called themselves Christians have been guilty of these various aberrations. The solution to the dilemma, however, lies not in repudiating the biblical perspective of man as the responsible steward of God's creation, but in reemphasizing it to a post-Christian culture that holds onto the forms but has forgotten the heart of the message.

The biblical perspective emphasizes the unity between man and earth by the creation account of man's formation from the dust of the earth. Although man is the crown of creation, he is given the responsibility to care for the created order. Commitment to biblical principles demands, therefore, both concern and appropriate action to preserve environmental integrity and to prevent pollution.

In an article in the *Journal of the American Scientific Affiliation*, Wayne Frair points to three main causes of our present ecological crisis, only the last of which has any direct correlation with a religious concern.[9] The first cause is simply ignorance; men have proceeded to do what seemed good at the time without realizing the ultimate damage to the ecology that might result. Even when men consciously do good, they may find themselves in this dilemma. Detergents to improve the quality of washing kill waste-destroying bacteria. Medical advances that extend the life span of the elderly accentuate the problems of population growth. Development of the internal combustion engine to make travel possible provides a major contribution to air pollution.

The second cause of the ecological crisis is inertia. Many of the customs and practices which today contribute to environmental degradation were initiated in a day when the problems simply did not exist. For many years the pattern of life in the United States was dominated by the push to the open lands of the West. The life-style appropriate for the frontiersman surrounded by unlimited resources and constant danger in his fight to survive in the midst of

---

[8] Lynn White, Jr., "The Historical Roots of our Ecologic Crisis," *Science* 155 (1967): 1203.

[9] Wayne Frair, "Ignorance, Inertia and Irresponsibility," *Journal ASA* 21 (1969): 43.

a hostile nature is not the life-style appropriate for a city dweller today. The manufacturing and resource utilization style of an earlier day often persists when greater sensitivity to the effects on the environment would call for a drastic change.

The third cause that Dr. Frair mentions is irresponsibility. It is true that in the pursuit of selfish interests many have acted irresponsibly and have forsaken the responsibility of being caretakers of God's creation. Unconcerned about the long-term loss to many other human beings, they have ignored the processes involved in the balance of nature and have interfered with that balance for the sake of their short-term gain. A social pattern that constantly calls for greater expansion, larger markets, and bigger profits seems to foster this kind of irresponsibility. An effective response to environmental degradation may require a radical change in our economic goals, as will our success in limiting the population. Such a change must grow out of the biblical perspective of the Christian faith, setting forth man's position as responsible caretaker of this earth.

Is There a Christian Economic System?

The world is divided today along many lines, but along none quite so clearly as on the appropriate economic system. The argument is frequently heard that a basic economic system is revealed to us in the Bible. Thus there can be no doubt that the Christian will be committed to private ownership of property and business, the free enterprise system, and the profit motive. Several principles can help establish perspective on this question.

1. No human economic system is derivable from biblical principles. Economic systems are by their very nature constructions of men and products of both use and culture. The fact that a certain economic practice was suitable for the people who lived in Bible times gives no necessary guidance as to what is biblical or Christian in today's situation. There are certain fundamental guides to life given in the Bible, however, from which we can judge and shape economic systems.

2. Any human economic system could work if men were perfect. If man were sinless, not ensnared in self-satisfaction but open and receptive to the needs and desires of others, then any economic

system he came up with would work just fine. If there were difficulties in the system, he would in time correct them in justice and equity. Once again, the main factor in the economic system's failure is the human ingredient.

3. No human economic system can actually work with imperfect men. No matter what system is devised, nor how perfectly it is planned, the actual operation will be corrupted by the self-centeredness of the human participants. The most successful systems are those that recognize clearly the potentiality of human good. Stressing the maximum of freedom while also taking full account of the potentiality of human evil, they have built into them a variety of checks and safeguards against a runaway of human selfishness. Our own governmental system with its three branches is an outstanding example of this kind of success.

The two principle economic systems in the world are *free enterprise* and *socialism*. Both of these are ideals, and it might be argued that neither really exists in pure form anywhere in the world today. A summary of some of the characteristics of these two systems is given in figure 5. The strengths and weaknesses of each are evident.

In a system designed for Christians along the lines of biblical ideals, the cooperative ideal of socialism seems more appropriate than the competitive method of free enterprise. The Bible constantly stresses the need to work together and to bear one another's burdens. It would seem, then, that a system that emphasized working together to achieve common goals for all members of society would be quite preferable to a system that emphasized competition between members of society. When every member of society works for the common good of all, with no one obtaining exhorbitant profits and no one suffering the degradation of poverty, it would seem that the welfare of all would be best served.

On the other hand, the biblical view of the nature of man apart from God in Christ tells us rather plainly that the above idealistic system will not work. Many will try to avoid their fair share of the work. Many will cheat to get more than their fair share of the results. If left in a purely voluntary form, the system would fall apart. Apparently even the early Christian community described in Acts 4:32 suffered this kind of fate. If this cooperative socialistic system is to work among real men, then some at least must be *forced* to

Figure 5

ECONOMIC SYSTEMS

The System	The Method	The Goal	Succeeds if	Fails if	Relation to Freedom
Free Enterprise	Competition	Profit	The successful show responsibility for the failures	The successful are selfish, stealing from the have-nots	Maximizes freedom from regulation; minimizes freedom to cope with failure
Socialism	Cooperation	Service	All work together for the common good	The lazy are selfish, stealing from the haves	Minimizes freedom from regulation; maximizes freedom to cope with failure

cooperate. Once again freedom must yield to human responsibility with all the associated effects that this has on society. Even the Apostle Paul said, "If any one will not work, let him not eat" (2 Thess. 3:10). Forced cooperation may enable the system to survive, but now the attractiveness of its ideal of service is somewhat tarnished.

Something must be offered to the individual which will stimulate him to participate and work in the system. What more effective method can be found than to appeal to his own self-interest, which after all is the dominant motif of his life if he is not committed to God in Christ? Thus the free enterprise system, by appealing to the self-interest of man and promising the reward of profit, actually gets him into action with results that do benefit many. But now the man who is successful has no reason to share with others. After all, his success is the result of his own hard work and foresight; why should he share with lazy indigents who weren't able to find their own success? Once again this freedom must be limited or the system will collapse; governments require that this man be *forced* to give some of his own gains for the help of the unsuccessful.

If there were a biblically based economic system, therefore, it would include some of the stimulation provided by the free enterprise system together with a strong psychological and legal provision for cooperation in general service. It would combine the biblical ideals for Christian cooperation with biblical reality on the nature of man. Without force, socialism would collapse and free enterprise would become unbearably inhumane, in both cases because of the intrinsic selfishness of human nature apart from Christ.

The Christian himself must remain uncommitted to any human system, holding himself free to move where God leads him at a given time and under a given set of conditions. There is a trend in economic systems, however, which accompanies the population growth and the increase in interpersonal interactions. The free enterprise system is best suited for an individualistic society where high value is placed on material gains; the socialistic system is best suited for a large, strongly interacting society where it is essential to retain some human values. Population growth has caused the world, and particularly the United States, to move continuously from an individualistic society to a large interacting society. In such a system, drifting of free enterprise toward socialism is required to maintain a society with humanitarian concerns, while drifting of absolute socialism toward free enterprise is required to maintain individual incentive. It is not too great a simplification to say that at the present time we see the former process taking place in the United States and the latter process in the Soviet Union. As time passes and ideological pressures decrease, a great deal of similarity between the two systems can be expected unless force is used to maintain their characteristic differences.

Racism

A difference between people, whether racial, ethnic, or religious, has always served as the basis for the stronger group to impose its will in an inhumane way on the weaker group. Man in rebellion against God needs instances that he thinks prove his own superiority; what better way than to determine that some other people will be inferior by definition? No scientific basis for racism exists, and against all such racism, the Christian faith stands adamantly opposed.

The Bible presents a clear picture of the human race as a whole —a unity. All men and women, regardless of race, national origin, or color have a unity in the fellowship of sin (Rom. 5:12), have a common blood stock (Acts 17:26), share in the common spiritual death (2 Cor. 5:14), and need a Savior (Gal. 3:22). Among Christians the unity is still greater—and certainly the relationships between Christians should be the model for all men. Segregation among Christians because of racism is unthinkable in the biblical perspective. James speaks out against the practice of showing deference to the rich and powerful members of the early church (James 2:1, 9). To place separations between Christians is a violation of the Christian faith; to make such separations is a violation if it is done on the basis of wealth and power, and it is no less a violation if it is done on the basis of skin pigments or national origin.

The message of the early church established beyond a doubt that all differences between men are swallowed up in Christ.

For in Jesus Christ you are all sons of God, through faith. For as many of you as were baptized into Christ have put on Christ. There is neither Jew nor Greek, there is neither slave nor free,

there is neither male nor female; for you are all one in Christ
Jesus (Gal. 3:26–28).

Here there cannot be Greek and Jew, circumcised and uncircum-
cised, barbarian, Scythian, slave, free man, but Christ is all, and
in all (Col. 3:11).

We are certainly constrained to add in practice, "black man, white
man, yellow man," to this list of differences dissolved in Christ.

The efforts to remove the evil of racism can have no stronger ally
and supporter than the Christian faith when it is lived in a biblical
perspective.

Violence and War

The question of participation in violence and war has plagued
Christian thinkers from the beginning. At various times in history
elaborate constructions have been made to define a "just" war, such
a war being one that the Christian community could endorse. Like
other problems involving individual responsibility, no universal prescription can be given. Certain guidelines can, however, be set
down.

For the individual Christian, the biblical position is clear. He is
exhorted to respond with love when evil is perpetrated upon him,
not returning evil for evil, but overcoming evil with good. The
Christian is not to seek revenge; blessing the enemy is to be his response to evil done against him.

Still, it is also clear that the Christian has the responsibility to
defend himself and those for whom he has been given responsibility.
For a Christian not to defend himself or those for whom he is responsible is a violation of his Christian stewardship of all things
before God. This defense, however, is to be made only in the sense
of restraining evil, with a minimum of injury to others, and without
hatred or desire for retribution against the guilty one. It is this responsibility for the welfare of others that makes absolute pacifism a
position that cannot be defended on biblical grounds.

Any participation of the individual Christian in an act of violence must therefore be related to an act of protection and must be
limited to the restraint of evil with a minimum of destruction. The
same constraints must guide any collective action of Christians,

whatever the involvement. Whether this be Christian action through a group of individuals in a democratic society, the development by Christians of principles to guide a state, or some other activity, such a group must be willing to accept injury without seeking retribution or to defend itself and those for whom it is responsible.

The same guidelines must also apply to any state whose leaders are attempting to act according to Christian principles. It is often argued that the ethic of love is intended for individuals, whereas it is the business of the state to concern itself only with justice. Justice is indeed a primary concern of the state, but this distinction between love and justice is a false one. Shall the state be only just and never merciful? Or, if the prime concern of the state is to maintain justice within its own borders, how shall this principle be applied to its international relationships? Who is to be the judge of justice when the state itself is one of the parties involved? The situation cries out for a court to dispense international justice so that individual nations may be free to treat one another in love and mercy. The basic responsibility for the general defense of the peoples of the world rests upon the collective, cooperative actions of nations through a League of Nations or a United Nations organization. The fact that these international forms of government show little promise of being effective in our time (and perhaps not in any time, given the characteristics of human nature) does not lessen the responsibility of the Christian today to assist and work toward whatever measure of success may be achieved.

The application of the Christian ethic to individual nations will require that, under particular circumstances, force must be used to restrain evil. The use of such force will be first through the joint efforts of nations in nonviolent actions, next through unilateral nonviolent actions, and only in the last resort, in the event of the immensity of the inhumanity exhibited, through unilateral warfare. This warfare, however, must concentrate on the defense of the injured parties and on the restraint of evil. It will not involve the bombing of cities, the development of weapons of death to kill entire populations, the proud exhibition of an enemy body count, or the call for humiliation or destruction of the aggressor. In almost every case, the demands of military strategy will be contrary to the demands of the Christian ethic. Although in principle the use of war as an extreme action in the protection of human beings can be defended for the Christian, the individual still faces an agonizing decision as to whether or not he can participate in any particular action of war actually carried out by the nations of the world.

Within the internal life of a nation, individual Christians may have to face similar questions. As a citizen of a democratic government, it is the Christian's responsibility to shape and influence government policy and action through the established procedures of a legal and orderly political system. Nevertheless, clear violations of human behavior may force an individual by his Christian convictions to act outside the normally accepted procedures of law and order. Such action is first through the joint efforts of individuals in nonviolent actions, next through individual and joint breaking of the law in nonviolent actions in order to test it, and finally, only in the last resort, because of the immensity of the inhumanity exhibited, through individual or joint violence. The participation in violence by an individual Christian should be such a rare occurrence as to be almost unheard of; by the same reasoning, the participation in war of a nation guided by Christian principles in a world with international controls should be a similarly rare occurrence. In either case, the participation in violence should be constrained at all times by the principles set forth at the beginning of this section.

These comments can be somewhat more specific if we apply them to guidance for foreign policy in the world situation today.

The present world situation suggests two practical courses of action that may be undertaken as alternatives in the future. If they are evaluated simply on the basis of previous history alone, neither may be considered to be particularly hopeful.

The first course of action is to continue in a buildup of armaments and instruments of warfare, with no foreseeable end in view, in the effort to maintain a balance of potential terror. The argument is that if the potential terror that can be generated by our side is equivalent to or greater than can be generated by the other side, the net effect will be a deterrent to the use of that terror. The justification given is that it is necessary for our country to defend itself against threatened attack from external enemies, and that there is no way to accomplish this without a continuation of the arms race.

The record of history indicates that any time two nations have continued to build up huge backlogs of potential terror, at some time this unstable stalemate has crumbled, perhaps under the influence of a third power, and the instruments of death have been regretfully put to use. The choice of the first course of action requires the hope that this record will not be repeated, that the continued buildup of arms will lead to a world situation where it will become unnecessary to use them.

The second course of action is to bring an end to any continued buildup of armaments and instruments of warfare, all chemical-biological warfare, all research aimed at counterinsurgency in other peoples' countries, and to restrict any militarily directed research to measures of defense alone. The nonaggressive defense of the country is a legitimate activity of the government and has a legitimate claim on the scientific talent of the country. Government support of scientific education of students is also a valuable contribution to the welfare of the country, but it may be questioned whether funds granted for projects directed by the military are the most appropriate way to achieve this educational goal.

By emphasizing restriction to purely defense activities, it is clear that we risk the possibility that other nations not following this restriction may increase their armaments to the point where their potential for terror exceeds our own. Choice of this second course of action requires the hope that other nations of the world will not take advantage of the possible inequity to enforce their will upon our country. History offers little support for this hope to be fulfilled. The justification for making this choice rests upon the conviction that the continued arms race can lead to nothing except global nuclear war, and that it is possible that some alleviation of international aggravation might be secured by a reduction in belligerent attitudes and actions. The same speech justifying the spending of more money on armaments, missiles, and bombs is made both by the secretary of defense in Washington and the minister of defense in Moscow, each claiming it is necessary to protect the mother country because of the buildup by the other.

How can a choice be made? It can be made by realizing that the choice offered is not really that between death and enslavement; it is between *killing* and enslavement. It should be clear that the extreme alternatives really are these. A deterrent can be effective only if the enemy is convinced that when the chips are down we will make use of our potential terror to retaliate in kind and destroy him, even if for no other reason than vengeance. If it is suspected that we will not retaliate, that we will not kill when the only motive can be that of global revenge, then any deterrent is disarmed. The whole deterrent-based argument is suspect. No Christian can push that final button.

The ultimate choice is between an alternative which is evil, and one which by historical standards is simply foolish. In such a case, the Christian is called upon to choose the foolish alternative.

The course of action that calls for the continued buildup of armaments for increasing levels of deterrency can, I believe, be labeled evil. There are at least three reasons for this judgment: (1) it commits a large fraction of human ingenuity, concern, and effort to the development of instruments of death and inhumanity, (2) it provides no basis for a resolution of the problems that appear to make the buildup necessary, but serves only to intensify the confrontation, and (3) it diverts into military hardware a large portion of the resources badly needed at home and abroad for the alleviation of human needs—poverty, sickness, and injustice. One cannot continue on such a course of action while at the same time consistently maintaining that one is trusting that God will set things right.

The course of action that calls for the end of a buildup of armaments and for a restriction of research to items essential to defense and the general welfare alone—together, of course, with that basic research into the nature of the universe that is the proper concern of science—can be labeled foolish. It is foolish because it assumes the possibility of an alleviation of international grievances deeply rooted in history and in national objectives, simply through the refusal of one powerful nation to seek to establish its will throughout the world by force. But if it is foolish, it is also a course of action that is completely open to the will of God since it is faithful to the constraints of his revelation. Here is a real challenge for Christian faith.

None of this discussion should be interpreted as being in any way an advocacy of isolationism. In internal politics, an unwillingness to be militarily involved in the rest of the world has become synonymous with isolationism. But this need not be the case at all, and is only the product of the close identification of foreign policy with military policy. A nation such as the United States must be involved in the needs and concerns of the rest of the world. Its willingness to be of aid, its practical sympathy for the needs of people in underdeveloped countries, its response to the need for counsel in areas of technology, medicine, and agriculture should be the hallmarks of foreign policy. Communism has a breeding ground in all those countries of the world today where desperate needs exist and where the powers-that-be are insensitive to these needs. Certainly it is both more Christian and more practical to seek to meet these needs through aid and advice than it is to support militarily those in power, who, in many instances, have no other claim to our support than their political opposition to Communism.

There is one other reality which makes ending the armaments buildup somewhat less foolish. The current world struggle is often depicted as a struggle between the forces of Christian freedom on the one hand and forces of atheistic dictatorship on the other; in fact, the world situation often assumes the form of a religious confrontation. In this context it is important to realize that Christian faith cannot be defended by force. When the focus of conflict is on whether or not an individual is permitted to be a Christian, at that point resistance by force becomes ineffective. Any attempt to defend the Christian faith per se by the use of force is doomed to failure. Even if the force is successful, what is preserved will no longer be the Christian faith. The biblical revelation makes clear that Christians are to expect persecution and suffering because of their faith; it gives no provision or example of avoiding that persecution by violent resistance. Certainly it is historically evident that the Christian faith has been transformed into something else whenever it has been defended or extended by force.

Consider the revolutionary impact of even such a minimal pledge by all Christians in the world as the following: "*In view of the unity of the Body of Christ, I will neither engage in nor support war or violence directed against any other Christian.*"

Situation Ethics

There is considerable discussion about the replacement of the old morality by the "new morality," about the replacement of legalistic absolutism by the adaptive law of love. As in most other controversies, the extreme positions receive the most attention because they are the easiest to define, as well as the easiest to attack and discredit by the opposition.

In its extreme caricature, the old morality is supposed to consist of a set of rules or laws, the meaning and application of which are spelled out in complete detail so that absolute right and wrong may be known without reference to any specific situation. The "new morality" is supposed to be devoid of any guiding regulations except those of love, which will prescribe the appropriate action as completely defined by the specific situation.

Neither of these extreme caricatures has much support in practice. The absolute commandment "Thou shalt not kill," for example, is interpreted to mean that it is all right to kill a cow, but not to kill a man, except in self-defense, in war, or in punishment for crime. To guide one's actions wholly on the basis of an undefined and unguided love is, in practice, impossible, for some code or system must be used in order to define what an act of love is in a particular situation.

The resolution of this difficulty in Christian faith is the same today as it has been in the past. It lies in the distinction between absolute principles and specific applications, and in the distinction between what is right and what is the lesser of two evils.

In Romans 13:10 Paul defines love as "the fulfilling of the law." Law and love are closely related, not antithetical. The law describes what it means to act in love. For example, the commandment "Thou shalt not commit adultery" describes what it means to act in love. To claim that an act of adultery was motivated by love is merely to expose one's ignorance of the working of this world. To commit adultery is always to treat the married partners involved as less than whole human beings. It is therefore always wrong for the best of reasons: it involves a denial of the worth of human beings.

At the same time, it is true that in the real world it is sometimes necessary for the Christian to do those things which he knows are wrong. Often his choice is not between loving and not loving, not between right and wrong, but between loving little and loving less, or between less evil and more evil. It is possible to have freedom in individual cases to choose the lesser of the two evils, the loveless choice over the destructive, within the framework of the Christian faith. What is evil is recognized as evil, however, even when it is chosen over the more evil, and what is loveless is recognized as loveless even when it is chosen over the destructive. For the Christian, the lesser evil and the loveless choice may be forgiven by God; it is not necessary for him to redo the whole system of right and wrong so that what is sometimes wrong is othertimes right.

The Christian, therefore, does not necessarily identify the proper choice in a specific situation with what is right, i.e., consistent, with the working of the world as the creation of God. The proper choice may be for an option which is not consistent with the working of the world as the creation of God, but the alternative to which is a choice which is even more inconsistent. Thus he strives for the wholly consistent approach at all times but recognizes that an imperfect world sometimes requires imperfect actions.

When the origin and function of biblical law and commandments are understood, any source of conflict disappears. Every biblical commandment, whether one of the Ten or from the Sermon on the Mount or elsewhere, is an expression of what it means to live in a wholly human way, to treat others in a wholly human way, and to respond to others in a consistent attitude of love.

Anti-Intellectualism: The Modern Romantic Rebellion

In chapter 2 we summarized briefly the nature of the romantic reaction against the rationalistic excesses of deism and an over-intellectualized approach to religion and life. Today we are living in a modern romantic rebellion which started when the first hippie decided to drop out of the mechanized society of modern technology and return to a simpler life of love and flowers.

A wave of anti-intellectualism is sweeping over the country, fed by the philosophical convictions on both extremes of opinion. The conservative forces are more and more anti-intellectual because they identify the university as the seat of radical dissent. Suspicious of higher education anyway, they are quick to relate protest movements with all that "highfalutin book learning." The radical forces are more and more anti-intellectual because they identify the establishment as the master at self-justifying rationalization. If a rational, logical approach to politics and economics has brought us to the present catastrophic state of affairs, then the time has come to follow "gut feelings" and forsake the misleading machinations of the intellect.

When one adds these considerations to those we have previously mentioned—the growing loss of scientific prestige and the growth of anti-intellectual influences in the church—it becomes evident that a very strong movement is alive. This movement contains many emphases that are good and necessary, but when carried to an extreme it threatens the foundations upon which a truly concerned approach to life's problems must rest.

In few areas is the growth of anti-intellectualism more evident than in the area of religion. The fastest growing Christian denominations are those that emphasize an emotional and experimental approach to Christian faith and minimize doctrinal statements or thought-out theological positions. Though religious interest in general is at a level not encountered in recent years, it is to a large extent determined to remain unrelated to the rational historical Christian faith. Every major newspaper carries a column on astrology with horoscope for the day; most of these are simply nonsense, to be sure, but the demand that placed them there is manifest. Eastern religious thought, with its denial of the value of the finite and of matter, attracts many with its meditational and mystical aspects.

Consider three elements of modern life: UFO, ESP, and LSD. Each of these is typical of many others by which people seek something more than just the meaninglessness of materialistic existence. For many people life is painful, for many others it is dull, and for many more it is painfully dull. As a result, they are lured by any evidence that the world isn't really all that counts, but that there is a mystical other world that man can contact, think about, react to, and enjoy according to *his* will.

The UFO affords a dramatic opportunity to escape the confines of this world. When man's bona fide exploration of space started, there were many opportunities for the ordinary man to enjoy vicarious excitement. But the more time passes, the more obvious it is that effort in space research is just as tiring, unromantic, frustrating, and even deadly as any other kind of dangerous honest effort. Landing on the moon has not changed human nature; money spent to shoot ships into space might better be spent here on earth. The UFO has the potentiality of fulfilling the desire for mystic excitement. If the UFO represents a secret and unknown mission, good; but if the UFO comes to us from the mysterious reaches of outer space bearing creatures who are not earth-bound, the possibilities for generating self-excitement have unbounded alternatives. These

UFO supposedly travel at fantastic speeds, are not limited by the usual laws of nature, and possess powers that no mortal man has. They are a resurrection of our childhood infatuation with fantasy— a marvelous and inexpensive escape from the dull painfulness of life as usual on the job in the riot-torn city of a constantly and pointlessly war-torn world.

Astronomers have repeatedly pointed out that there is no evidence for life on the nearer planets, that there is no evidence that any possible UFO has had an arrival pattern consistent with coming from a nearer planet, and that the time required to travel from any body outside of the solar system is inconsistent with the trip being made. No matter. The UFO offers contact with the mysterious forces of the universe. It is not likely to be given up until something real takes its place.

Extrasensory perception (ESP) and its more or less popularly related associates—psychokinesis, clairvoyance, prediction of the future, and communication with the dead—offer perhaps an even more dramatic opportunity for man to enjoy a life different from everyday experience. Scientific research has been conducted on ESP for some time without coming to any satisfactory resolution. No unambiguous, scientifically acceptable proof has been established for a direct mind-to-mind contact or for a control of mind over matter in a laboratory situation. Such effects may indeed exist, but if they do, they are the extension of natural properties of the universe and will come to be understood in terms of natural reproducible and controllable phenomena. In no case will they prove to be critical evidence for the existence of a supernatural, transcendental, or spiritual mode of existence.

The strong appeal of ESP is that it can be interpreted as the first step toward the establishment of the reality of a spiritual world, particularly a spiritual world that will take away man's fear of death and his living responsibility to God. Men are freed from all the pressures of this responsibility, from obedience to his commandments, from acknowledgment of his Son, from action in accordance with his will. They are so freed because quite independent evidence exists that there is for everyone a fairly pleasant life after death after all, no matter what the Bible or Jesus Christ had to say about it.

The basic attraction of LSD and other mind-expanding drugs is quite similar. Here is a promise of contact with new dimensions of life, an opportunity for experiences denied to the ordinary person in the pursuit of this dull and meaningless life, an opportunity to experience and see "God" without fulfilling the requirements of obedience that God has revealed to us. It is the answer to the universal human dream of what religion *should* be like: a religion of ecstatic mystic experience separated from the daily responsibility of obedience to God. The effects produced by LSD and other such drugs result from biochemical action of the drug on the sensory perceptions of the individual and on the working of his brain. In no way do these effects reflect or give evidence for the reality of an independent spiritual or transcendental mode of existence. One might as well argue that the ordinary dream provides such evidence, with a lot less risk to the individual.

As seldom before in recent years, men are coming to the place where they recognize and admit a basic need in their lives. They need to know who they are and what they are doing here. They need to reestablish the way in which they are related to the Creator and his universe. They will try anything that promises satisfaction without cost. What a challenge exists for the Christian to make known to them that the only real satisfaction of their needs has been provided in the person of Jesus Christ.

Science as Service

Science offers an opportunity for service. This is an opportunity with special significance for the Christian scientist.

The Christian scientist is called to serve the Christian community particularly by participation in education and in propagation. Through education he has the job of making sure that the Christian community has an accurate understanding of the limitations and of the potentialities of science. There are as many caricatures of science in the Christian community as there are of Christianity in the scientific community. He is responsible for building an understanding of the differences between pseudoscience, science, and scientism. The ability must be developed to discriminate both against pseudoscience, the attempt to use scientific form without scientific integrity to defend Christian ideas, and against scientism, guilty of the identical error in attempting to discredit

Christian ideas. He has the opportunity of using the scientific perspective on the relationship between objective reality and natural laws to combat the prevalent tendency to subjectivize and relativize all experience and values.

The Christian man of science is also called upon to be the possessor of "beautiful feet" (as in Isa. 52:7 and Rom. 10:14–17) as he assists in the propagation of the gospel. The church still lags far behind in its utilization of modern means of communication for bringing the gospel to that vast majority who will never (humanly speaking) be found inside church walls. Missionaries at home and abroad have constant need for help from scientifically knowledgeable people for the solution of daily problems.

It is also a valid thesis that the development of science is a necessary Christian response to the existence of need in the world. The Christian confronted with need and suffering can make no other response than to alleviate it. The fact that human nature will pervert the best in life does not mean that the best should not be sought. When science in service to mankind is viewed as a redemptive instrument on the natural levels in the hands of men committed to Christ, the purpose and practice of science is established in the context where it belongs.

If, therefore, the Christian response to human need requires the development of science as one way to meet that need on the natural level, Christian men of science have a double responsibility. First, they must make certain that the pursuit of science is directed toward the aid of those in need, and, second, they must see that possible evil effects of scientific advance, inevitable in our imperfect world, are counteracted and neutralized.

Summary

If there were ever days with the signs of the biblical "last days," we are living in them now. Patterns of behavior and development that have been appropriate for thousands of years must now be changed. Our attitude toward the earth, toward population growth, toward utilization of natural resources, toward economic expansion, toward war as a means of settling international disputes—all these are being called into question. And the need to change so that we are able to live in new times with new approaches is imminent. At the same time, certain problems are not new at all, but are as old as human nature itself. For these problems of spiritual alienation and rebellion, only the old solution of reconciliation with God through Jesus Christ is effective. One of the greatest challenges we face is how to apply this solution to the new situations that confront us.

In this chapter I have tried to show the results of integration of science and Christian faith, of research and revelation, in my own life, as I have considered a number of the pressing problems of our day. I suppose if there were a unifying theme it would be the exhortation to avoid extremes. The belief that all of the evil in the world can be associated with a particular institution or system leads to the unleashing of self-righteous destruction. The belief that science provides the only path to truth and our only hope for the future leads to the disillusionment that turns to irrationalism. In the church, traditionalists and innovators represent extreme perspectives which, if held as absolute positions, do not contribute to the overall health of the church. Modern man has the responsibility to tread a middle path. He must not on the one hand see modern man as unresponsive to all spiritual approaches nor on the other as unresponsible to take over those choices to which God has brought him. In face of the need to stem population growth, we must avoid both the extreme of unconcerned continuation on the current path and the extreme of unlimited abortion and euthanasia without regard for the value of potential or remembered human life. We must avoid the fallacy of considering either the free enterprise or the socialistic system as the perfect economic system. In ethics we must avoid both the extreme of inflexible legalism and the extreme of uninformed subjectivism. In perspective, we must avoid both the overintellectualized dehumanizing rationalism that reduces human beings to things and the anti-intellectual subjectivism that reduces human beings to feeling but not thinking animals.

Finally we need to view science less in the category of end-in-itself or as foundation for military activity, and more in the category of a service to the human race. We need to remember that science has *a* role to fill in the development of the world, not *the only* role. We need to remember that scientific developments can deliver us from many of the problems now facing us if we really want to use them, just as they have delivered us in the past from such scourges as beri-beri, scurvy, pellagra, rickets, dysentery, typhoid, cholera, and tuberculosis. Who would give up penicillin and streptomycin, television, rapid transportation, and release from physical labor?

The Christian involved in science has additional opportunities. He is in a position to bridge the gap between the Christian community and the scientific community. He is the only one who knows from the inside what it means to trust oneself wholly to God in Christ and at the same time what it means to evaluate properly the potentialities of scientific investigation for an understanding and control of the natural world. If he does not undertake the role of reconciling these two communities, there is no one else able to do it.

Topics for Discussion

1. Christians living at the time of the American Revolution were sharply split over the appropriate Christian action. Discuss what the probable dividing issues were and how they arose. What position would you have taken then? Does your position now depend on the fact that we won?

2. Consider examples from your experience where statements of an anti-intellectual character have been made from both the political right and left. What would be the natural consequence of following the implications of such statements?

3. How can scientists make their own humanity and the human factors in science more evident to the public?

4. Discuss the modern counterparts of the Pharisees and Sadducees, using for guidance Mark 12:18–27 and Acts 23:8 for the Sadducees, and Mark 7:1–23 and Luke 18:9–14 for the Pharisees. Do you find a little of each in yourself?

5. There has been talk about freezing the bodies of individuals upon death so that they can be preserved until a cure for their disease is known. Then they can be thawed out, cured, and given a new lease on life. Should Christians allow this? Why, or why not? What would happen to their souls in the meantime? Would you like to do it?

6. It may soon be possible to control the sex of an unborn child

by appropriate medication. Should Christians make use of this possibility? How about control of the IQ of an unborn child? How about cure of a physical or mental defect by pre-birth treatment? How do you decide what to allow?

7. Is modern man more or less controlled by societal influences than his grandfather? Can any society exist without controls?

8. Do you believe that people should have the freedom to commit suicide? To starve to death? To watch while others starve to death? Would you consider it a punishable crime for a mother to refuse to feed her child? When does freedom have to give way to regulation?

9. Did you ever have a Times Square on New Year's Eve crowd experience? If population is not limited, what is to prevent the whole world from becoming like that? Would life be worth living? Is it selfishness or responsible stewardship to work to prevent such a result?

10. If we were to accept the thesis that an unborn fetus is only a potential human and not an actual human, a one-minute-old baby would also have exactly the same description except for certain critical physical changes in breathing and blood supply. Is infanticide any worse than abortion? Why or why not?

11. Should abortion be allowed in particular cases where to give birth to a baby would result in disastrous social or economic consequences for the baby as well as for others? Why or why not? How does this differ, if at all, from abortions for reasons approved by the American College of Obstetricians and Gynecologists?

12. If the life-sustaining apparatus needed to keep a "living vegetable" with irreparable brain damage alive were critically needed to sustain life in other cases with a chance of recovery, what would you choose to do?

13. One scheme to encourage birth control is to give to every married couple permission for two children. Subsequently such permissions could be exchanged or bought and sold between couples. What do you think of this scheme? Would it work? What would you do with the couple where the wife is pregnant with the third child?

14. Should there be any Christian objection against voluntary sterilization? How about compulsory sterilization after two children?

15. Does your charcoal burner on the patio contribute to air

pollution? Are you going to keep on using it? What will make you stop using it? Do you think it makes any difference?

16. What would happen in our system if a young man went to his boss and said, "I like the job I have right now and would like to spend my time on other things rather than work for advancement. Please don't consider me for advancement."? What should happen?

17. Would you work less hard if you knew that you could never get more than 20 percent higher salary than you are making at the moment? Why, or why not? Should you?

18. There is a song from the musical *South Pacific* that says children must be taught to hate. Do you think this is true?

19. Could you push the button that would mean death to 140,-000,000 men and women living in the Soviet Union?

20. Is it always wrong to lie? Why, or why not? Would you ever deliberately lie? Why, or why not?

21. It is sometimes claimed that seance experiences in which dead friends or relatives are supposedly contacted through a medium constitute direct evidence that life after death exists. What do you think of this evidence? Suppose that the word from the other side was to the effect that Jesus was just another one of the people there and not someone of any particular importance. What would you think of such comments? Would they affect your view of the evidence?

22. American Indian tribes have used peyote weed for years as a hallucinatory drug in religious ceremonies. If such drugs without harmful physical effects become available, should Christians make use of them? Why, or why not? How about the Christian use of such drugs as caffein, aspirin, tobacco, and others?

23. Faced with the reality and the deadliness of cancer, does a Christian researcher in this field have any option except to seek a cure, even though he knows that success will aggravate the population growth problem?

Bibliography

The following books, some of which have been referred to previously in notes in the text, provide source material for the topics discussed in this book.

Anderson, J. N. D. *Christianity: the Witness of History*. London: Tyndale, 1969.
———. *Christianity and Comparative Religion*. London: Tyndale, 1970.
Augenstein, L. *Come Let Us Play God*. New York: Harper & Row, 1969.
Barbour, Ian. *Christianity and the Scientist*. New York: Association Press, 1960.
———. *Issues in Science and Religion*. Princeton, N.J.: Prentice-Hall, 1966.
Beck, S. D. *Modern Science and Christian Life*. Minneapolis, Minn.: Augsburg Publishing House, 1970.
Berger, Peter. *A Rumor of Angels*. Garden City, N.Y.: Doubleday, 1969.
Bonhoeffer, Dietrich. *Creation and Fall; Temptation*. New York: Macmillan paperback, 1967.
———. *Letters and Papers from Prison*. Rev. ed. New York: Macmillan, 1967.
Borgstrom, G. *Too Many: A Study of the Biological Limitations of Our Earth*. New York: Macmillan, 1969.
Bronowski, Jacob. *The Identity of Man*. Garden City, N.Y.: Natural History Press, 1965.
Brown, C. *Philosophy and the Christian Faith*. London: Tyndale, 1969.
Bube, Richard H., editor. *The Encounter Between Christianity and Science*. Grand Rapids, Mich.: Eerdmans, 1968.
Clark, R. E. D. *The Christian Stake in Science*. England: Paternoster, 1967.
Collins, Gary. *Search for Reality: Psychology and the Christian*. Wheaton, Ill.: Key Publishers, 1969.

———, ed. *Our Society in Turmoil*. Carol Stream, Ill.: Creation House, 1970.

Coulson, C. A. *Science and Christian Belief*. Chapel Hill, N.C.: University of North Carolina Press, 1955.

Davis, W. H. *Science and Christian Faith*. Abilene, Tex.: Biblical Research Press, 1968.

Dillenberger, John. *Protestant Thought and Natural Science*. Garden City, N.Y.: Doubleday, 1960.

Du Noüy, Pierre L. *Human Destiny*. New York: Mentor Books, 1947.

Dye, David. *Faith and the Physical World*. Grand Rapids, Mich.: Eerdmans, 1966.

Elder, Fredrick. *Crisis in Eden: A Religious Study of Man and Environment*. New York: Abingdon, 1970.

Friends Service Committee. *Who Shall Live?* New York: Hill and Wang, 1970.

Gilkey, Langdon. *Maker of Heaven and Earth*. Garden City, N.Y.: Doubleday, 1959.

Green, Michael. *Runaway World*. Chicago: Inter-Varsity Press, 1968.

Greene, John C. *Darwin and the Modern World View*. New York: Mentor Books, 1963.

Heim, Karl. *Christian Faith and Natural Science*. New York: Harper & Row, 1953.

Jaki, Stanley L. *The Relevance of Physics*. Chicago: University of Chicago Press, 1966.

Jeeves, Malcolm A. *The Scientific Enterprise and Christian Faith*. London: Tyndale, 1969.

Jones, D. G. *Teilhard de Chardin*. London: Tyndale, 1969.

Kitwood, T. M. *What Is Human?* Chicago: Inter-Varsity Press, 1970.

Kraft, R. W. *The Relevance of Teilhard*. Notre Dame, Ind.: Fides Publishers, 1968.

Lack, David. *Evolutionary Theory and Christian Belief*. London: Methuen, 1957.

Lever, Jan. *Where Are We Headed?: A Christian Perspective on Evolution*. Grand Rapids, Mich.: Eerdmans, 1970.

Lewis, C. S. *Miracles*. New York: Macmillan, 1947.

———. *The Problem of Pain*. New York: Macmillan, 1962.

Maatman, R. W. *The Bible, Natural Science, and Evolution*. Grand Rapids, Mich.: Reformed Fellowship, Inc., 1970.

MacKay, Donald M. *Christianity in a Mechanistic Universe*. Chicago: Inter-Varsity Press, 1965.

Mascall, Eric L. *Christian Theology and Natural Science*. New York: Longmans, 1957.

Mavrodes, G. I. *Belief in God: A Study in the Epistemology of Religion.* New York: Random House, 1970.

———, ed. *The Rationality of Belief in God.* Englewood Cliffs, N.J.: Prentice-Hall, 1970.

Moberg, David O., *Inasmuch: Christian Social Responsibility in 20th Century America.* Grand Rapids, Mich.: Eerdmans, 1965.

Monsma, J. C. *The Evidence of God in an Expanding Universe.* New York: G. P. Putnam's Sons, 1959.

Montgomery, John W. *History and Christianity.* Downers Grove, Ill.: Inter-Varsity Press, 1964, 1965.

Plantinga, Alvin. *God and Other Minds.* Ithaca, N.Y.: Cornell University Press, 1967.

Polanyi, Michael. *Science, Faith and Society.* Oxford: Oxford University Press, 1954.

Pollard, William G. *Chance and Providence.* New York: Charles Scribner's Sons, 1958.

———. *Man On a Spaceship.* Claremont, Calif.: The Claremont Colleges, 1967.

———. *Physicist and Christian.* Greenwich, Conn.: Seabury Press, 1961.

Ramm, Bernard. *The Christian View of Science and Scripture.* Grand Rapids, Mich.: Eerdmans, 1955.

Rookmaaker, H. F. *Modern Art and the Death of a Culture.* Chicago: Inter-Varsity Press, 1970.

Russell, Bertrand. *Religion and Science.* Oxford: Oxford University Press, 1961.

Schaeffer, Francis A. *Death in the City.* Chicago: Inter-Varsity Press, 1969.

———. *Escape from Reason.* Chicago: Inter-Varsity Press, 1968.

———. *The God Who Is There.* Chicago: Inter-Varsity Press, 1968.

———. *Pollution and the Death of Man: The Christian View of Ecology.* Wheaton, Ill.: Tyndale, 1970.

Schilling, H. K. *Science and Religion.* New York: Charles Scribner's Sons, 1962.

Sears, J. W. *Conflict and Harmony in Science and the Bible.* Grand Rapids, Mich.: Baker Book House, 1969.

Smith, C. U. M. *The Brain: Toward an Understanding.* New York: G. P. Putnam's Sons, 1970.

Spitzer, W. O., and Saylor, C. L. *Birth Control and the Christian.* Wheaton, Ill.: Tyndale, 1969.

Stace, W. T. *Religion and the Modern Mind.* Philadelphia: Lippincott, 1960.

Teilhard de Chardin, Pierre, *The Phenomenon of Man*. New York: Harper Torchbooks, 1959.

Thielicke, Helmut. *How the World Began*. Philadelphia: Fortress Press, 1961.

van der Ziel, Aldert. *Genesis and Scientific Inquiry*. Minneapolis, Minn.: Denison, 1965.

————. *The Natural Sciences and the Christian Message*. Minneapolis, Minn.: Denison, 1960.

Vaux, Kenneth. *Subduing the Cosmos: Cybernetics and Man's Future*. Richmond, Va.: John Knox Press, 1970.

Whitehead, Alfred N. *Science and the Modern World*. New York: Macmillan, 1926.

Wooldridge, Dean E. *Mechanical Man*. New York: McGraw-Hill, 1968.

Yarnold, G. D. *The Spiritual Crisis of the Scientific Age*. New York: Macmillan, 1959.

Index

For further reading

SHAPING YOUR FAITH. By C. W. Christian. A guidebook which explains what theology is, why it is essential to faith, and how it grows and develops out of the believer and the church. Answers such questions as where theology comes from, how to understand the questions it raises, how to "do" theology. #98002 (quality paperback).

THE BECOMERS. By Keith Miller. A helpful and insightful look at what happens to a person after he or she becomes a Christian. Realistic, honest, and full of hope, for people who "are in the process of becoming whole as we reach out with open and creative hands toward work, people, and God." #80321.

THE WONDER OF BEING. By Charles H. Malik. A compelling defense of the Christian faith, taking issue with modern philosophy's overemphasis on subjectivism, idealism, and verbalism, all of which place knowledge ahead of existence. Dr. Malik calls for contemporary Christians to recapture the sense of wonder at the mystery of the world's independent existence, affirmed by Jesus Christ. #80342.

COME TO THE PARTY. By Karl A. Olsson. An invitation to a celebration of life. Describes the author's pilgrimage from the world of academe to a life-style of honest relationships and real humanity. Tells how you can recognize and affirm your own spiritual gifts and the gifts of others as an indispensable part of living. #98001 (quality paperback).

THE EXTREME CENTER. By Nels F. S. Ferré. Here in Dr. Ferré's last book (published posthumously), are the riches and realities of the gospel; treasures from the Old and New Testaments; sermons first preached in a rural church in Japan, a university church in India, at Cambridge and Harvard Universities or in a rural Iowa congregation. #80255.

THE LETTER AND THE SPIRIT. By Rabbi Robert I. Kahn. Can a book on ethics used several thousand years ago be applied to today's moral dilemmas? Rabbi Kahn says yes and draws striking parallels between the principles and spirit of Hebrew laws in biblical history with those in contemporary society. #80297.

VIOLENCE: RIGHT OR WRONG? By Peter W. Macky. Shows that to understand violence you need the insights of a variety of disciplines. A close look at biological, psychological, sociological, historical, and biblical materials leads the Christian to ask himself: What is my role to be? Dr. Macky points out that the answer lies in implementing Christ's teachings in your personal situation. #80309.

WHO AM I? By Ralph T. Overman. A scientist suggests that real faith is the means for discovering your identity. In this book, you'll see that the only meaningful way to validate your existence is to find out how to fill your emotional needs for relationships with other people and God. #90003 (quality paperback).

GOD, THE DISTURBER. By Alan Walker. Internationally acclaimed minister reaches to the very heart of things: looking at war and racism with prophetic judgment and concern; delving into the questions of the role of the Church in urban situations; searching for the role of the faithful Christian in national crisis and personal conflict; calling to mind God's active influence in mankind's current situation. #80328.